AF394505

A LONG TIME COMING

Love great sportswriting? So do we.

Every month, Pitch Publishing brings together the best of our world through our monthly newsletter — a space for readers, writers and fans to connect over the books, people and moments that make sport so captivating.

You'll find previews of new releases, extracts from our latest titles, behind-the-scenes interviews with authors and the occasional giveaway or competition thrown in for good measure.

We also dip into our back catalogue to unearth forgotten gems and celebrate timeless tales that shaped sporting culture.

Scan the QR code and join the growing Pitch Publishing reader community today.

Andy Bargh

A LONG TIME COMING

The Inside Story of Scotland's Journey Through the 2026 World Cup Qualifiers

First published by Pitch Publishing, 2026

1

Pitch Publishing
9 Donnington Park, 85 Birdham Road
Chichester, West Sussex, PO20 7AJ
www.pitchpublishing.co.uk
info@pitchpublishing.co.uk

Set in Adobe Caslon Pro

Typeset by Pitch Publishing

Cover design by Olner Design

Printed and bound by CPI Group (UK) Ltd, Croydon, CR0 4YY

The authorised representative in the EEA is Easy Access System Europe OÜ,
Mustamäe tee 50, 10621 Tallinn, Estonia gpsr.requests@easproject.com

A CIP catalogue record for this book is available from the British Library

ISBN 978-1-83680-509-0

Papers used by Pitch Publishing are from
well-managed forests and other responsible sources

Contents

Acknowledgements

THE PROCESS of writing this book – from being given the green light by Pitch until its submission – lasted 97 days, with the writing component done in just more than a month. My previous book, *A Nation Again: The Inside Story of Scotland's Journey to the European Championship*, was written over 21 months. Time-wise, actually quite comparative to the two starkly different qualification journeys I've now written about. Although the subject matter is fairly similar, this has been a completely contrasting challenge. The list of people to whom I owe a few drinks and will be entirely grateful is significant because without their consideration and understanding, there would not have been enough time to scramble these 70,000-odd words together.

Firstly, my wife Alex. Thanks for supporting and encouraging me to meet this head-on in the weeks before our wedding. For being my *vent-bearing-executive* while you were swamped making sure our day would be so special and memorable. Love you xx(x).

Thanks to Mikey MacCallum, Ciaran Cameron, Chris Stenhouse and Lewis Irons as well for telling me it was possible to get from A to B between the start of December and March, and my parents for always supporting me and leaving their door open for me to come home and work in the comfort and solitude of my old bedroom.

Thanks to Pitch Publishing for agreeing this could be done and allowing me the opportunity to write again about one of my biggest passions.

Luckily, during my work as a football commentator and as the creator and host of the *Hampden Roar Podcast*, I have met a number of Scottish football folks who can sometimes trim a few degrees of separation and generously put me in touch with relevant people. There are also elements of luck, such as being a former team-mate of a close friend of Kenny McLean.

So, thanks to Del Esplin for making that happen, as well as the aforementioned Lewis, Calum Brown, Doug McNeil and Lee Miller for making introductions. The media and communications teams at Brentford, Bournemouth, Hearts, Hibs and Rangers were open-minded and a pleasure to deal with. I'm also grateful to Luke Shanley, Liam McLeod and Amy Canavan for sharing their memories of following the team – passionately and professionally – throughout the Nations League and World Cup qualifiers.

Most of all, as if I, or we, weren't appreciative enough for that night in November, thank you to Ryan Christie, Nicky Devlin, Lyndon Dykes, Lewis Ferguson, Ben Gannon-Doak, Craig Gordon, Grant Hanley, Aaron Hickey, Kenny McLean, Lennon Miller, Lawrence Shankland and John Souttar. Without their cooperation – be it from home, after training, in a hotel before a match or during a dog walk – you wouldn't have this book to read.

Each of the boys were understanding of the time-sensitivity, enthusiastic during our conversations, generous with their time and candid in their recollections. Like us all, some have better memories than others (one player asked who was in our Nations League group after the Euros!), but no topics were off the table and I feel very fortunate to have had the chance to reminisce with them.

And thank you to you, the reader, for taking the chance on this and deciding to give it a bash. I hope you find it written fairly and humorously, praising when deserved, critical when necessary and above all, an enjoyable read. This story isn't smooth, but when are they ever?

Chapter 1
Euros Exit

SOME SCOTLAND players sunk to their knees with enough desolation to forge a crater. Their pulsating pursuit of progress to the Euro 2024 knockout stages was over. Relentless for 90 minutes, a Scottish siege in Stuttgart should have brought an opening goal for Steve Clarke and the side to savour, but saves here, a post there, Hungarian deflections and their bodies on the line thereafter was a survival mission to admire as they begged Scotland to cease and desist. Hungary's winner in the 100th minute allowed them to live with hope on three points for another few days, but Scotland were out on one. Among the deflation, some solace could be found in the lack of regret. Granted, regret in the factual conclusion of the group, but with the performance in this must-win game? How could one possibly wallow when it was God Damn Rotten Luck's fault that we didn't find the back of Hungary's net before they found ours with the game's final kick? On any other sunny, summer's day in Stuttgart, that would have been three or four to Scotland. History would have been written by the first Scotland team to reach the knockout stage of a major tournament. Defeat snatched from victory's jaws, again!

Ultimately, only the first sentence of that paragraph can stand up in court.

Must-win, it was. After being mauled 5-1 by the Germans in the tournament's opener, Scotland refused to flatline against the Swiss and drew 1-1 in the north-west. Winner takes all in game three, and faith had been kept. Supporters crammed into trams to proceed to the MHP Arena and for hours before the game we queued for bratwursts and beers. *Murdered down in Munich, one point in Cologne, three points here in Stuttgart, and we're never going home!* The pint cup with the host stadiums printed on it was sought and kept as a souvenir. The atmosphere was genuinely joyous, as it usually is; like the start of a spring-break horror film, with teens leaping off the boardwalk without the faintest idea of what lurked beneath and the devastation that would soon unfold. This was a Film4 repeat.

Must-win, it was. Anybody unfamiliar with the evening's context would have leapt to the conclusion this was the group's dead rubber or perhaps even a pre-tournament friendly accidentally arranged three weeks behind schedule. Victory imperative, Scotland's first shot on target came in the seventh minute of a chaotic second-half stoppage time. Kevin Csoboth hit the post, that aforementioned shot from Grant Hanley was saved, Callum McGregor was prevented from pulling a point-blank trigger with a last-ditch tackle and Csoboth scored from the subsequent counter-attack; the latest goal ever scored at a European Championship. A point would have kept Scotland interested in the tournament for a couple of days, but two would ultimately have sent them home with how other results developed. Three points and a goal difference of minus three wasn't even enough for Hungary to get through in the end.

Must-win, it was. Reflecting on the Euros in 2021, captain Andy Robertson advised there would be 'no regrets' this time. Hanley's rather tame shot from 16 yards was only Scotland's fourth goal-bound shot across the three games. There were two instances at the tournament of a team failing to have a crack during the first half of a game. Yes, you don't need me to write it. Their total of 17 efforts is the joint-fewest by a nation since the group stage was introduced at the Euros in 1980. Alongside them, Northern Ireland, who had the smug satisfaction of a means to an end by reaching the last 16 eight years previously.

Must-win, it was.

Lack of effort would be an unfair stick with which to beat the boys. A dearth of invention among these clever, forward-thinking players was apparent. Ingenuity and incision were as scarce as the efforts on goal – probably the primary reason for it – as Clarke's side pondered on the Hungarian shade of the halfway line. Scotland didn't expect Hungary to operate with the handbrake off, but they certainly didn't anticipate it being pulled on the edge of their box with a bus that could accelerate from zero to 60 on the counter. The opposition had done their homework. All they needed to do was watch the lifeless friendly against Northern Ireland at Hampden in that year's spring; asking Scotland to break down a low block is often like asking primary school children to solve the Pythagoras equation. In the first ten minutes of the game, Scotland had 80 per cent possession across the park. At full time they could shrug shoulders at a share of 75 per cent across our own and the middle thirds of the park and 62 per cent across the field, our second-highest in major tournament history. Big whoop.

David Moyes was on punditry duty for BBC. Scotland's possession gave a 'false sense of security' in the game, he said. Identifying McGregor and Gilmour, he urged Scotland to play forward with more intensity through the thirds. Ryan Christie came on in the 83rd minute and ended up playing almost 20. His admission echoes the observations of Moyes and the vast majority of those watching it unfold on screens or live in Stuttgart:

> It was a strange game with what was on the line, and I felt this against Switzerland as well – neither team really wanted to open themselves out to try and win the match. I suppose you can get that at tournaments in international football. You don't want to find yourself 2-0 down at half-time. We got into the changing room at 0-0 thinking it was there for us but we hadn't really created anything. A sticky game, we fell on the wrong side in the last minute.

'Don't play with the fear of failure. Play with the expectation of success,' is Clarke's motto for his approach with his Scotland squad. He prophesised his boys would play with *swagger* and before the tournament criticised the 'Negative Normans' who 'talk ourselves down'. Like Christie, Grant Hanley is another who struggles to explain this 85-minute exception to these rules.

> Teams can cancel each other out in those games. With the nerves and pressure they aren't the best to watch from a fans' point of view, but from a players' one it is about staying alive and in the game to get something at the very end. I just remember it being tight and tense.

In a sense, I get it. There are few things in my life I'd rather have than a Scotland cap. Given the chance, would I have the balls to actually do it? To be brave? To be bold? To have the courage to play the pass that might be intercepted and incite the wrath of those I am desperate not to disappoint? To take the shot from 20 yards instead of letting someone else fire high or wide?

I will never proffer the Scotland squad let *us* down in Germany. Anyone who walks out a tunnel in a blue jersey and plays until their face is the same colour has my support. There can be no denying their efforts, hopes and dreams. Perhaps the nerves referenced by Hanley and Christie relate to a fear of letting *us* down as a by-product of losing, but I do believe – because they have shown what they are capable of – they didn't do *themselves* justice when it mattered. They didn't play with the belief that they could beat Switzerland and Hungary aside from the first 20 minutes against the Swiss. This is no dissertation, but I can't help but feel drawn towards the inferiority complex associated with *us* as a country.

Austria topped a group containing France, the Netherlands and Poland. Georgia beat Portugal to reach the knockouts. Unbeaten Slovenia were knocked out on penalties by the Portuguese in the last 16. Slovakia overcame Belgium and were two seconds from sending England home at the last 16 stage before Jude Bellingham scored an overhead kick. Albania threw punches at and connected with Italy and Croatia before a narrow loss to Spain ended their hopes of progression. There go the population arguments. We scored one more goal at this Euros compared to the previous one. An own goal. That was Clarke's threshold for humorously – but really demeaningly – pointing at progress for us. Asked about our bluntness and lack of creation going forward, he responded, 'It's probably not the night to speak about that, because I'm sad.' His tones were as confusing as they were insulting.

Kenny McLean came on for Scotland in all three games. In Stuttgart, he entered the fray in centre midfield with seven minutes to play before Andy Robertson was taken off on the edge of stoppage time, meaning he also filled the left-back hole after Hungary rampaged down that side a couple of times – hitting the post on one occasion – because Scotland had so many bodies forward.

> It was desperate in the end. The Swiss are very good, but we went and took them on and saw we could be at this level. Knowing we could do that and then only show it in stages – ten minutes here and there – isn't consistent enough. Against Hungary, maybe there was something in the back of our minds that a win would take us there, so maybe we wanted to stay in the game. It was like Hungary dared us to break them down. We'd planned to go toe-to-toe with them but when they set up deeply we didn't adapt well enough. That was totally on us and we need to take responsibility. There's only so much info and tactics the manager can give us on the pitch, but the impetus has to come from us. We hoped they'd come out more but they sat in and we didn't show enough to break them down. Maybe the Germany result impacted that and we left

it a bit late to have a right go. We should have taken
the game to them more.

Among the fury a narrative developed that *had* Scotland subjected
Hungary to an onslaught and lost, fans would have ticked the
slightly disappointed box rather than *extremely* on their feedback
form. It's all hypothetical and each to their own opinion but if it
simply had not been our night in front of goal in Stuttgart – much
like the picture painted in this chapter's opening paragraph – I
think the acidity of the defeat would have slightly diluted. Hearts
would have shattered all the same but heads would have remained
more balanced. It would have been in the 'Typical Scotland'
bracket. This loss didn't quite feel like it belonged there among
similar sorrowful stories of the 21st century and beyond.

It would be erroneous not to circle the simply unfathomable
decision not to award Scotland a penalty in the 78th minute.
Watching it back now is not easier to digest. The VAR not advising
referee Facundo Tello to take a second look at Willi Orbán
thundering into Stuart Armstrong as he set himself for a shot –
with nobody between him and the goalkeeper – is worthy of head
scratching to scar the scalp. Hungarian manager Marco Rossi even
admitted his team were lucky in that particular incident. A distinctly
and understandably rattled Steve Clarke led the barrage at full time,
rightfully questioning the decision but strangely portioning some of
the blame on the referee's Argentine nationality.

He demanded an explanation from the authorities while each
fan wished for a queue to personally depose him. In mitigation he
had to plan without the possibility of selecting Aaron Hickey, Lewis
Ferguson, Lyndon Dykes, Ben Doak or Kieran Tierney. The first
couple were out with long-term injuries, Dyksey and Doaky were
ruled out just before the squad travelled to Germany, and KT had
torn his hammy against the Swiss. However, with the match moving
turgidly and with no distinct signs of improvement, he seemed
reluctant to roll the dice. James Forrest hit a fruitful stride in the

final few months of the season at Celtic, but even with the absence of Ben Doak didn't get further than a warm-up on the sideline.

Lawrence Shankland played 47 games for Hearts that season, scoring 31 goals and winning PFA Player of the Year. He'd scored in the tournament warm-up game against Finland at Hampden and in Georgia to rescue a draw at the end of 2023. He played half an hour, give or take, across the group stage, coming on in the 76th minute against Hungary.

> I can see the tactical side from the manager when we discuss the opposition. We expected them to be different to how they played on the night so it sprung a bit of a surprise for the full team. I want to play as big a part as I can on the pitch and give something to the team, but I've been in the national team long enough and understood my role going into the tournament and that there was a high chance that would be the part I'd play with the way things were going.

There is no right or wrong way to support Scotland while following the team, whether you are a moaner, cheerleader, shouter or nail-biter. Support the team how you feel comfortable in doing so. Everyone has views on what is appropriate, helpful or understandable – including the players, which is expanded on later in the book – but the rulebook is as short as the Tartan Army's songbook these days. If one follows Scotland to see the team play well and win, continue as you see fit. If one prioritises going to games for the social aspect, to visit new cities or to learn about different fans and cultures, the prerogative is theirs to do so. Both reasons can exist strongly together, but one will always matter slightly more than the other to each individual.

The importance you place on each side of that fence should dictate the pride or condescension felt when opposing fans whose countries vaulted the group stage shower us with compliments in defeat.

It's nice but, in my opinion, contributes to the inferiority complex that has troubled Scotland for some time. We laugh, we sing, we drink. We joke that we'll win it because we're scared to say what we really think. Rivals might run scared in a drinking contest but largely, we are not seen as a serious football nation. Enter German World Cup-winning captain and Euro 2024 tournament director Philipp Lahm, who mused in *The Guardian*: 'The Scots did everything right. Even in cities where they weren't playing, they infected everyone with their good humour. They used this tournament to celebrate with others. It's not just the caterers who will miss them. I've been asked what bothers me most about this Euros. I said that the Scots have already gone home.'

Thanks, Phil, but we were absolutely dreadful. This well-meaning patronage – which pretty much made headline news – came with a hair ruffle and pat on the backside while we shuffled to airports and train stations. Does it matter how the football went? 'At least they liked us while they pumped us,' a close friend of mine said dryly and insincerely after a chat with some Germans following the first game, while social media was flooded with pictures of Scots drinking Munich dry in the Marienplatz or roaring the anthem in the Allianz.

Performance schools, meaningful minutes for youngsters, the priority of PlayStations after school; there will be no laborious post-mortem of Scotland's Euro 2024 endeavours across the following pages, but the mise-en-scene is important before them. A voyage into Nations League 'A' was imminent and Scotland's almost winless run would reach just more than a year. Not completely as a collective, but pundits and fans wondered if – some ascertained that – Steve Clarke had taken this Scotland squad to their limit under his leadership. How sufficiently could he and the players give themselves a shake in the top bracket of the Nations League and be ready for the World Cup qualifiers, which would start in March if Scotland were directly relegated from our division. With one win in 12 games – 2-0 against Gibraltar before the Euros –

matches against Portugal, Croatia and Poland were around the corner. Forgive the conclusion jumping, but those clashes hardly felt like fertile ground for confidence. This Scotland squad would have to rediscover it one way or another.

Chapter 2
Poland and Portugal

TWICE UNDER Steve Clarke, Scotland have strung a sequence of results together that caused fans' drink of choice to rise from half full to overflowing with bubbles. In the second half of the 2022 World Cup qualifying campaign, Scotland won six games in a row to propel themselves to the delayed and doomed play-off against Ukraine, before the Euro 2024 qualifying journey saw Scotland ransack 15 points from five games to soar into unassailability. Teams such as Spain, Norway, Denmark and Austria were all beaten alongside the types of hopeless fodder that used to sneakily lay banana skins on their turf as we disembarked aircrafts in Tórshavn, Chișinău and Tbilisi.

The contradicting run already requiring arresting had been exacerbated by the winless Euros, but with the Nations League offering six, albeit difficult, matches across ten weeks, focus was firm and vision fixed solely on the opportunity and challenges ahead over the autumn. Not only from the national team manager, as expected, but the Scottish media as well.

Another lie to start a chapter. I won't do it again.

Steve Clarke seemed to have gone into hiding after returning from Germany, although this probably wouldn't be an accurate description. He didn't feel he had anything from which to hide. In Londonian suburbia, Clarke wasn't surrounded with or brought down by the blowback from the summer's failure. A week before the shitshow in Stuttgart, SFA President Mike Mulraney stated on television, quite unequivocally, 'Qualifying can't be enough for Scotland,' and described Steve Clarke as 'perfect' for the job. A Member of Parliament had not been caught snorting lines off a prostitute's tits here, but accountability and professionalism matter. Members of the media pestered the SFA with requests, perhaps pleas, throughout July for a press conference and the ability to extract explanations from the horse's mouth. Allow the cycle to move on. A bit of closure was what everyone needed, eh?

Why did you persist with the 3-4-2-1 shape when Kieran Tierney was injured? Why did you appear uncertain to make in-game changes before the Hungary game entered the latter stages? Why did the team struggle to make an impact in the final third? Did you not feel James Forrest's pace and directness or Lawrence Shankland's finishing ability would have improved our chances in that situation? Do you feel that an apology to, or degree of empathy with, the Scotland fans who travelled around Germany is appropriate considering how sourly the group stage developed?

At his squad announcement press conference, Clarke wasn't having it.

Interrupting BBC Scotland's Chris McLaughlin, who had proffered this chat was a chance for reflection and was in the middle of explaining he'd spoken to some deflated, angry fans before the presser, Clarke objected, completely unironically, with, 'How many did you speak to? Name quite a few, how many? Ten, 20?'

'There's always going to be criticism when you don't achieve your targets so if that criticism comes to me, that's fine, I can take it,' he followed. 'I think you have to look at the build-up to the tournament. It wasn't smooth, we lost a lot of players through injury. I think what we've shown is if we're missing one or two key players we're not as strong a side as we would be with those players in the team.'

His impatience for these events is well known but such a rebuttal was unlike him, and as a spectator my judgement is criticism bothers him more than he would like us to believe. The whole exchange carried an uneasy whiff and was a difficult watch on the socials. After replying with a straightforward 'no' when asked if he had considered that it was the right time for him to move on from the gig, he was questioned for reasoning other than injuries on what went wrong for Scotland.

'Too many little things' was the predictable platitude. No expansion on what those vague fragments were.

So why do you want to continue, Steve?

With an initial snigger, he simply said, 'My contract.' Some severity came afterwards: 'I've always said I'd love to go to a World Cup with my country. I've got a group of players who are determined to go to a World Cup with their country, and for some of them it'll be their last chance. It'll certainly be my last chance. There's your motivation there.'

Sky Sports reporter Luke Shanley was one of those hoping this inevitability would have been avoided with a debrief weeks earlier.

> It was interesting. I remember speaking to Ian Maxwell and he said, 'Yeah, we'll review it [Euro 2024].' That's in relation to the location, training, the management side and football side of things. Clarke was calculated with his thinking; he's quite clever with it because whatever he says after the Euros, everyone will still be annoyed. He can't slaughter his players and if he makes excuses, people will say he's just making excuses. He was in a no-win situation, but from a media point of view it doesn't go away. So when he announces his squad for the Nations League, people just want to talk about the Euros while he's probably moved on. He's got to think about the games, injuries and the goalkeeping situation whereas we just want to speak about the Euros. I get that he wanted to move on but it has to be put to bed as well. One thing I've learned about Steve Clarke is

that he'll do everything on his terms. Sometimes that's a good thing. How many managers have we witnessed in the past getting bogged down in what the media or fans say? Steve has his own mind, and to his credit that stubbornness can work really well for us. He doesn't get caught up in the goldfish bowl and can take a step back, but sometimes we probably just want him to put his hands up and say it wasn't good enough.

Perhaps conversations took place to find private rationale – but after being described as Mr Perfect in advance, Clarke didn't owe his employers an explanation to be played out in front of the gallery. Anything he did say at the presser would be for the appeasement of fans. Belgium boss Domenico Tedesco took the opposite approach and displayed some humility that week, apologising for blaming local police in Stuttgart for holding up their team bus before their bore draw with Ukraine that preceded a meek exit to France in the last 16. Tedesco took responsibility for his tactical decisions, substitutions, opinions in adversity and above all, remorse at the outcome.

Clarke must have thought such sentiments weren't necessary or wouldn't be helpful. Or both.

The fact Scotland were readying for League A of the Nations League was of huge credit to Clarke, proving pretty much nothing but steady improvement over his six years as decision maker. They approached their first barn dance with the big boys without the key players affected by long-term injuries – Aaron Hickey, Lewis Ferguson and Kieran Tierney – but contained some fresher faces, regardless of age.

Zander Clark, Angus Gunn, Robby McCrorie; Grant Hanley, Max Johnston, Scott McKenna, Ryan Porteous, Anthony Ralston, Andy Robertson, John Souttar, Greg Taylor; Ryan Christie, Ben Doak, James

Forrest, Ryan Gauld, Billy Gilmour, John McGinn, Kenny McLean, Scott McTominay, Lewis Morgan; Ché Adams, Tommy Conway, Lyndon Dykes, Lawrence Shankland.

Fans quickly crunched the numbers. Four centre-backs! Five inclusions was the norm. Jack Hendry had dropped out to be replaced by John Souttar while Tierney and Nathan Patterson's injuries and Liam Cooper's unemployment were easily explainable. *This must mean a change from five at the back!*

Much like your ex's perfume, the smell will now be permanently associated with heartbreak. The whiff of something new was exciting.

Adding to that excitement was Ben Doak. The Liverpool winger – who completed a season-long loan to Middlesbrough shortly before the camp began – was (and still is) the great hope. His pace and directness was an asset unavailable to Scotland since Ryan Fraser's involvement dwindled a couple of years earlier. Moving to Merseyside with a buzz cut, slight figure and a moody, adolescent demeanour, the now 18-year-old arrived for international duty bursting out his cocoon with biceps stretching his hems, a sleeve tattoo between them, a flowing fade and a sense of belonging. He was yet to be baptised at international level, but his absence among the Euros squadron was almost as painful for us as it was for him.

> My first session with Liverpool after my rehab was the last training session of the season. I wasn't expecting to get picked for the Euros. I just saw it on Sky Sports at the training ground. It was a bit mental. I did well and enjoyed myself, wasn't expecting anything really, just enjoyed being there, but my knee had swollen up after the flight. It went away really quickly and I was actually able to train normally about a week later, but I

think they'd rather have taken a player who was fit and ready than someone who hadn't played a game. I fought my corner. I was feeling alright. It was a problem I'd had throughout my rehab because of the nature of it with my meniscus (cartilage), but the docs didn't want to take a chance so I got sent home. My knee just hadn't fully adjusted to the demands of training yet. It was tough; being out for so long, getting picked and then smacked down to earth a week later.

Doak's fitness-dependent call-up was a foregone conclusion. The clamour quota had been filled in the direction of Ryan Gauld. The Vancouver Whitecaps midfielder, 28, had often been the debatable absence in squads over the last four or five years having consistently impressed in Portugal for Farense, even being included in the league's Team of the Year in 2020/21 when his side were relegated. He joined Whitecaps at the end of that season as one of the club's Designated Players – a rule that allows three players per squad to be paid beyond the salary cap – and immediately continued creating and contributing after his life-changing move.

Clarke insisted over the years when questioned that Gauld was rarely far from his thoughts. A dreary loan at Hibs from Sporting Lisbon in 2019 closed some minds as far as his international credentials went; he didn't seem to have fulfilled the undeniable potential shown during his breakout at Dundee United in 2013 that encouraged Sporting to buy him for £3m. Those in the Tartan Army who sought footage of his offerings on the Portuguese and Pacific coasts were quite loud in their declarations that Gauld should be involved. One announcement after another, his omission was as unfathomable as it was disgraceful from Clarke. The conspiracy that the more Gauld's inclusion was demanded, the less likely the manager was to pick him was cited as the only possible explanation for such absurdity.

He arrived in Glasgow with nine goals and 11 assists in MLS that season (the campaign starts in March) and the potential solution to the deprivation of someone willing to thread a needle in the final third, be it as a central attacking midfielder or someone drifting in-field. Those numbers were nothing new; more than 100 goals and assists in the last five seasons give serious credence to his call-up and the Gauld fandom's cries.

'He's a creative player, slightly different to the type we have got. It will be nice to have a look at him up close and personal,' said Clarke. Strangely, though, his inclusion was met quite quietly by those who demanded it; a bit like a howling child being given the toy they've been desperate for only to see them ditch it two minutes later. Nonetheless, his potential debut was intriguing and exciting, and perhaps made more likely because of the absence of a squad regular.

Callum McGregor had announced at the start of the Scottish Premiership season that he'd had enough with international football at 31 years old. After 63 caps, his decision was 'the right one at the right time'.

He'd played 54 games the previous season for Celtic and Scotland. Since Clarke became manager in June 2019, McGregor had missed two squads through injury and didn't feature in only three games in all the ones he made. He's in the history books as a major tournament goalscorer for Scotland thanks to his fizzer against Croatia in 2021, scored in both play-off shoot-outs against Israel and Serbia, and was spoken about as 'Clarke's boy' among SFA circles, with the manager immediately warming to McGregor's approach to training when his tenure began.

'Throughout my career, I wanted to make myself available for Scotland at all times and whenever selected, give the absolute maximum possible to help the country and represent the supporters with passion and pride,' said Scotland's – now former – number eight. 'Appearing just once would have been a dream come true, so to achieve 63 and be inducted into the Roll of Honour at 50 caps is something I could only have dreamed of as a young kid.'

Clarke lauded McGregor's dedication and influence, and conceded his disappointment at the decision – which he understood. It was the first official international retirement of his tenure.

Interestingly, McGregor's relentless schedule and fitness concerns weren't directly referenced in the SFA's press release as the main factor in his thought process. It was the natural conclusion to reach, but off-record whispers circulated that he had allegedly become fairly disillusioned with the Scotland set-up and the preservation of his body was a convenient and relative parallel that made sense. It came as a surprise to the squad members, some of whom found out through natural breaking news alerts. Either way, his departure meant there would be an opportunity for someone to make a central midfield spot their own for the Nations League.

The unfamiliar faces of Gauld and Doak were joined by one-cap Tommy Conway, who went to the Euros, the relatively inexperienced Lewis Morgan and uncapped Max Johnston, while Ryan Jack and Stuart Armstrong began to be phased out of selection. Injuries notwithstanding, Clarke had squeezed the Febreze post-Euros. In total, 11 of the boys who went to Germany were not involved.

Forrest, Taylor and McCrorie all eventually withdrew with injuries, as well as Ché Adams. The *Scottish Sun* reported that Adams was fit and available but had opted to stay in Italy to continue settling in to his new surroundings in Turin. He signed for Torino on a free transfer at the end of July and hit the ground running with a goal in their win over Atalanta. Clarke was asked about the accuracy of this. 'The club informed us he picked up a knock against Venezia. I can probably get you the email if you like.' I don't believe anyone took him up on the offer.

The fragrance would change around the technical area as well as the Lesser Hampden training pitch. Uncapped duo Josh Doig and Connor Barron were given a chance to impress, while Jon McCracken had the chance to train with the keepers. Forty six-cap James Morrison left his coaching role to focus on the same one he held with West Brom and was replaced by Alan Irvine, who would focus on attacking phases of play. Graeme Jones, the SFA's performance director, was about to become Hearts' sporting equivalent after less than a year in the job.

Unlike Alan Partridge schmoozing with BBC Commissioning Editor Tony Hayers, Clarke didn't tie himself in a knot with his aim for 'evolution not revolution' during the Nations League campaign to be in 'better shape' when the World Cup qualifiers started in either March or the following September. Along with Andy Robertson at the presser a few days before the Poland game, there was only room for a party line of positivity. 'Since the Euros, not one person has come up to me and said he or she was disappointed,' said assistant John Carver. 'They've actually said it's been a great journey and hopefully we can continue that. That gives you a little bit of a lift, the fact people are saying that.' Got to take him at his word, I suppose. More concerning, ahead of six games against top-quality sides, was what followed: 'I think people are realistic. Let's not forget how big our nation is. It's a wonderful place up here but we're not a huge country when it comes to football. We are in the eyes of the fans and players but what's the population?'

A journalist replied, '5.2m.'

'So it's not a huge population.'

Genuinely depressing. There is so much more to this topic and the Scottish football psyche. Enough for a book in its own right.

John McGinn was more candid during the camp, admitting disappointments 'never leave' him. 'I still think about getting relegated with St Mirren.' The kind of honesty that has endeared him to the fans for more than ten years.

Clarke was complimentary of the inexperienced players that galvanised the squad and gave the place a 'breath of fresh air'. The opportunity for a reset was upon us. Perhaps it was what Poland needed too; they were knocked out of the Euros even quicker than Scotland, losing their first two games against the Netherlands and Austria before drawing with France.

Persisting with three centre-backs against Hungary while Kieran Tierney was injured was more of a trunk than a stick with which to beat Clarke. It's not necessarily a defensive shape – see Bayer Leverkusen under Xabi Alonso or Ruben Amorim's Sporting Lisbon – but the pegs must fit the holes. The edges weren't sufficiently rounded now and Clarke's opinion aligned with the vast majority of Scotland fans.

In a 4-2-3-1 formation, his team for the Nations League opener against Poland read: Gunn; Ralston, Hanley, McKenna, Robertson; Gilmour, McLean; McGinn, McTominay, Christie; Dykes.

Robertson became the seventh player to reach 75 Scotland caps, ten and a half years since earning his first, which came in a 1-0 friendly win in Warsaw. Hampden was around 5,000 short of full, probably thanks to the five-match package sold at the start of the year. Those not in attendance but keen to watch tuned in to ITV4, with rights-holder Viaplay scaling back their UK operations and struggling to agree a sub-licensing deal with BBC Scotland or Premier Sports.

Kenny McLean's opportunity to start an important game in central midfield was a rare one. Known as a closer in the ranks – someone who is brought on to help Scotland protect what they have – he knew this was timely ahead of a huge 2025.

> I played quite a bit under Clarke when he first came in but the midfield kept getting stronger so he used me on the left a lot of the time. He's always been very transparent with what he wanted me for. Normally it was to come on and be a bit more defensive, but when things like McGregor's retirement and Fergie's injury happen you need to take advantage. Everybody is always desperate to play their preferred position; there are no issues for me coming off the bench but I want to show the best of myself. The middle of the park is more about control of the game and we have quality

players going forward, so my thought is how do I get
the ball to them as quickly as possible.

It wasn't an ideal start for him or Scotland. Poland led after seven minutes. McLean and Gilmour were surfing different waves, coughed up the ball, and six seconds later it was in the back of Angus Gunn's net. Sebastian Szymański thundered it in off the left post's base from nearly 30 yards.

Poland didn't look great; Scotland looked alright. McTominay had a goal bearing a striking resemblance to his winner against Israel in 2021 ruled out for an accidental handball to bring the ball under control. Not much else happened in the half; Dykes sliced a brilliant chance at the back post, and the likelihood was Scotland would trail by one at the break.

The Polish spark wasn't coming from Robert Lewandowski, Piotr Zieliński or goalscorer Szymański, but rather nippy Roma winger Nicola Zalewski. He epitomised the type of player for which Scotland yearned. Brave, quick, direct, skilful, confident; totally threatening. The aforementioned characteristics took him into the box just before half-time, where Anthony Ralston clattered him. The Celtic right-back knew it and sat on the turf contemplating the consequences. Not a single team-mate fought his corner. Stonewaller. Lewandowski rolled it to his left, Gunn leapt the opposite way; 0-2 at the break. Boos at the break.

Scotland passed the ball around nicely, probed with some intent, struggled to break down the opposition defence, and didn't take advantage when they did. It was the typical tale of their 2024 so far.

Twenty seconds into the second half, Gilmour stepped forward and with two red shirts throwing themselves at him, rifled a low drive through the forest and into the net. It was only his second career goal, and his second for Scotland, who felt a gust on their backs now. On the hour, Shankland was brought on alongside two debutants: Doak and Gauld. The latter looked tidy, the former brimming with intent on his first competitive game since December, becoming the youngest debutant since Tierney in 2016. Fifteen minutes after crossing the line, he contributed to Scotland's equaliser. McTominay tapped in after Doak found Ralston's underlapping run to the byline. McTominay's goalscoring exploits continued, Ralston atoned for his clumsiness on the stroke and Doak had provided a spark. Not that it was a big deal or anything for him.

> I felt relaxed and wasn't expecting to play. I was just happy to be there. Fortunately I came on and painted a decent picture of myself and made the right decision [to pass to Ralston], but it wasn't difficult, it was a simple pass.

Scotland's goals had been scored by the two protagonists of the Scottish transfer story of the summer. Napoli gave the pair life-changing moves to the Amalfi Coast's gateway, with Antonio Conte familiar with Brighton's Billy Gilmour from his time at Chelsea and Scott McTominay seen as the driving, box-to-box goalscoring midfielder to push Napoli towards another Serie A title. His performances for Scotland in a similar role, rather than the more restricted one he often occupied at Manchester United, made him a rather attractive proposition at less than £30m. He admitted he owes Clarke for changing his perspective on football a few days before he scored four goals in the games against Cyprus and Spain, at a time when United games usually kicked off with him watching from that weird, brick-wall dugout.

'The manager and I sat down and he said I didn't look happy, that I didn't look like I was smiling around the place,' McTominay said when he picked up his Scottish Football Writers' International Player of the Year award for 2023. 'I spoke to my family, my girlfriend, and they all said the same thing. Sometimes you just need to enjoy football and play with a smile on your face. Not everything is the end of the world if you're not playing so well. Ever since that meeting with Clarke it has lifted a weight off my shoulders. He wanted to see the kid who was happy whenever he first came on the scene and was playing every week.'

Scotland had never beaten Poland in a competitive game and five of the last six meetings had ended in a draw. The ascendency was Scotland's now. They looked like they might win from 2-0 down for the first time since the 40s. Nothing to fear. Clarke was all-in on the jackpot. Playing with the expectation of success.

Poland broke in the fifth of eight added minutes. Zalewski, to be specific. Darting down the left side of the box and waiting for the cavalry to catch up, he sought an angle to do something. Hanley had him shadowed; Zalewski was about to either run out of room or the pitch. Then Hanley's impulses malfunctioned. He lunged. He gave away one of the most obvious penalties Hampden will ever see. His hands were on his head in regret while he was still in the midst of his tackle. He knew; like the trusty family dog that instinctively bit the new neighbour. Zalewski squeezed his penalty under Gunn. Poland had won, Scotland had lost. Played well, but lost. One win in 13. Against Gibraltar. Hanley contemplated what he'd done.

> That was a low moment. I thought I'd dealt with the situation really well. Zalewski was quick but I moved my feet and kept him outside me. The best possible scenario was to keep him wide and put him down an alley that's difficult to score from. The decision to dive in was … I dunno. I think I actually had a decent game so I felt I could get a toe in and win the ball. Maybe if I hadn't played well I'd have been safer or more reserved, which would have served me better. It was a rush of blood to the head and a bad decision.

This was undoubtedly a troubling incident for Hanley but was far rarer than some would have you believe. Naturally on this occasion, it incited a rather savage mob to amplify their opinions. He doesn't chill out in the evenings by putting his feet up by the fire and searching his name on social media, but he knows what errors of judgement like his against Poland can lead to.

> The reality is there are only a few opinions that matter. Firstly, mine. I'm as honest as I can be with myself and a fair judge on things I've done; nobody is as harsh on me as I am. Secondly, the manager. He's got to tell me what he thinks, and what he thinks decides whether I play or not. I learned quickly that whatever the narrative or what the press are saying needs to be put to one side. If you can look yourself in the mirror and know you're being honest with yourself, that's the most important thing. I've never had social media. The things young players see now, and how they speak about what people are saying about them online, is mad. They're taking the opinions from people who are nowhere near as qualified to judge performances. It's human nature to focus on negatives, but it's not something I've ever lost any sleep over. You have to have the balls to deal with pressure. Gordon Strachan used to always talk to us about having the balls to play for Scotland; we'll get pressure and stick but we are the ones with the bottle to try and perform for our country. The beauty is there's always a game around the corner to put things right.

All three goals were completely avoidable from a Scottish perspective. Two penalties and loose possession in midfield preceding a cracker. The pattern was worrying; 17 goals conceded in eight games across 2024, with a trip to Lisbon next.

Clarke was happy with the performance. Most of *us* were, to be honest. There were enough encouraging signs. He agreed his side were punished for daft mistakes, thanked the fans' loyalty, praised the debutants and advised they 'win as a team, lose as a team'.

As a team under Clarke, Scotland had responded well to adversity on a number of occasions. After what the manager anointed 'the lowest of the low' in Moscow following a 4-0 defeat in 2019, Scotland embarked on a nine-game unbeaten run culminating in the Euros play-off final a year later. After the disappointment at the Euros, Scotland strung six wins together during the World Cup 2022 qualifiers to reach the play-offs for Qatar. That subsequent tie against Ukraine ended badly, but Scotland then quickly won Nations League promotion and started their Euro 2024 qualifiers with five uninterrupted wins.

Just under a year ago, Scotland and their hordes swarmed *La Cartuja* in Seville with a completely genuine belief of beating Spain. Now, they were booked in for the Gods in the Estádio da Luz with the hope of keeping the result respectable.

Portugal had won 20 of their last 24 matches in their home country. Scotland had lost 12 and won two of their last 17 away games against countries ranked higher than them. They had only played Portugal twice in 30 years – noncompetitive – with their World Cup qualifier in April 1993 ending in a 5-0 defeat and manager Andy Roxburgh confessing, 'A team died out there tonight.'

They returned to a modernised version of the same stadium in search of a resurrection of their own to continue the trend of recoveries after setbacks. Unfortunately for them, their journey was a bit more prolonged than they'd have liked. The charter flight touched down into Beja military airport just shy of 100 miles outside of Lisbon. They arrived at their hotel a couple of hours later, meaning dinner was eaten just on the pm side of midnight. Ryan Christie was whisked off upon touchdown to fulfil his media duties and spent the next hour and a half in a car with his manager and a few members of the SFA's media team. 'There's not much chat in the cars, I'll be honest!', laughs Christie.

Ben Doak's substitute appearance at Hampden on Thursday whetted – nay, flooded – the appetite for more. One of his first involvements was to drive more or less 40 yards forward with the ball before being swarmed by a few concerned Polish men. Hampden had been starved of his electricity. *Unleash him!*

'He's certainly not ready to play 90 minutes at this level,' said Clarke. 'We will try to bring him along slowly over the next couple of years. Hopefully he progresses and becomes a big player for the country. But we have to protect the boy.'

Spoiler alert: Konstantinos Karetsas.

Doak didn't make the XI and neither did any of Thursday's subs. He selected the same lads who stood for the anthem at Hampden. The only alteration was McGinn and Christie switching sides. The most caps among a Scotland starting XI in history: 493.

Exactly a year since their last competitive victory, in a 4-2-3-1 formation, Clarke's XI read: Gunn; Ralston, Hanley, McKenna, Robertson; Gilmour, McLean; Christie, McTominay, McGinn; Dykes.

Scotland may have lost against Poland, but they managed something they didn't against Hungary – turn up. The supporters did as they always do. As they settled behind the protective netting in the stadium's away end, the gaps between the highest row and the stadium's roof offered them a stunning view of the sunset over the city's skyline. Ideally, not a visual representation for this Scotland squad's cycle just yet.

After seven minutes against Poland, Scotland believably trailed. After seven minutes against Portugal, they unbelievably led.

Wearing the minty-yet-blue away kit, Gilmour floated in a deep free kick, which McGinn nodded to Robertson just outside the left edge of the box. Pressed by Bernardo Silva, he passed it to a loitering McLean. His first-time cross was measured to utter perfection for McTominay to stroll on to and thump his header into the net. The fans at the other end of the stadium began falling over themselves in disbelief. Christie, Dykes, Hanley and McKenna almost gave themselves whiplash by checking for the flag. There was no need for one, and with a knowing look from Icarus, Scotland had an early advantage. Scott McTominay had his tenth goal in a year and a half after managing just one in his first three and a half years of involvement.

The bear had been prodded. António Silva missed a header from six yards, Gunn dived quickly to stop Rafael Leão's shot from sneaking in at the near post and also blocked a Diogo Jota header with the Liverpool forward looking destined to score. Scotland remained brilliantly organised and resilient, with Portugal forced wide, and were helped by a quality performance from Gunn. They'd scored with their only shot on target; Portugal had scored with none of their 16. That fact called for the half-time introduction of Cristiano Ronaldo, who'd scored his 900th career goal a few days previously against Croatia.

It wasn't he who scored the equaliser. Bruno Fernandes struck a fairly flimsy shot from the edge of the box, which Gunn reached easily. Unfortunately, he pushed it into the side netting rather than around the post. Portugal had probed at times reminiscently to Scotland in the summer. It was a pity this was how they sourced parity. The ball whizzed past McLean's shins en route.

> We have a lot of video meetings now where the manager talks and gives us all the information he can on opponents. It's about the whole team shape; how we break-down their play, work as a whole unit, how we stop them if they break our striker press, how do our defenders react if they get past the midfield? Against teams like this we have to be hard to beat, stay compact and try to anticipate what's going to happen.

Portugal pushed but Scotland weathered the storm, with Gunn atoning for his weakness at the equaliser by thwarting João Félix three times. He magnificently anticipated Felix's finish in a one-on-one, leapt to parry his powerful downward header and most impressively sprung to his feet to punch the ball away with Félix millimetres from heading in on the goal line after Ronaldo hit the post.

Gauld came on in the city he once called home. He trained with João Palhinha, Bruno Fernandes and an adolescent Rafael Leão while with Sporting and is fluent to the extent he could catch up with them in their native language if he wanted. He ran on with Conway. Perhaps Clarke thought there could be room to exploit while Portugal chased a second.

Dykes was given a breather after 72 minutes. Nights like these are long for him.

> Occupying the centre-backs as much as I can is my main job. I want to score goals, but we have a lot of goals from midfielders arriving into the box as well, so my role can be to take centre-backs out the way with front-post runs to leave space for guys like McTominay and McGinn to arrive and have a simple finish. Serbia feels like a long time ago now, and we've changed in certain aspects, but when I'm playing for Scotland I should occupy the centre-backs to make the midfielders' job much easier. I like making sure a defender knows he's in a game. Defensively, I'm trying to block their central midfielder the best as I can. For example, against Spain it was my job to force the ball away from Rodri. It's a graft.

Scotland's winless run would continue with the referee's whistle at 1-1, but the narrative would shift immensely. Talk of firing bullets at our own feet would subside for a shower of compliments for the resolution shown against one of the world's best. Paris Saint-Germain, Manchester City, Manchester United, Liverpool, AC Milan and Chelsea are just a few examples of the clubs employing the lads who started for the hosts.

The one on Paris Saint-Germain's quite small payroll is Nuno Mendes. With three of the 90 to go, he skinned Lewis Morgan and sent one down Quality Street. Gunn was distracted by Jota's slide and McKenna dozed off for a second; long enough for Ronaldo to get himself into position to tap-in the ball and snatch two points from Scotland. His 32nd international goal in four years. McKenna pinched the bridge of his nose. McGinn stared at the grass with hands on hips. Gilmour looked like he was literally trying to tear his hair out. Ronaldo did his stupid little celebration. It was a severe kick to the stomach for Scotland.

Scotland were now on their longest competitive winless run in the history books. However, comparable to Thursday's match, Steve Clarke was chuffed with his team's performance and was adamant his players deserved something tangible and reminded the press his team were in 'part of a cycle'.

Kenny McLean remembers the regular reminders about the bigger picture:

> There was a lot of disappointment after that game. In the next camps we analyse things and Clarke and the staff show us what we did well and need to do again. We work to get those habits ingrained. It's important not to let isolated moments deflate us because you can easily find yourself getting lost in what wasn't good. Robbo always seems to find the words after disappointing games, to know what to say and what we need to hear.

Lyndon Dykes expands a bit further:

> We had a chat after the Euros to separate what had happened during the summer. There was a real mindset change from the Euros into the games that would lead us to the World Cup qualifiers, to realise what we had

the chance to achieve and get back on a winning run step by step. At the start of camps Clarke would have meetings with us to compare us to the top teams and how we can be one of them. We look at things like box entries and number of crosses, have markers to hit, and at the start of the next camp will see how we did and set a new goal. I don't think football should be stat-led; it's a free-flowing game but they can tell us part of the story. There was always going to be a sticky patch but I knew with the team, manager and fans it wouldn't last forever. In the Nations League games we were competitive and looked the part. Sometimes it just doesn't go your way.

The Scottish defence had dug in so deeply at the Estádio da Luz there was a risk they'd miss their flight home by the time it took them to clamber from their trenches. This battle was over, but the Nations League war – and Scotland's own personal one – had just begun.

Chapter 3
Croatia and Portugal

THIS WAS the way of it now; 23 days after Scotland's plucky Portuguese excursion, the Scottish FA's media team pressed post on their squad graphic for games three and four in the Nations League. A trip to Zagreb in Croatia and a visit from Portugal were now within a fortnight. A torturous string of conclusions needed to be nipped long after the bud had developed. The boys would only play four league games between camps, which is a few too many as far as they're concerned. They count down the days until their reunion as soon as the previous one ends.

A significant number of them had the near monthly merriment removed from their schedules through injury. John McGinn's thigh strain narrowly took him out of contention, and Scott McKenna was nursing his hamstring in the same canoe. McGinn had played 35 consecutive games for Scotland since the 2-0 defeat in Copenhagen in September 2021, with this only being the third squad with his absence since Clarke took charge. Jack Hendry, Kieran Tierney, Nathan Patterson and Aaron Hickey were all unavailable as well. Five regularly picked defenders couldn't contribute.

Hickey's situation had become desperate. At 22 years old now, he hadn't played in almost a year after suffering an injury in training initially expected to keep him out for roughly 12 weeks; A *4C* tear of his hamstring, meaning there had been a complete rupture of a tendon, which attaches the muscle to the bone. A leg brace for two weeks, crutches for another couple, then a slow but sure rehab with increasing intensity to fortify the muscle. Movement quality and range of motion comes first followed by strength building, succeeded by running. Hickey barely got halfway through the process.

It was around the six-week point I felt something. I tried to carry on with the rehab by taking a few steps back, but I was passing a football and just thought, 'Fucking hell.' I got another scan, which returned with bad news that I needed another operation. The same surgeon did it, but throughout my second rehab I just knew something wasn't right. Simple things like lifting my leg were causing me problems. Eight weeks after that second surgery, I had a ball at my feet, did a backheel and felt my hamstring 'go' again. I needed a third surgery. I thought, 'This cannot be happening to me.'

The sight of him training with Brentford during summer 2024's pre-season warmed the cockles. They were frozen over by Brentford's sudden confirmation at the end of August that Hickey would miss the majority of the campaign because of the extensive care needed following his third admission. A three-month setback would cost him almost two years of his career, his trajectory significantly flattened. Around the time of his initial injury, a Google search of his name produced news articles with clubs like Manchester City and Bayern Munich in the headline. This was devastating for a young player of such promise and professionalism.

It was very tough for me. I had come close to coming back and then had to get back into a brace and use crutches. I'd wake up, go into training, do some rehab and strength training, then go home and sit on the couch. I was by myself the majority of the time. Anyone who was in that situation would struggle, big time. A lot of time alone, wondering if I'd ever get back to full fitness or how long it would take. It felt out of my control because it had happened a few times. I just wanted to be able to run outside and be in amongst it with the boys. After the second surgery I thought there might be a chance I could get into the Euros squad, but as time went on I knew I wasn't making it. That was a very low point. Watching the tournament from home was probably the worst part of all.

With the injuries affecting selection, Clarke invited a few boys to training who probably thought their chance would not arrive for another few years – or never – as well as someone who thought their days were done. Prospects such as Lennon Miller, Lyall Cameron, Max Johnston, Josh Doig and David Watson, who may have been extended a handshake, were left to the use of Scot Gemmill and the under-21s ahead of their important Euros qualifiers against Belgium and Kazakhstan.

> Craig Gordon, Angus Gunn, Jon McCracken; Nicky Devlin, Grant Hanley, Liam Lindsay, Ryan Porteous, Anthony Ralston, Andy Robertson, John Souttar, Greg Taylor; Ryan Christie, Ben Doak, James Forrest, Ryan Gauld, Billy Gilmour, Andy Irving, Kenny McLean, Scott McTominay, Lewis Morgan; Ché Adams, Lyndon Dykes, Lawrence Shankland.

Nicky Devlin, 30, was part of, and scoring for, the Aberdeen team whose domestic record at the start of October read 'played 12, won 12'. Granted, half of those games had been in the League

Cup against opposition beneath the Premiership, but Aberdeen were flying under their new Swedish manager Jimmy Thelin. Between being called up and arriving at Glasgow's Blythswood Hotel, Devlin scored in Aberdeen's thrilling 3-2 win against Hearts. Celtic's Ralston hadn't played in a month. Nicky had crossed the threshold for a call-up, ten years after being released by Stenhousemuir for a lack of confidence and 15 years after having to return home early from an under-19s camp because he had his higher English exam.

> The biggest thing for me were the nerves at not really knowing anyone apart from Lyndon Dykes. You get added into a group chat for each camp where the schedule and timings get posted, and Lyndon's was the only number I had saved. That was a bit surreal. The boys made me feel like I'd known them for ages, and one of their biggest strengths was genuinely feeling like they worked with each other every day. Boys weren't keeping themselves to themselves in different groups. I didn't know how they'd be with me, but I couldn't speak any higher of them. Once Jack McKenzie had been called up, McTominay came and sat next to us at dinner and he was brilliant. He was asking us about Aberdeen and was really interested in our fine list up there because it's got forfeits on it. He'd never heard of anything like that. We were telling stories and he was buzzing over it. Kenny McLean was great as well. We have a mutual friend and he made sure I was sound. I think loads of stuff tied in for me at the same time with the injured lads and how well we'd started the season at Aberdeen. I wouldn't have had the recognition if we weren't doing so well. I scored against Hearts the day before we met up as a squad, so that was a good conversation starter with a certain goalkeeper!

Preston's Liam Lindsay and West Ham's Andy Irving were called up for the first time as well, but Devlin's inclusion – plus a delayed invitation to training for his club-mate Jack McKenzie – followed a slight trend of Clarke trusting Scottish Premiership players to make the step up during moments of depletion. Guys like Paul Hanlon, Paul McGinn, Stephen Kingsley and Andy Considine all fit in that bracket, while Declan Gallagher and Stephen O'Donnell made historic impacts. I was there when McKenzie was informed assistant John Carver had been at Pittodrie to watch him against Hearts. His smile almost touched both sides of the tunnel. He and Devlin were now both in the players' group chat for the first time. Craig Gordon was re-added after being kicked out a few months previously.

Remember Andy Murray being ushered into a care home following his first-round loss at the Australian Open in 2019? His admission earlier that week that if he wanted to carry on he'd need a significant hip operation – possibly resulting in his retirement that year – induced the Aussies to conduct themselves with nauseating levels of on-court sycophancy and be the ones to retire him through presumption. *Should get a few likes and retweets for this! Oh Andy, love me!* Being forced to hear repeated congratulations on his achievements and publicly digest a montage of his highs despite telling interviewer Mark Petchey, 'Maybe I'll see you again, I'll do everything to try,' was a tough watch.

Gordon was given a summer send-off he didn't particularly ask for in the pre-Euros friendly with Finland at Hampden. Left out of the Euros squad after recovering from a broken leg, he was privately presented with a commemorative jersey bearing the number 75 – the number of caps he wasn't supposed to add to – before being brought on for the final 20 minutes of the game. 'There's only one Craig Gordon!' chanted the jovial Hampden crowd. It didn't go well.

Two minutes later, he was beaten fair and square by a low header. With five minutes to go, he misjudged a cross and his fists connected with the Finnish striker rather than the ball. Penalty, goal, and a 2-0 lead gone.

> That was an emotional night. I was probably too emotional to play actually, thinking this is the last time I'll play for Scotland at Hampden, knowing I was going to be coming off the bench. It doesn't happen very often that the whole narrative is about me; the whole build-up was really strange. It was difficult to focus on playing in the game, but I wanted to have that last moment. I wasn't happy about being left out the Euros squad but the manager was very upfront with me. He said I hadn't played enough matches compared to the others [Gunn, Kelly and Clark]. I was never going to agree with him, but I realise he had a difficult decision to make and I was the one to miss out.

Like Murray, Gordon told Clarke and his team-mates that he hoped this wouldn't be the last they'd see of him. The reality of time escaping no man and his Scotland career not culminating with a major tournament appearance was painful. In 2021, he was David Marshall's unrequired deputy. Now stuck behind his inferior club-mate, he was just allegedly unrequired. He found a few days' serenity on Lake Como to be able to saunter without anybody congratulating him on a Scotland career he hoped hadn't finished. At the start of the following season, the 41-year-old reclaimed Hearts' number one jersey and came out of a retirement that never was.

> It was nice to get out the country and get my head around what had happened; that the boys were all going to Germany and I wasn't going to be part of it. A nice trip, just very calm and quiet.

An important member of the squad returned but a crucial member of the coaching staff moved on. Set-piece coach Austin MacPhee's dad was unwell and he combined his role with the same one he held with Aston Villa, meaning family time was scarce. A reluctant departure but the right one.

Croatia's exploits at major tournaments are as enviable as they are intriguing; Five World Cups since we departed France '98 – including a final and another semi – along with six European Championships and seven group stage advancements between the tournaments. We were booted back over the German border having failed to achieve that for the first time.

There are two types of jealousy. The type in which one can't stand the success or circumstance of another and so it must be diminished or damaged because it's unattainable for the envious. Or the type in which one is inspired by the success or circumstance of another and so they strive to match or surpass those achievements through hard work.

I feel compelled to reiterate that no thesis will follow this context, but around a month before the visit to Zagreb, the Scottish FA published a rather alarming internal report that used data to confirm what most Scottish football stakeholders could see with the naked eye. Youngsters get fuck all game time.

In this study, they said Scottish football is 'significantly underachieving its potential' in youth development compared to countries of a similar size. They reference the Croats as a leading nation for developing youngsters who will almost certainly contribute to the national team as they enter adulthood. 'This has got to be a country to look at and maybe mould ourselves on a little bit,' said our manager. Montenegro and North Macedonia were two improving examples among more prominent ones such as Norway and Denmark.

How easy it would be to copy Croatia's homework is a matter of debate, but it certainly extinguishes the population argument. Scotland has around 700,000 more men than Croatia and as such plenty of boys interested in and good at football. Former manager of the famed Dinamo Zagreb academy, Ivan Kepcija, was quoted in the findings as emphasising 'technical repetition is the foundation of everything we do, which is why we are successful not only in football but in all sports in which we participate'.

The foundation of everything we do. The Scottish FA's research identified 'insufficient' player development at an early age. The kids are up against it from the first whistle. It also found a gap between under-18s and first-team football and a lack of support for players transitioning between those stages. So the young men are disadvantaged as well as the children. Clubs were also judged as operating myopically with barely any long-term strategy in place. Chandler Bing might say, 'Could we be any worse at developing young players?'

Stenhousemuir assistant manager Brown Ferguson produced some stellar work at the end of the 2024/25 season and in a fascinating Twitter thread shone a bright yet rather dim light on the ignorance or indifference of the Scottish Premiership clubs, revealing an average of 3.2 per cent of players who started across the league each week were Scottish and under 21 years old. That's four of the 132 across 12 teams. Only 7.8 per cent of players who started games were part of the youth pathway at the club employing them, and that included Craig Gordon and Liam Kelly who had left Hearts and Rangers before returning years later. Aberdeen and Celtic did not start a single Scot under 21 years old throughout the entire season.

Rijeka, Dinamo Zagreb and Hajduk Split were separated by two points at the end of the previous Croatian league season, with Rijeka claiming the title on goals scored. This is how much prominence they gave to their youngsters throughout those months.

- Fourteen natives at Rijeka aged 23 or younger played during the campaign, with six of them playing 20 games or more.

- Dinamo Zagreb trusted 15 Croatian lads aged 23 or younger throughout the season, including seven teenagers. Four 20 or 21-year-olds played at least 30 games.
- Fifteen Croats aged 21 or younger played for Hajduk Split, with four of them (including 16-year-old Bruno Durdov) making at least 30 appearances.
- Sixteen-year-old Fletcher Boyd played 18 minutes for Aberdeen at the end of 2023/24 and scored two goals. He played fewer league minutes the following season. Now he's 19 and is playing in Premier League 2 for Aston Villa's youth team.

Merited or otherwise, the inclusions of the 40 years-plus Gordon, 30-year-old Devlin, and 28-year-old Lindsay for the first time – to go with Gauld and Morgan's recent introductions in their late 20s – was no coincidence in relation to all this. That was a debate for a not-so-distant other day, perhaps after summer 2026. In the here and now Scotland had three points to steal in the Croatian capital, to smack down the reasonable assumption two defeats in Zagreb and back in Glasgow were following in the slipstream of the opening two.

Suitably hydrated from the local Pan lager – tallying at a tenner for four – the Tartan Army arrived at the odd Stadion Maksimir in the embers of a beautiful day's sunshine. Ambling or *tramming* to the east of the city, almost the exact equivalent of Glasgow City Centre to Celtic Park, there was no need for any second layers; arms were burned in almost 30°C October heat. Interested eyes glanced towards the youth match on the adjacent astro while vendors sold more Pans, and friendly Croats – including the family of Osasuna striker Ante Budimir – accumulated pictures with men in kilts while one of ours dished out teacakes to policemen and children.

A royal blue running track surrounds the Maksimir pitch with a separated and exposed quartet of stands even further from play than the ones that form Hampden. The main stand wasn't open for business because of safety concerns incurring from an earthquake 50km outside the city in 2020, turning the viewing experience at home into a strange one and contributing to an attendance of only 21,700. The last time Scotland played there in June 2013, they won 1-0 thanks to a Robert Snodgrass winner. Grant Hanley earned his seventh cap.

Those watching from home were doing so on YouTube. ViaPlay hadn't agreed a sub-licensing deal with BBC Scotland, ITV or anyone else and wanted to save some money. 'It's a disgrace the Scotland games aren't free-to-air!' the middle-aged man usually shouted at the cloud. 'It's a disgrace the Scotland games are free-to-air on YouTube!' the middle-aged man now shouted at the cloud.

In a 4-2-3-1 formation, the XI in Zagreb read: Gordon; Ralston, Souttar, Hanley, Robertson; Gilmour, McLean; Doak, McTominay, Christie; Dykes.

Doak became the youngest player to start a competitive game for Scotland in almost 60 years, Adams was still recovering from illness, and two Euros omissions were starting only three games later. A rib injury had rendered Angus Gunn useless; Gordon was in and so was Souttar, after watching the Euros in Portugal with his family.

> I was disappointed to be left out for the Euros but I'd got injured towards the end of the season so still had that going into the camp. I think I'd only played one game in the qualifiers for it, so the squad was settled. We shook hands and that was that. I said I'd fight to come back, that I'd go away, work hard and do my best. There were no hard feelings.

His inclusion was music to the ears of his central defensive partner, Grant Hanley.

He's one of the best centre-backs I've ever played with. He has absolutely everything you could ask for. Without his three Achilles injuries I think he'd be playing for a top Premier League club. That I went to the Euros and John got left out is absolutely mind-blowing to me. I'm really grateful for those opportunities. It could have been really different. I spoke to Soapy [Souttar] a wee bit for advice during my recovery, but I had a lot of complications. John was younger so that helped his recovery, but because I was already into my 30s my ankle was quite knackered.

Ah yes, I should explain. Hanley ruptured his Achilles tendon against Blackburn Rovers in April 2023, not long after playing 90 minutes in the 2-0 win against Spain. It's an injury Souttar had to recover from on three separate occasions between 2017 and 2021. A rehab process lasting nine months took Granty into 2024 and the Euros were closer than the horizon.

I got back into the team at Norwich, but I struggled to find form and confidence. I was questioning everything. Would I get back to a level where I could compete? There were times along the way I wondered if I'd get back at all. It's tough to find it in yourself to keep going. It was on my mind that I wouldn't make it to the Euros. As soon as we qualified that was my motivation, but I really struggled with my form and couldn't really move properly; something wasn't right with my ankle. I wasn't able to move freely and when you're carrying pain your decision-making changes. A big part of my game is being aggressive with front-foot defending, so having an injury like that at my age was having too much of an effect. I took a decision to step away from the team and see some specialists until I felt improvement and felt like myself. I owe the manager a huge thanks for putting his trust in me when I hadn't really played.

Scotland's literal status or prestige as a League A side wasn't as relevant as the by-products that came with retention or relegation. Firstly, a run of form was required with which to build momentum ahead of the World Cup qualifiers starting in March or September 2025 – month dependent on the Nations League outcome because of potential play-offs. Secondly, but just as importantly, their pot for that qualification draw would be dictated by their run of results and subsequent placing in the group. Stringing some points together would trigger a few dopamine hits, but the long-term effects couldn't be ignored.

If Scotland finished first or second in this Nations League group, they'd remarkably be a Pot 1 side for December's World Cup qualifying draw. If they sustained their place in League A through winning a relegation play-off, they might hold on to their second seeding. If Scotland were relegated, they would very likely become a Pot 3 side knowing only one country would qualify automatically from each World Cup qualifying group.

A group Craig Gordon wasn't really expected to participate in with the bulk of it a year away. The same sentiment was relevant in the here and now, yet here he was strapping on the gloves again, this time as the oldest player to ever start a game for Scotland at 41 years and 286 days old.

> I didn't want to close the door on Scotland because you just never know. I'm aware there aren't too many Scottish keepers around that are playing first-team football in top leagues so I thought I was always one or two injuries away from being called up. I always thought there was a chance. I didn't think it would happen that quickly, but everything aligned and I was

the one who managed to profit having been on the other side of it with the Euros.

Starting to put a few points on the board was kind of important, from whatever angle one assessed it. Once Marcelo Brozović was recognised in retirement with a home shirt bearing the number 99 (why not just play one more game?), the pleasantries were done.

Scotland were recognisable. Tidy in possession, hardly sweating but not forcing the opponents to perspire either. Not much to report at the half-hour mark other than, 'Yep, we don't look too bad.'

The issue, reminiscent of the Euros but with the added context of playing away to Croatia, was that we didn't look like scoring a goal. Thankfully Croatia were ready and willing to sign off on our permission form, with the type of defending that could have sealed Scotland's dismal fate in campaigns across the last couple of decades.

Gilmour won the ball in midfield and gave it to McTominay, who gave it to Doak. The kid made Joško Gvardiol think twice – more on that later – and delivered with his weaker left side. It wasn't his best cross and Petar Sučić was in a comfortable position to clear – something I'm sure he'd much rather have done than the near-fresh air shot that ensued. After his inadvertent slice, Christie was the beneficiary and into the net it rolled via a three out of ten attempt at a clearance from Duje Ćaleta-Car.

> I think I'm lucky I got the credit! I had been on a bit
> of a dry spell though so I was happy to chip in. My
> shooting boots haven't really returned at my club!

Christie's self-awareness is accurate. His goal against Serbia was almost four years ago. Since then he'd scored a penalty against Republic of Ireland in 2022 and in the pre-Euros friendly against Gibraltar. Doak's role in the goal had to be commended; Joško

Gvardiol didn't seem to have him under control. Mario Pašalić was booked for cutting down the teen as he started a counter-attack. For once, Scotland had a player who was willing and capable of taking defenders on.

> I know we don't have a lot of players in my position whose game is doing what I do. I go into a match thinking, 'How can I impact this in a way no one else can?' and that's always what I've been able to do. I've got weaknesses in other areas, but that's what I'm good at and I'll use it as much as I can.

Croatia nullified Christie's goal three minutes later. Nice goal; a cross-field pass, an intelligent knock-down from Ivan Perišić and a well-placed finish into Gordon's bottom right from Igor Matanović. It was 1-1 at half-time, during which Scotland supporters behind the goal digested and discussed the breaking news of former First Minister Alex Salmond's death.

Scotland's backs were gently kissing the wall in the second half, but Croatia were largely limited to shots from distance. Luka Modrić, recently 39 years old, was delightful yet dastardly. Grabbing the scruff, he advanced through Scotland's half, megged McTominay and missed Gordon's left post by less than a foot.

Scotland's midfielders had to confront quite the array during the group. Poland's Piotr Zieliński and Portuguese trio Bruno Fernandes, Vitinha and Bernardo Silva pose differing, severe challenges. None of them as harrowing as Old Luka's. McLean was in the heat of battle.

> The one I couldn't anticipate was Modrić. He's one, two or three steps ahead of everybody on the pitch. If you try and press him, he knows you're coming before you've even started and will stick the ball round the corner. Sometimes it's like he doesn't do too much

to stand out, but when you see him up close you just think, 'Wow, he is special.' Bruno Fernandes was good as well. He took the game to us in the second half in Lisbon.

Modrić ignited the move that resulted in Croatia's second goal. He sprayed the ball 40 yards to Perišić, who found a yard behind Robertson. Ajax's Borna Sosa met the cross, Gordon repelled, Andrej Kramarić nodded in the rebound. Gah!

Scotland showed some glimpses of being able to get in behind, but their lack of killer touch held them back. A sharp move through the thirds led to Christie wasting a one-on-one, while substitute Gauld showed why his inclusion could be handy, with a crafty first-time dink over the top that offered Adams a sight of goal as the clock struck 90. Adams's angle was tight and his lob dropped wide. I don't think any other player in the Scotland team would have attempted the pass.

Clarke's side were brave on the ball. They passed with intent rather than indolence and had the hosts concerned for the welfare of two precious points. They perhaps deserved ones of their own for their September exertions, and leaving Zagreb with one wouldn't exactly have been thievery. Scotland attacked in the fifth of four added minutes. Croatia struggled to clear, McLean backheeled the ball past a few of them, and Adams was racing Kristijan Jakić to get there first. The striker touched the ball onto Jakić and it trundled in a la Dykes in Oslo. Croatia pressed the big red button under their desk. VAR arrived, and three minutes later Adams was in cuffs charged with offside and the points were returned to the hosts. Correct decision. The players were completely crestfallen. Clarke told the boys he was happy with their performance. They'd been a few inches from taking a point in the home of a nation that reached a World Cup final six years ago and a semi-final in 2022.

'LLL' read Scotland's Nations League form guide, but the reality wasn't as black and white. 'We tried to play, tried to create chances. On another night we would've got what we deserved. There's so much disappointment in the dressing room that it's probably better to wait until we get back to Glasgow to analyse the game, but I feel like we're on the right path,' said Clarke. 'A full squad, fit and healthy would be a help.'

That last admission is an interesting one. Clarke is normally quite cautious with the timing of his substitutions, but using all five isn't uncommon. Only Gauld and Adams were trusted to contribute in Zagreb. The head count of the players unavailable to, or not picked by, the manager would provide a stern test for the XI that took Croatia to the wire: Clark; Hendry, McKenna, Tierney; Patterson, Ferguson, McCrorie, Hickey; McGinn, Armstrong; Shankland.

I take Clarke's point, but I was personally left feeling quite sorry for guys like Morgan and Irving. The boss's admission essentially confirmed they were there to make up the numbers for the time being. If you're good enough to be called up to train with your country, doesn't it mean you're good enough to play? 'It's very difficult to get the balance right between throwing players in to an international game when maybe they haven't felt that level,' said the man who makes the decisions. Like a graduate job advert demanding three years of experience in the field.

Scotland weren't out of their depth. They had been competitive and restored credibility against Poland, Portugal and now Croatia, but if they didn't win any of their next three games their record would stand at one win in 18 matches – again, it came against Gibraltar. Could Clarke and the Scottish FA crack on into 2025 with that backdrop? There was a slightly weighted division among supporters that Clarke had either maxed out his overdraft or should be given benefit of that turgid year's doubt. 'I want to see out my contract. I want to go to the World Cup,' was the manager's feeling on all that.

Doing that weird thing we do when we say *you* when we mean *we*, Clarke added: 'I feel as though I'm repeating myself. There is a process you have to go through. You're playing at the top table against top teams. Maybe the results aren't going to go for you but we have to believe in what we're doing. The players understand where we are in the process, they understand what we have to do to get results.'

Process isn't a word among the managerial lexicon that softens supporter anxiety, but some context was perhaps starting to develop in Clarke's favour after the first three Nations League games. Anything but defeat against Portugal on Tuesday would turn over a new leaf. Another hiding might feel like two steps back after half of one forward. We'd never suffered five straight losses in our 152-year history.

Thanks to Portugal coach and former Motherwell midfielder (did you know?) Roberto Martínez's friendship with St Mirren chief executive Keith Lasley, Portugal trained at the SMISA and then frolicked in the swimming pool at their Cameron House digs. This was their first competitive game at Hampden since 1980 (4-1 thanks to Dalglish, Gray, Archibald and Gemmill), although both sides kept a clean sheet against each other at Ibrox in the 1994 World Cup's qualifiers. Something like that would do again. It would be Ronaldo's first, and probably last, time on our hallowed turf.

Scotland's players had a light recovery session on the Sunday before some shaping and video work on what is now bureaucratically known as 'matchday minus one'. Phases of play, specific tactical instructions, set pieces; the finer details. Clarke responded with caution about 'overhyping' young Scottish players when asked on the likelihood of Ben Doak starting. Not necessarily a dig at the wee man's potential, but more about protecting him from the glare. 'Don't put too much pressure on him. He's a young man.'

Adams's immune system had done its job. He was the only change. Clarke's XI read: Gordon; Ralston, Souttar, Hanley, Robertson; Gilmour, McLean; Christie, McTominay, Doak; Adams.

Scotland should have led after three minutes. McLean pinged one for Doak, who had switched sides from the start with Christie, but there was no room for him to exploit past João Cancelo near the byline. He gratefully accepted Robertson's arrival, and the captain curled a peach to McTominay who leapt with no one near him in an almost identical position to the one he made the most of in Lisbon. Down Diego Costa's throat. Scotland would struggle to carve a clearer opening. Christie had a sniff on the edge of the box 20 minutes later but didn't find the purchase. Amid Portuguese passing and possession, Scotland had created more than them so far. They didn't enjoy many forays for the remainder.

Portugal absolutely bopped Scotland. The speed of thought, precision passing and razor movement among their midfield was incredible. Scotland could barely breathe at times. They'd win the ball and regurgitate it within three passes. Far more concerned about any risk rather than reward, they defended their box well and Portugal's chances were of the *half* variety. Ronaldo was jeered every time he touched the ball. Doak was encouraged every time he did.

Realistically, what did we expect? Hardly the other end of the spectrum. However, Scotland had shown they were better than hanging off the ropes back in March in the Amsterdam Arena. Pressing and passing the Netherlands off the park for an hour was celestial. Then the hosts scored a second goal and beat us 4-0. Then we were abysmal against Northern Ireland. Then Germany beat us 5-1, from the tardy seeds sewn in the spring.

Bernardo Silva, Rafael Leão and Rúben Neves were all brought on at the hour. Gauld and Morgan replaced Christie and Doak, for whom it was a frustrating night with his back predominantly to goal. Gauld showed intelligence and care of the ball. Portugal's growing urgency caused some carelessness, but they continued to lap on Scotland's edge. Ronaldo shot wide before Leão dropped a shoulder and almost ruptured both of Ralston's ACLs. Fernandes's close-range shot from the subsequent cutback was outrageously stopped and clutched by Gordon as Ronaldo scurried for a rebound. Less than five minutes to play.

He bent over and got in my ear to let me know, not quite in these words, that I was rather fortunate to have saved that one. He wasn't very happy. There was a feeling among the players and fans that we were getting stuck in, grinding it out, doing what we could to stay in the game and maybe get a set piece or counter-attack to get our noses in front. For me, I have to try and slow things down as much as possible because I'm taking in so much information at once. When they're attacking I'm checking every individual player, predicting the next pass, reading body shapes and angles, anticipating what is likely – who is in the best position – thinking about my own position, wondering if I can get out to cut-out a through ball or need to retreat. The ones who score the most have a habit of hitting the ball early to take advantage of a goalkeeper; they can pick you off at any given moment so I have to be constantly aware. I feel the international level get higher, even just at training. McTominay is excellent at it.

A point almost sealed, Clarke turned to Nicky Devlin to replace a cramped-up Ralston, his family in the stands bursting with enough pride to send shockwaves around the stadium. Four months ago, he was among the Scotland support in Cologne with his son. His purpose was to stop Leão from creating or scoring a winner. In the 92nd minute, he threw himself at the winger's close-range shot like he was taking a bullet to his vest. Robertson clenched his fists with arms outstretched. Gilmour skipped in celebration. Souttar patted the sub's chest. He had made a tangible contribution in his five minutes, but it was nearly so much longer.

At half-time all the subs go into the indoor warm-up area and use the bikes to keep their legs ticking over, but Tony had hurt himself in the first half so I had to go into the changing room to watch the tactical stuff on video because they were considering taking him off. I went out onto the pitch with the sports scientist to make sure I was ready to go and then basically spent the entire second half warming up because they'd told me to stay out. I was knackered by the time I came on! It was surreal, aye. I remember at one point the ball got played down their left and I was running back; Leão looked like he was about to cross so I gave Ronaldo a wee shove to push him into an offside position, then Leão turned back and I could feel Ronaldo staring at me out the corner of my eye. I felt like he was thinking, 'Why did you just touch me?' First game, up against one of the best players ever. After the game, I did get a buzz that I'd helped the lads. They'd put in a power of work throughout 90 minutes and it's because of the timing that people remember my block. If he was a little bit further out he might have chopped me, but with how the ball sat up for him, how close he was and the time of the match, he was always going to hit it. I just flung myself out in front of it and hoped it didn't hit my hand. I didn't realise until after the game how high my arms were in the air. I was thinking, 'Imagine I'd come on and given a penalty away.' I was marking Rúben Dias from the corner after I blocked it. I've never wanted someone to head clear a ball so much in my life!

Scotland held on and the fans showed their appreciation. The winless run continued but the losing streak had been stopped and no resented history was made. The concession of late goals against Finland, Hungary, Poland and Portugal had typified Scotland's year. Quelling one of Europe's strongest squads in tandem with one of the greatest goalscorers of all time was an itch that needed skin-breaking. Ronaldo's strop at the referee's decision not to allow Portugal to take a corner they won when the added time was already over was an unrequired cherry. This had been a good night for Scotland. A great night for Souttar and Hanley.

> The clean sheet against Portugal was a huge confidence boost for me. I was having a difficult time and not playing a lot of football with Norwich yet coming away with Scotland and playing. The manager [Johannes Hoff Thorup] didn't really fancy me when he came in. He started me on the first game of the season but took me off after an hour and I barely played again. He never gave me a reason but football is a game of opinions and that can happen. Giving away the penalty against Poland was another knock to my confidence while it was tough at Norwich, so the Portugal result was a big point in my career to keep me hangin' in there for a bit longer.

Win, lose or draw as a team, but Clarke gave the two of them a mention in his post-match presser as well as Gordon. 'It's the first time in a while I have celebrated a save.' Since Belgrade in November 2020, perhaps?

'Their goalkeeper was incredible,' said Roberto Martínez with a dose of PR. Portugal had three shots on target. This was a point gained by an organised Scotland team that played with desire and belief.

Croatia and Poland drew 3-3 elsewhere, and with Scotland off and jogging there was all to play for in the group.

Chapter 4

Croatia and Poland

I REMEMBER quivering while writing *A Nation Again: The Inside Story of Scotland's Journey to the European Championship*, over the prospect of putting some wellies on and getting knee-deep in the shit and structure of Scotland's first Nations League campaign.

What a folly. This international break for Croatia (home) and Poland (away) requires a hazmat to safely comb through.

With one victory (Gibraltar) in 16 matches, Scotland had gathered a point from their four League A games so far. Two remained, with significance in the direction of all eventualities. What mattered most to you? Seeing Scotland perform well again? Scotland just winning a game of football? Staying in League A of the Nations League? Leaping into Pot 2, or even Pot 1, for the World Cup qualifying draw the following month?

A four-part domino effect from the first bullet point would be ideal!

In 18 months, Scotland's FIFA ranking had plummeted from 30th to 51st and they sat at 25th in UEFA's rankings – e.g. the highest-ranked team in Pot 3. The tough friendly fixtures, not winning against sides like Georgia, Northern Ireland and Finland, the summer's smashed bottle and the autumn's fine margins were all biting us on the backside. *Well, well, well, if it isn't the consequences of our own actions!*

Portugal led on ten points, Croatia had seven, Poland had four and Scotland had one. We didn't need to win both games to avoid bottom, providing Poland lost to Portugal on matchday five. Some sights were set higher than that with the mathematic possibility we could match Croatia's points tally and skip past them into second place, and with it a Nations League quarter-final and a place in Pot 1 for the World Cup qualifying draw!

Remarkably that was just as, or more than, likely an outcome rather than finishing third in the group and progressing from Pot 3 to Pot 2 thanks to the deficient results of teams like Norway and Czech Republic.

Head-to-head was the first decider for sides tied on points. The ideal scenario was beat Croatia by two goals on the Friday night and forage a win by any means necessary in Warsaw on Monday. A win or draw for Croatia would take them out of our grasp and mean we'd only have third place to achieve with a win against Poland. It would almost certainly nullify our chances of sneaking into Pot 2 because we had to keep our end of the bargain and hope others faltered. Even if we won both our games, we weren't really in control of this outcome.

To be continued … but that'll do for now.

Lewis Ferguson, Aaron Hickey and Kieran Tierney's long-term injuries hadn't healed by early November, but KT and Fergie were close to a return. Angus Gunn had played his part earlier in the group but the injury that got in the way of his October inclusion was still an issue. A few important players were fit.

Clarke's squad read: Craig Gordon, Robby McCrorie, Ciaran Slicker; Nicky Devlin, Grant Hanley, Jack Hendry, Scott McKenna, Ryan Porteous, Anthony Ralston, Andy Robertson, John Souttar, Greg Taylor; Connor Barron, Ryan Christie, Ben Doak, Ryan Gauld, Billy Gilmour, John McGinn, Kenny McLean, Scott McTominay, Lewis Morgan; Ché Adams, Tommy Conway, Lyndon Dykes, Lawrence Shankland.

A gang of Scotland's vital players were thoroughly enjoying their domestic seasons; Christie had emerged as an energetic, box-to-box midfielder under Andoni Iraola at high-flying

Bournemouth; Robertson was part of a Liverpool team that was beginning to run away with the Premier League; McGinn had recovered from his slight hamstring injury and was captaining Aston Villa in the Champions League; Adams had settled well and was scoring for Torino; Gauld had just finished the MLS season on ten goals and 14 assists; and Doak was bringing fans to their feet on a weekly basis while on loan at Middlesbrough, where his team-mate Conway was scoring at a rate of one in two.

Most excitingly, McTominay had quickly become a fans' favourite for Serie A leaders Napoli. Three goals, including at San Siro against Inter, expedited his rise to prominence at the Maradona. It was exotic, romantic and fun. His travel companion Gilmour hadn't managed to secure a starting spot yet.

There were also players not flourishing at their clubs. Ralston's start for Celtic against Dundee just before the squad announcement was his first league appearance since the end of August; Hanley had played 17 minutes for Norwich since the opening weekend of the season; Hendry hadn't been registered to play domestically by Al-Ettifaq; Dykes was coming off the bench here and there for Birmingham City and Shankland had scored once in 18 games after netting 31 times during the previous term. He was struggling to shake a shit summer.

> Naisy and the staff at Hearts asked me if I was having a bit of a hangover after the Euros, but it was hard to put a finger on it. There was some disappointment. After two seasons in a row with 30-odd goals and being taken to the Euros, there was a lot of talk about transfers and big moves. I don't care what anybody says, you hear about it and it does play on your mind. I needed to get over it as quickly as I could. The club's struggles didn't help either. The recruitment wasn't good going into the season and in the end we just had to find ways to win. Dropping me a bit deeper was putting all hands

on deck to help the team. I took a fair bit of stick throughout the season and it would have been easy for me to leave Hearts behind, but I wanted to go back and show I hadn't fucked it off. When you run your contract down you give yourself the opportunity to see if there is anything out there, you never know with football. I've seen some players get moves and thought, 'How?!' It's a hard situation to be in.

McGinn's aforementioned return was a curious one. He hadn't produced his best stuff for Scotland for a little while and hadn't scored a goal from open play since we last won a game, although he did bury a penalty in the weird competitive-yet-not-really 3-3 draw with Norway a year ago. Clarke adores him. He's the media's best friend. He makes his team-mates laugh. His name is sung by supporters. His addition to the starting team would require a casualty from the impressive performance against Portugal.

With creative license, Clarke said he had been struggling to sleep while trying to solve the problem that's often portrayed as one managers would like to have. One tight call was loosened slightly when Adams was removed from the equation after limping off during Torino's game against Fiorentina the weekend before the boys were due to rendezvous. So ... Dykes, Shanks or Conway?

Sifting for a first Hampden victory since Georgia were soaked through the previous June, Clarke's team read: Gordon; Ralston, Hanley, Souttar, Robertson; Gilmour, McLean; Doak, McTominay, Christie; Conway.

If Adams was fit, the XI would have remained unchanged. Conway was the beneficiary and made his first start. Scottish strikers had scored two competitive goals in two years; Dykes in Norway, Shankland in Georgia. This was a huge opportunity for Tommy. McGinn on the bench was a surprise – he'd played four games for Villa since his recovery – but his international form couldn't command a start right now. Clarke later admitted he felt

Christie and Doak did too well in the spaces vacated by Croatia's wing-backs in Zagreb to justify dropping one of them.

Scotland like to start strongly at Hampden. They didn't. Croatia's pawns moved two spaces while the hosts preferred just the one. Andrej Kramarić woefully dragged a shot after being set up by McLean's brain fart and Luka Sučić blazed one when the target shouldn't have been missed. A few let-offs after five minutes, and another a couple later.

Gordon was the cover star for the evening's match programme, depicted as a superhero soaring through outer space with fists punching asteroids into further oblivion. He instead conjured the powers of Mrs Incredible to deny Kramarić, somehow stretching an elastic leg sufficiently to poke the striker's shot around the post with his studs before it could squeeze inside his near post. Fifteen minutes in and Scotland weren't sure where to look. The quiet support were doing so through spliced fingers. Then, a spark.

Gvardiol had been afforded a glimpse in Zagreb of Doak's ability and determination. A lesson learned, the winger was afforded far fewer inches in which to operate a month later. The young Scot had to adapt. Feeling Gvardiol's breath on his neck as Conway's pass reached him on the right, he flicked the ball through the hasty Croat's legs and scurried towards the box. McTominay met the cutback but saw his shot parried. Doak's illumination was enough to suggest there could be light at the end of this tunnel.

> I did okay against Gvardiol in Zagreb, gave him a bit of bother and went past him a few times. All it takes is getting by somebody once. They can tackle you as much as they want, but I just need to do well once. They need to do well for 90 minutes. He came into the game at Hampden more aggressively and in the first 15 minutes was giving me a torrid time, but all I had to do was that flick and then everything opened up for me cos he knew he couldn't get too close either. All it takes is that

one moment. That's why I could never be a defender, to be flawless for 90 minutes. We attackers can make mistakes because we're trying things to score goals.

One of those mistakes came at the start of a second-half counter. Gilmour's pass fed wee Doak, who had a simple square for Conway as they reached the edge of the box. He didn't properly catch his pass and Croatia numbed the buzz with an easy interception. Doak punched the floor. His Middlesbrough team-mate should have been celebrating his first international goal.

I'm usually quite good at washing off my mistakes. You'll see me get frustrated but they'll never stop me from trying again. My end product and decision-making have been the biggest things to learn. I know I've got the quality but it's about where and when.

By this point, Croatia were down to ten. Petar Sučić, one of the Dinamo Zagreb youngsters referenced in the previous chapter who would sign for Inter Milan at the end of the season, was sent off just before half-time for receiving two yellow cards. The first was fresh cashmere but putting his studs onto John Souttar's knee for the second was a more severe misjudgement. Modrić told the referee what he thought of it. Yellow for him as well. And another for one of the Croat assistants as the teams headed down the excessive tunnel.

Scotland had to seize this game now. The contextual difference between a 0-0 while being teased by Portugal's superstars and concluding the same result with a man advantage for 45 minutes in what was a relatively scrappy game at home to Croatia is important to note. The charge against Steve Clarke's 2024 iteration of Scotland was that they didn't take responsibility to actually go and win games of football. The Nations League campaign had started to build a body of circumstantial evidence in the manager and squad's favour, but they'd have to enter a guilty plea if they didn't improve in the second half after a scruffy first.

With the aim of helping Scotland progress more quickly from their own third into the middle one, Clarke brought on Scott McKenna for Hanley. The defence was now more balanced with a left-footer carrying the ball forward on that side. McGinn also warmed up to a slightly higher temperature than somebody expecting to sit on the bench for much longer normally would.

He was brought on with 25 minutes to play along with Gauld and Dykes. Onto a stage on which the orchestra was still being conducted by Luka Modrić, whose effortless ability to find space and repel advancing Scots with his soothsaying was magical. Although I wonder how often Gauld replays his nutmeg of the Croat legend.

The atmosphere had an edge borne from nerves. Doak was exhilarating at times but the hope of a home goal didn't appear to be a promise. Croatia wasted a few counters and created more openings than Scotland, whose lack of invention and cutting edge was painful. The cohesion was stilted, at best. The only option was to keep feeding Doak's hunger. A step-over, a drop of the shoulder, a burst of acceleration; he was like the Tasmanian Devil and was making the world's most expensive full-back in Joško Gvardiol look like a clown. It wasn't McTominay, Robertson or Gilmour who seized the scruff. It was the teenager. Any butterflies in his stomach had used all their energy when he sang Backstreet Boys' 'I Want It That Way' after a golf day at Turnberry for his pre-Euros initiation. He was revelling in his first Hampden start.

With four minutes remaining, he blurred past Manchester City's left-back and saw his powerful shot parried. John McGinn careered onto the rebound and stroked a deflected winner into the top corner. It was going in anyway. Thumb and index finger around his eyes, McGinn took off towards the north-west corner and a point towards Doak recognised the boy's impact before he punched the air. The vice-captain arrived at the corner flag and screamed into the carnage before him. He was now level on goals with Ally McCoist. Another Scotland match had been decided with a pivotal moment in the embers. The winless run was over.

In contrast to Euro 2020, Scotland approached the Croatia match with a different mentality after their competitiveness in the first four games of the Nations League. Dykes explains:

> They outplayed us at Hampden the last time. There was an underdog look at it during the Euros, but this was the third time we'd played them in total. We had a few new faces and freshened it up. It's actually a release to get to an international camp with the boys. We were desperate to get a win under our belt and kick on and we used our experience together with that mentality to get the win. We got Doak in the team and he's a much more direct winger than a wing-back, so that gave us an outlet with a bit of youth and speed. He fitted in straight away with the squad and his different qualities have helped us.

Christie was determined for that kind of night:

> That win had been coming. It was something we could take so much positivity from and it flips the script on the group after it had been going the other way. We wanted a deserving result to lift spirits and get Hampden onside and it felt like that.

Beating a team – well, ten of 11 – who'd been to semi-finals at the last two World Cups? The performance was still a bit concerning as far as quality, not determination, goes. Maybe Scotland enjoyed some luck that had deserted them earlier in the group.

'My first thoughts are we can play better,' said Clarke. 'Better with the ball and more clinical when we get to the final third of the pitch.'

With some rare candour, he offered he still felt 'uptight' and that pressure hadn't been released. 'You're always waiting on that low blow that's affected us a few times recently.'

After regular talk of protecting Ben Doak, who didn't quite grasp he was receiving a standing ovation on his way to the dugout after being subbed, Clarke also admitted his performance reassured him the teen was 'good for now', not a year down the line. What catharsis for the support!

A deep cleanse helped McGinn as well, who had settled a personal score with his demon after his costly miss against the Croatians at Euro 2020, when he missed the ball at the back post to put Scotland 2-1 up. 'I've personally gone back to that about 70 times,' he'd said in the summer. 'I should have went with my head.'

And on to Warsaw.

After picking up their first competitive win in 14 months, Scotland could somehow hijack a place in Pot 1 for the World Cup draw in a few weeks, never mind just give themselves a chance of staying in League A. Securing that survival could lead to a play-off in March against a League B runner-up, while second would bring a place in the Nations League quarter-finals, but few people seemed genuinely arsed with that. The prospect of boosting our World Cup qualification chances as a top dog took precedence.

This was the required constellation in the Polish skies:

- Scotland must beat Poland.
- Croatia must lose to Portugal.
- Scotland must win by two goals OR Croatia must lose by two goals.
- Scotland score three more goals than Croatia – e.g. Poland 2-3 Scotland and Croatia 0-1 Portugal.

Incredibly, a 2-1 win for Scotland and a 1-0 win for Portugal would give us and the Croats an identical record across six games, and second place in the group would be decided on the *ninth* tiebreaker rule: away wins. A defeat or draw would confine Scotland to relegation. The permutations for that were succinct. A draw would only be enough to sneak into Pot 2 for the qualifying draw if one of Czech Republic, Norway, Slovakia or Romania stumbled against much weaker opposition in their final games.

For League A survival and a commended position in Pot 2 for the World Cup qualifiers, Scotland had to win combined with one of the developments out of our hands.

I commentated on this game for Viaplay's YouTube channel – remotely done from their Stockholm HQ – and the wall behind the monitor was surrounded with A4 pieces of paper and arrows explaining current states of play and each domino effect. It was kind of like an FBI office without the mugshots.

In Zagreb and Lisbon, kick-off was preceded by foot soldiers drinking and dining al-fresco on cobbled streets and squares; fluttering saltires are the regular Bat-Signal from 100 yards or more that your like was here. In the Polish capital, with temperatures around 5°C, the streets were quiescent. Opening a door to one of the many honeypots found by the bees released a welcoming din within. The scattered taverns and vodka bars were packed with Scots, some of whom enjoyed Poland's relaxed smoking laws.

The Nations League had probably done its job at a base level after the Euros. Do Steve Clarke's Scotland believe they can, and will they prove they can, compete with teams they are striving to cause problems for at major tournaments?

Yes.

Relegation to League B wouldn't be an embarrassing episode; floating between the top two divisions is Scotland's level. That circumstance wouldn't be met with anything other than a shrug of the shoulders and more pints, provided it wasn't a pollutant after a doing from the Poles. That condition would blow the balloon towards the drawing pin.

Play well, compete, maybe win and at full time we'll cross whatever bridge it is. The general understanding needed a campaign or three, but the *glorified friendlies* movement had settled. We might not have obsessed over it the way that actual qualification campaigns dictate our limbic systems, but most fans understood the assignment and ramifications of our Nations League matches.

And so did the players?

> The Nations League … I have my annoyances. I'll never complain about playing international football, but even still I'm at a point where it confuses me with all the outcomes for pots. It's worked in our favour in the past but then you get promoted into League A, which is supposed to be a good thing but everything around it felt like the opposite. There was less to be achieved or won and it was a tough period to get through.

Ryan Christie is candid. Qualifiers are much simpler to follow. I asked him if he knew what the eventual outcome of the Poland game would mean for the squad.

> I don't know if we needed more of an explanation, but as players we often don't know what's fully at stake. We knew we were trying to stay in League A, we're not going to set our stall out as 'let's win the Nations League'. For overall standings and pots I think it would help us out to understand more. But hey, it's more games for Scotland, so that's a good thing.

The Polish press had Michał Probierz's peg hanging by a thread. They'd conceded three goals in each of their last three games and not kept a clean sheet in ten. Portugal had already won the group after walloping his side 5-1 in Porto and gave key players Ronaldo, Dias, Fernandes and Silva some time to chill out. They fielded a bit of a second string in spirit, not in name, and should still make Croatia work for any points. Poland would have to field some replacements against us but not because Probierz was feeling generous; Bobby Lewandowski, Jan Bednarek, Sebastian Szymański and Bartosz Bereszyński were all injured. They'd been in League A of the Nations League since it started in 2018.

Some of the narrative in the build-up to this international break revolved around Ryan Christie getting the chance to play in the same position in which he was impressing for Bournemouth, but McLean and Gilmour had the deeper midfield positions locked down for now. In the end, McGinn replaced him. Scotland needed at least one goal and McGinn's nose was on the trail again after his dry spell.

With the temperature descending towards freezing by the back of 8pm, fans felt the wind take a blade to their skin as it whipped across the Vistula River outside the stadium's west bank; the exposed stairwells offered little protection as the Tartan Army ventured far beyond Row Z again.

Back in March, Scotland showed they could travel to a tough venue and control a game of football. 'Scotland should have won 4-0,' said Rafael van der Vaart after watching his country win in the Amsterdam Arena by that score. 'It was unbelievable that Scotland didn't score,' said Dutch boss Ronald Koeman. 'We can't keep doing this,' said Andy Robertson.

Well, boys, you've taken Portugal and Croatia until the final minutes. Go one step further in Warsaw.

Clarke's XI read: Gordon; Ralston, Souttar, Hanley, Robertson; Gilmour, McLean; Doak, McTominay, McGinn; Dykes.

Scotland had struggled for months with corroding sides happy to snigger at the onus weighing them down. How about it then when Doak locked eyes with Gilmour, who took four Poles out the game with one through ball. The winger resisted the urge to make a beeline for the byline and rolled it to the arriving McGinn, who passed the ball into the left corner from 16 yards with his weaker right. The mud from the trail was all over his nose now. Cue a captivating game of football.

End to end; Karol Świderski enticed celebrations before half of the crowd realised he'd hit the side netting in a one-on-one,

Gilmour struck the bar from around 30 yards out, Adam Buksa should have found the net but Gordon extended that leg again to quell, McTominay had his own one-on-one saved and then drilled a shot off the post from the edge of the box. It was enthralling. Scotland carried the promised swagger that was absent at the Euros. At the breaks, we led and Croatia were down 1-0. As it stood, Scotland needed one more goal to finish second and be a Pot 1 side for the World Cup qualifying draw.

John Souttar magnificently prevented an equaliser at the start of the second half by sliding in the way of the ball after Jakub Kamiński beat Gordon. The type of intervention associated with match-winning in stoppage time. The chances of this game finishing 1-0 were slimmer than the side of a fiver.

True enough, Poland equalised on the hour. No keeper on God's green earth was stopping Kamil Piątkowski's wonder strike from the 18's apex. Still rising as it flew into the stanch, it packed enough power to wipe out life on said planet. Scotland fans defended their eardrums as one of the loudest home roars they'd ever heard rebounded under the Stadion Narodowy's closed roof.

The doors slid when Dykes had a header well saved at the same time Joško Gvardiol – who'd been dealing with the paltry talent of Rafael Leão in contrast to Ben Doak – equalised for Croatia. Scotland had to score again and hope Portugal scored two, or vice versa. Late goals or incidents had settled four of the five games in the Nations League so far. Be it in the Balkans or not, this felt like it was going to the wire as well.

Although consequences for Scotland weren't as severe, this was a must-win game of football and they had approached it in a divergent manner to the summer's equivalent against Hungary. The team illustrated self-belief and intelligence. A caveat was that Poland attacked Scotland and *a fortiori* we had more room in which to navigate and exploit, in comparison to Hungary hunkering down for the evening in Stuttgart.

As stoppage time approached, evidence was crystal that Scotland wouldn't be gatecrashing Pot 1, but one more goal would turn the campaign into a six-game success. Like a pensioner who'd wandered out his nursing home, John Souttar caressed a De Bruyneish cross as the minutes became seconds and Andy Robertson – on his 80th cap – headed in a thing of beauty at the back stick to give Scotland the win. His first goal since his screamer in Clarke's bow against Cyprus.

Because of the way the ball struck the post, bounced off the back of the net and ended up in Nicky Devlin's arms, many in the distant away end initially thought it was the right-back who had scored a sensational winner on his second cap. Even the match director was confused, managing to orchestrate shots of Devlin, the coaching staff's celebratory huddle and the delighted travelling support but none of Robertson as he ripped over the turf towards the bench, knocking the wind out of Doak as he arrived. McLean sprinted to join the scrum.

> That was a hell of a moment. We had Poland pinned back at times and put them on the back foot, so I think we deserved that. I've not seen Soapy cross a ball like that for a long time! I was just inside him after passing it to him; I wasn't expecting him to cross it. When a centre-back is crossing the ball from 35 yards in injury time it shows the intent we had to win. I was buzzing for Robbo because he's been an incredible captain for us over the years. Think he just about did half a lap of the pitch afterwards.

Dykes was among the melee:

> When you see us celebrating a moment like that as a group, you see how happy and together we are. We'd been playing well but not getting results, so two clean sheets against Portugal and Croatia showed we were going in

the right direction and helped build momentum. We put blood, sweat and tears into games and sometimes it doesn't work, but for an important goal to stay in the top group, you could see the joy for everyone.

Souttar saw five centre-backs go to the Euros while he watched on TV. He'd now started four games in a row with his goal-line block and last-minute cross vital to the night's outcome.

> That was a mental game. I remember it being really enjoyable to play in, Poland were a good side. It felt end-to-end and I remember them scoring an unbelievable goal. The last-minute goal showed our togetherness, that's what we're all about. Me being forward like that in the last minute doesn't happen very often for Scotland. The bench were shouting at us to keep on going and it was a great header from Robbo. The pitch wasn't actually great that night, but it was a great atmosphere in a really cool stadium.

The head coach glistened as he congratulated his players on the pitch at full time, but his brow had furrowed by the time he sat in front of the press. Put the footage on mute and you'd be forgiven for assuming Scotland had suffered another disappointment. 'The more you play at this level, the more you learn how to win the games and we've proven that,' he said, traditionally starving the press of access to his happiness.

Clarke's reluctance to repent after the summer had sharpened pitchforks. After six encouraging performances against serious operators, they were blunted. Not that he was intimidated in any case. 'Evolution not revolution,' he'd said at the end of August. Actions speak louder than words – certainly louder than Steve Clarke's – and with a change of shape and the emergence of a whippet co-existing with a will to win, there was demonstrable improvement over a couple of months. Like the response after summer 2021 and the play-off against Ukraine the following year, Steve Clarke and Scotland had shoved adversity to the side.

A few issues had their full beam on; a dependency on Doak for incision was one that could be leaned on as a solution to a problem, but a reliance on a keeper in his 40s and picking a striker from a not-so-vast array who don't score many goals were complications requiring resolutions within a year. What do Sweden, Norway, Slovenia, Denmark, Czech Republic, Poland, Greece, Ukraine and Serbia all have in common? *That* thing that we don't.

Ours bring differing qualities to the fore that are valued in certain circumstances. In my opinion, Scotland have performed most impressively under Clarke with Dykes up front, yet Shankland is the best finisher available to us. On 18 caps at the start of 2026, he was on the same number that Kris Boyd finished with. Leigh Griffiths achieved 22. I make that 58 appearances between the three most lethal finishers available to Scotland in the last 20 years. Shankland, who came on for Dykes in Poland with 25 to play, is comfortable with his place in the squad.

> Lyndon, Ché and I are all different. Lyndon is good in the air, can flick it on and likes the ball played up to him with players around him and I back him all day to win them. Ché is more athletic, has a stronger build, likes to take it into feet and run the channels, whereas I prefer to link-up and play between the lines. Maybe in terms of what we do as a whole that doesn't suit the team so I can see why the manager leaves his options open. It's a good problem to have, but as long as I'm among it I'll be happy.

Scotland had kept their end of the bargain but other required results the next day didn't fall in their favour and they were confirmed as a Pot 3 side for the World Cup qualifying draw. A draw that would have been approached a few months ago with trembles and trepidation could be giddily and curiously anticipated. Key players – for the squad if not the XI – would be back by its beginning if not for the Nations League relegation play-off in March; KT, Fergie, Hickey, Patto and Gunn.

Supporters threw their Monzo cards around the taverns in the warm afterglow of a late Scotland winner, the moments of which are as priceless as the pints in the Polish capital. Three unbeaten against Portugal, Croatia and Poland, with two clean sheets and two late winners as part of the fun and games. Optimism couldn't be confused with denial.

Chapter 5
World Cup Draw

STRUCTURES AND logistics are constantly changing as FIFA, UEFA and their global equivalents continue to mangle the footballing calendar at their whim. However, one thing remains certain … everyone loves a group stage draw!

The modern norm for qualification campaigns we were accustomed to saw groups of six with a few breaks in autumn, one in spring, one at the end of the season and then a few more for the business end in that autumn. Players suffering injuries – even serious ones such as ACL ruptures or leg breaks – would get the chance to contribute to the lengthy process in which fitness and club form heavily impacted selection. It's a marathon, not a sprint!

You can flip that cliché now. The development of the Nations League and its concurrence with the major tournament qualifiers narrowed the windows. Six games over ten weeks would potentially decide Scotland's automatic qualification for USA, Canada and Mexico, their reliance on a play-off or their seventh consecutive desolation. Either that, or eight games with knackered players enduring the first couple in June.

The longer process was conducive to constructing tension. If Scotland lost a game after the clocks had gone back, they had to wait for almost five months to right a wrong. Who would hit a stride and command a place the next time the squad gathered? After England beat us 3-0 at Wembley in November 2016, I distinctly remember my impatience for Slovenia at home and the introduction of Stuart Armstrong to the team. Martin's winner that night, oh yes! Only 20,000 were at Hampden.

Although Scotland ended the Nations League with a refreshing change of tune, those three results weren't enough to break the fall from the chronic year-long tumble before them. The repercussion of three wins in 17 games was a place in Pot 3 for the World Cup qualifying draw. No play-off parachute could be deployed if Scotland were to finish where their seeding suggested they should; only the winners of each Nations League group would have that in their back pocket.

Participating in League A directly before a World Cup qualifying group carries no strategic benefit for Scotland besides exposure to playing the strongest teams on the continent. This is because Nations League group *winners* secure the back-door play-off spots for the tournament, should they not finish first or second in their group.

Participating in League A directly before a Euros qualifying group benefits Scotland because the play-off places drift down the leagues in a ranking form. The majority of League A nations will qualify for the tournament anyway by finishing first or second in their group, so any that failed in that regard have a play-off by the virtue of their participation in League A. It's all a way for UEFA to ensure there are as few skid marks as possible at their showpiece.

I'll try and keep the minutia to a minimum. There was a strong chance Scotland wouldn't know their Pot 1 opponent until the tax year-end. The Nations League quarter-finals were arranged for March and the four winners of those ties were guaranteed to be drawn into groups of four not five, because they'd be playing in the Nations League finals at the end of the season and so couldn't start their campaign until September. They would be drawn from Pot 1 as 'loser of play-off X' or 'winner of play-off Y'. It is realistic to suggest a team could be willing to sack-off their Nations League quarter-final if they knew losing would result in an easier World Cup qualifying group.

Teams participating in the Nations League promotion/relegation play-offs – like Scotland – *could* be drawn in a five-team group to begin in June, but the chances were very low. If we were to be drawn into such a group, it would contain only England or Switzerland as the top seed because of the permutations above. If either of them were drawn into a four-team group, we would be as well.

The draw was arranged for 13 December. Three weeks previously we discovered who we'd be playing in the two-legged Nations League play-off in March; visiting one of the runners-up in League B – Turkey, Ukraine, Greece or Austria – before they returned the favour a few days later.

Ukraine were probably the preferable draw despite our play-off heartbreak against them in 2022; they only won twice in their Nations League group and didn't get out of their group in Germany. Austria reached the last 16 of the Euros – beating the Netherlands in their group – and were performing well under Ralf Rangnick. They pumped Norway 5-1 in the Nations League. Turkey have an aura and were an own goal away from taking the Netherlands to extra time in their Euros quarter-final, but they were second to Wales in their Nations League group.

We hadn't played Greece since the Euro '96 qualifiers. They lost on penalties to Georgia in their Euro 2024 play-off final (I urge you to seek the footage on YouTube for vociferous scenes) but found a groove in their Nations League campaign, only finishing second to England on goal difference, whom they beat at Wembley. You probably couldn't slot a Rizla between the sides, all considered. They'd all provide a tough game, as Clarke would be sure to remind us.

Greece, it was. Fresh opponents to observe and a new city to experience.

To the World Cup qualifiers then. Qualifiers for a World Cup with 48 teams!

That was 16 more teams in total – a mental dilution infringing on participation medal territory – but only three more spaces to be grasped by UEFA nations. A rise from 13 to 16, so a third of the teams at the tournament would be European. Each of the 12 group winners would qualify automatically, and the runners-up would enter the play-offs.

With the quality among the Pot 1 lot and our place as a Pot 3 side, the working assumption was Scotland would probably be in competition for second place in the group. A best-case scenario was probably Switzerland, Austria or Denmark (1), Slovakia, Romania or Wales (2) and Latvia (4). A worse-case one looked like France, Spain, England or Germany (1), Turkey, Greece or Norway (2) and probably Kosovo (4). Something in between felt like Croatia, Belgium or Italy (1), Czech Republic or Sweden (2) and take your pick from the fourth pot – let's say Belarus.

It's quite easy – and very Scottish – to be the raincloud spotter ahead of a draw and fear the threat of the challengers, but I say this with confidence having spoken to journalists and commentators from the countries who subsequently drew us; we were the Pot 3 team others wanted to avoid.

Among nations like Republic of Ireland, Georgia, Finland, Albania and North Macedonia, opposing fans looked at our section and thought, 'Please not *Scotland*.'

Our fate was in the hands of big, sexy Fernando Llorente, whom I've always resented for demonstrably mopping his brow in relief after he scored Spain's third goal in a Euro 2012 qualifier at Hampden after we had come from 2-0 to equalise. Wanker.

'Scot-LAND,' he proclaimed after unfurling the FIFA-branded paper. Group C.

The loser of the Nations League quarter-final between Denmark and Portugal would be our top opponent; generous.

Greece were the new Israel. They were our Pot 2 opponents and four of our eight competitive fixtures in 2025 would be against them. Tough draw.

Belarus completed the quartet. Six games over ten weeks. All in all, it could have been better or worse. If Portugal dealt with the Danes, Scotland could approach this group with a realistic aim of automatic qualification. If Denmark pulled off a shock, it could be a photo finish for the play-off between us and the Greeks.

Ryan Christie didn't watch the draw – they rarely do – but recalls his initial thoughts:

> I remember thinking we had a good chance, that it could have been worse. With the games being compact we could hit the ground running and put ourselves in a positive situation. I remember the groups being longer and tension building towards the final games if you're in with a shout. I think there's an argument for both sides for what's better. This format means we could batter it out and stay on a rhythm to see ourselves through to qualify, but previously from one summer through to March or the next season the country might be in a bit of transition. So three points you get the previous year could be just as important but you might not get picked to go to the tournament. The gap between the November and March breaks is so long. I love being able to see the boys each month at the start of the season; they're all my mates so I don't mind the shorter window at all.

The fixtures fell charitably as well. Away to the top seed then Belarus in September. Greece and Belarus at Hampden in October. Athens for the penultimate one and the top seed at Hampden to finish. Nine points from the first four games would surely put Scotland's destiny in their own hands, for a play-off spot at least.

Say your *orações* for the Portuguese. While we played our future qualifying opponents in March's Nations League play-off, we'd be almost as concerned with the outcome of their quarter-final with Denmark. That would probably dictate if we admired the sunrise or were pre-occupied by the storm warning.

Chapter 6

Nations League Play-Off First Leg

A DEFEAT and relegation to League B probably mattered less than the fashion in which that hypothetical scenario happened. A narrow loss after a couple of competitive or competent performances with portrayals of attacking capability as well as defensive solidity against a formidable Greek side wouldn't spray much herbicide on Scotland's green shoots. A hammering would land Scotland on a snake sliding more than just a couple of squares back.

As briefly referenced in the previous chapter, staying in League A would be beneficial not for prestige but essentially guaranteeing a play-off spot for Euro 2028. Anyway, that's for another book; what really mattered in March was avoiding a complete disruption of the momentum built by performances and results in the Nations League.

It was headway Clarke and the players had done well to generate. Scotland weren't the juggernaut they became at the start of 2023, but the autumn's propulsion left sufficient wind with which to sail to Piraeus. And the BBC had agreed a deal to show the games until summer 2026! Football for everyone! Things were pretty good.

The Scottish media beast is rarely fed by Steve Clarke. There are few headlines on his watch, so he must have woken up on the right side of bed on 11 March, willingly giving the hounds a sniff.

'I'll go on percentage – 75 per cent,' he responded to a probe on how sure he was that he wouldn't be Scotland manager beyond 2026. He'd already said after the Euros that he'd run his contract down, but these were the first words close to confirmation that he wouldn't be fussed about an extension. The remaining 25 per cent seemed to rest on if he could tick two blank boxes: qualify for the World Cup and do well at the World Cup. 'Maybe somebody will persuade me to stay,' he said in relation to that hypothesis. 'But at this moment in time, I'm happy to run my contract down.'

The admission wasn't enough to unsettle the squad members. They revere their boss but had the stresses of club football and a tournament to qualify for. A likely farewell with Clarke at the end of that year or the following summer wasn't going to keep them awake at night.

I doubt it was weighing on Clarke's mind either. He'd negotiated two contract extensions – I'm sure with handsome pay rises – in the near-enough six years he'd been in the job. If he didn't get to the tournament, his concern might be the offering of a new contract rather than the rejecting of one.

A more pressing complication was the impending absence of the boy wonder. Ben Doak's thigh injury required surgery. It was unclear if he'd play again that season. He didn't. After his impact in the Nations League, this void couldn't be overstated. To a lesser degree of importance, Lewis Morgan and James Forrest were also injured.

Dykes was also out with a long-term issue. The striker suffered a partial tear of his Achilles, which badly affected his soleus muscle, located between the heel and calf. He also wouldn't play again that season. While on holiday before pre-season, the striker used the Las Vegas Raiders' training centre for a final push with his rehab thanks to their owners also being in command at Dykes's club, Birmingham City. Not injured but not selected was Lawrence Shankland. He'd struggled for scoring form at Hearts all season. Angus Gunn had hurt his hamstring jumping over an advertising hoarding. Poor Hickey was still months from playing because of his injury, while a fit Nathan Patterson seemed to be equidistant at Everton with his manager David Moyes demanding he 'step up' if he had ambitions to play.

Clarke's squad read:

> Craig Gordon, Liam Kelly, Cieran Slicker; Grant Hanley, Jack Hendry, Max Johnston, Scott McKenna, Ryan Porteous, Anthony Ralston, Andy Robertson, John Souttar, Kieran Tierney; Ryan Christie, Lewis Ferguson, Billy Gilmour, John McGinn, Scott McTominay, Lennon Miller; Ché Adams, Tommy Conway, Kevin Nisbet, James Wilson.

Tierney and Ferguson were finally fit while mightily impressive Motherwell midfielder Lennon Miller and Hearts attacker James Wilson earned their first call-ups at 18 years old. The latter had shown promise in flashes throughout the season including a last-minute equaliser in the Edinburgh derby, but his inclusion was time sensitive because of his eligibility for both Irelands. Clarke referenced his speed, which might be necessary given nobody else in the squad possessed that attribute. He was still a pupil at Balerno High School, where his street cred could barely have been higher.

Miller's international integration was a foregone conclusion. His dad, Lee, was capped thrice in the late 2000s, but Miller Jr – who had already captained his club on several occasions – is expected to cruise into the Roll of Honour by his mid-20s. Operating with grace, versatility and maturity, he is a delight to watch in possession.

> I never thought at all about being in the Scotland squad that season. I was getting my pictures taken with a flag before training for an under-21s call-up and during my warm-up somebody came up to me and said, 'Well

done.' I said thanks, presuming they were talking about the 21s, then someone else said it, and someone else, and I was thinking, 'This is strange, these people don't normally congratulate me.' I ran over to our physio and asked him to show me the first-team squad list and I was in complete shock when I saw my name. It was completely out the blue and a brilliant feeling. I was car sharing with Stephen O'Donnell at the time, so I had loads of questions for him about his memories and training and all that and he told me they were a brilliant group of boys. I was quite nervous to meet everyone, I'm not really the loudest guy and would be around people playing in the Premier League every week.

Lewis Ferguson was 25 years old. Any inference of him being part of the *next generation* had to be binned. He was named Midfielder of the Season shortly after he tore his ACL against Monza in April 2024, which cruelly whipped his seat on the plane from under his backside. He tried to play on for five minutes before accepting his knee was *wobbly* and *unstable*. It was a frustrating absence, but he only had 12 caps and wasn't a starter for Scotland at that point – certainly not in his preferred position. Often deployed on the left, he had played five consecutive international games (two starts) before his cruciate ligament rupture but probably wouldn't have started the matches at the Euros. Now back in the Bologna team since mid-December, a player performing to a level as consistently as him had to be living in the international stage's present, not waiting for the day after tomorrow. Box-to-box, prepared to seize a shovel and with an eye for goal, he was keen to make his mark:

I was always in squads by that point but not playing as much as I wanted to. It was all about patience for me; biding my time and continuing to work hard and show the manager what I could do. I was getting some more minutes and that was the best season I'd had at club level, so it was a tough one to take because the Euros had been in the back of my mind since we qualified in November. I felt really good, was playing great football and the timing couldn't have been worse. It was really hard after thinking there was a good chance I would play, so it gave me that extra motivation for 2025.

There was a crackling fire causing the smoke about a new addition to the striking department. Steve Clarke had been seen watching Ipswich Town striker George Hirst, and two goals – one of them in front of Clarke's eternally unimpressed gaze – in the weeks leading up to the play-off convinced the head coach he was worth a look at Lesser Hampden. Given the decade-long dearth of a goalscoring striker to rely on, supporters could be absolved for camping outside Hampden waiting on wisps of white smoke confirming Clarke, Carver and co had anointed a would-be marksman. For now, the charcoal truth of Hirst's call-up was confirmed after the squad had gathered because of a delay in some paperwork. He'd have a chance to make the striking position his own but that was definitely a matter of if rather than when. 'He brings us a different dimension,' said John Carver, who also referenced a similarity to Dykes, whose injury accelerated the necessity for the 26-year-old's presence in the camp. Son of former England international David and eligible for us through his grandfather, he had four goals that season, two in the Premier League, and was getting ten minutes here and 15 minutes there.

You might remember earlier in the book I skirted around the notion that Scots suffer from an inferiority complex and ambition – or at least public displays of it – results in scorn or castigation. Mind you, it wasn't really the wider fanbase that made a big deal out of what young Lennon Miller said when asked about the confidence in his ability to slot in at international level …

'I'm confident in my own ability. There's loads of unreal midfielders in there and I'm just going to try and learn as much as I can from them. I'm obviously not going to go in and be the best player there, but I believe that I could, maybe, in a couple of months be the best player there. I think that's how you need to think as a football player – you need to want to be the best.'

The headline read: 'I could be Scotland's best within months'.

They'll talk you up, Lennon, and tear you down at the first opportunity. He was about to win the Scottish Football Writers' Young Player of the Year. Is it any wonder players often shrivel under these spotlights and clubs feel compelled to rehearse stock answers with players before they joust?

> It wasn't ideal. I was going into my first camp, some of the senior players could read a headline and think, 'Who does this boy think he is?' That's the total opposite of what I am like as a person. It got taken the wrong way … I got called up for my country, said the wrong word and everyone was all over it. It was a long question and I'd given it quite a short answer, so I felt a bit of pressure and just added a few extra words to it. Saying 'a few months' might have been a bit ridiculous, but I do want to be the best player. I'm ambitious and will keep being that. I don't want any limits as to what I can do and what we can do as a country.

Carver strangely concluded that Miller needed 'guidance' and has 'got to learn' before ambiguously adding 'there's nothing wrong with being confident' and 'the headline might have been taken out of context'. Make your mind up, John!

McGinn took a humorous approach when he was asked to opine on Miller's 'audacity', drawing on an experience he had during his maiden call-up while a Hibs player. Charlie Adam – then of Premier League Stoke City – questioned why a player from the Scottish Championship was being called up, leading to experienced members of the squad affectionately testing McGinn's resolve by asking him why he was in the squad. McGinn went to bed that night after being turned inside-out on the training pitch by Shaun Maloney and doubted his credentials.

'As the sessions go on, as you get more experience, you get more comfortable and you start to express yourself more,' McGinn reminisced. Referring to Miller and Wilson, he added: 'They are not here to make up the numbers. They are here to take our places if they, eventually, are better than the ones who are here. He definitely has the ability to do so and so does James.'

Thankfully Clarke had the teenager's back: 'I've been told to put Lennon in the squad for 12 months. As soon as we put him in there's a little bit of negativity. I think it's wrong that he's criticised for wanting to improve. What's wrong with wanting to be the best? I'm amazed there have been two or three days' headlines about it because, for me, it's not a headline story.'

I resent – and perhaps contradict – myself for including a few hundred words on this pathetic tale, but it illuminates a particularly embarrassing facet of our landscape and aligns with the national psyche, which – I believe – holds the country back on-and-off pitches, fields and courts.

Tradition is important, right? The last dance at a wedding is 'Loch Lomond'; New Year's Day means it's steak pie on the dinner table; the winner of the Masters hosts a dinner with all the previous winners a few days before the following year's edition and chooses the menu himself (cool as fuck); signing for a new club or being brought along on international duty for the first time means you'll sing a song in front of your new team-mates. Steven Naismith managed to evade detection at each club he played for until he was prepared to pay a 'serious' fine at Norwich to abstain. Jordan Henderson abruptly left a Liverpool team dinner and night out to avoid the responsibility and happily paid into a kitty as well.

I was chuckling listening to Miller's recollection of his performance, particularly imagining Wilson's panic:

Personally I think it should be banned from football! I remember it clearly. We were having dinner at the Blythswood then I started hearing the cutlery off the glasses. George went up first with loads of confidence and was brilliant. James went up next and couldn't get the lyrics up on his phone, so he had to borrow one of the other boy's phones to sort that, then I sang 'The A Team' by Ed Sheeran. I was nervous as anything and was just relieved once I'd finished it and knew I'd never need to do it again. One of the worst things in football but unfortunately it has to be done!

'That was alright, maybe in a few weeks you'll be the best,' teased McGinn as Miller walked back to his seat.

The Greeks had a few teenagers who'd earned their first call-ups as well. In contrast, 18-year-old Christos Mouzakitis of Olympiakos and Genk's 17-year-old Konstantinos Karetsas were paraded as the 'future of Greek soccer'. Karetsas (more on him later) was born and raised in Belgium but committed to the country of his parents' birth. The owners of a local wine bar enthused about his emergence to our foot soldiers. If he'd quoted similar to Miller at a press conference, I have a feeling (based on lived experience in the industry) he would have been championed and celebrated by our media.

The Greeks were up for it. The Euro 2004 champions were 20 years beyond their finest hour but a new generation, boasting far greater promise than the one that chimed in Portugal, were on the precipice. The match in the Athenian suburb of Piraeus, taking place at Olympiakos' Georgios Karaiskakis Stadium, had seen unprecedented demand for tickets. The Hellenic Football Federation had taken the decision to move games from the 70,000 capacity Olympic Stadium to one nearly half the size purely on the basis that the atmosphere would be more intimidating for opponents. Progress before profit.

Scotland fans expecting some spring warmth were disappointed in that regard. It was quite cold. It was raining. The scrupulous security measures outside the ground meant many fans' entry was delayed with only two guards on shift to check our lot's passports. Probably still quicker than trying to get into Hampden's west stand before kick-off after 7.15pm on a match night.

Tierney's return posed an interesting conundrum. He'd made 11 appearances for Arsenal (two starts) in almost three months since recovering from the torn hamstring suffered against Switzerland. Could a fit player of his quality be left on a bench? Scotland's revival coincided with a change of shape to the 4-2-3-1 shape from the 3-4-2-1 and, crucially, the availability and form of Doak. One is a left-back, the other is a right-winger, yet they probably couldn't exist on the same field.

With Robertson as captain, Tierney would only start as an LCB as part of the formation that served Scotland well at the start of the 2020s. Doak is a winger and would hardly be selected as a wing-back in that system or ahead of McTominay, McGinn, Christie or even Ferguson behind the striker. He could probably only thrive in the now trusted 4-2-3-1 shape, in which there was little room for Tierney unless Clarke wanted to drop a bomb by playing him at right-back or on the left of a centre-back pairing. With Doak out, would Clarke revert? Who knew. What we did know by then was that Clarke's mind was a tough one to read.

'The team has been good with a back four,' he said. 'We changed the whole way we approached the Nations League. We went with four, it worked. It worked well because we also had a little outlet on the right with the pace of Ben Doak and we didn't have the option of putting Kieran into the team. It's given me a lot to think about.'

Clarke kept the shape. His XI read: Gordon; Ralston, Souttar, Hanley, Robertson; Gilmour, McLean; McGinn, McTominay, Ferguson; Adams.

Christie was suspended and Fergie was in for his first competitive start; a predictable selection on this occasion and the result of UEFA's ridiculous ruling that two yellow cards received over six Nations League games should carry the same suspension as receiving two in the same game. The experience Ralston had procured over the last year meant he kept his place over Sturm Graz's Max Johnston despite playing only twice since Hogmanay. Likewise for Hanley who had signed for Birmingham City in January but couldn't buy more than five minutes as a sub. One minute against Stevenage, two against Lincoln City, one against Reading, one against Bradford and five against Charlton were how he'd kept his match-ready legs warm. He'd played 114 minutes of league football that season in comparison to 500 for Scotland. Scott McKenna was playing 90 minutes in La Liga every week for Las Palmas and was part of the team that beat Barcelona and held Real Madrid.

> My international credentials come into my thinking whenever I move club. I'm not daft, I know I've not exactly got another decade in me, so I'm trying to stay in there for as long as I can. It doesn't always work. I'm probably defending myself more than anything here but experience has a lot to count for. Robertson is a good example this year at Liverpool; he's played almost every game for Scotland since Steve Clarke came in and there are no doubts about whether he'll play or not. There's a lot to be said for caps and experience in big games, plus everyone is really professional these days. It's not like lads who aren't playing are in the pub and eating burgers every day. The lads look after themselves and are ready. I'm grateful to the manager for showing that trust in me.

The sun hadn't been out over the Greek capital but Hanley basked in this particular Piraeus heat. Scotland have picked up a few narrow victories around Europe in my lifetime but I don't think they've had to defend their box as diligently to protect a lead since McFadden scored in Paris in 2007. Craig Gordon was relatively quiet on his 80th cap; it was the lads in front of him who stopped the ball reaching him too often.

Scotland started assuredly by keeping possession quite nicely, winning the ball in promising areas and repelling any Greek advances without all their hands being required on deck. A final ball was lacking but the team had a bit of purpose. This was decent.

The first half of Scotland's Nations League group stage was full of the narrative-friendly hard-luck stories that shouldn't be confused with rotten decision-making but often are; rash tackles, ball-watching and poor finishing belong in a different bracket to misfortune. We have had our share of genuine hard-luck stories: McTominay's disallowed free kick in Seville, Patrik Schick scoring from halfway in the Euro 2020 opener, the ball taking a few deflections before bouncing off the post into Lewandowski's path in the last minute at Hampden in 2015, Czech Republic winning a fraudulent penalty and equalising in stoppage time in a vital Euro 2012 qualifier at Hampden. Scotland must have let their Karma Clubcard rack up the points. They spent pretty much all of them in one evening.

Scott McTominay muscled his way into the Greek penalty area, slipped, and accidentally planted his studs onto the ankle of right-back Lazaros Rota. Penalty to Scotland. A truly dumbfounding decision that would result in a VAR intervention and rightful reprieve for Greece.

Nope, penalty to Scotland. Thirty-two minutes played.

With green lasers blotting his face, McTominay nestled it to the keeper's left and he maintained his one-in-two scoring record for Scotland since he scored against Cyprus in early 2023. The hosts were furious, as would we have been.

Greece shifted into a higher gear and started peppering Gordon's goal, but their efforts were high or wide. Adams hurried a shot after being passed the ball by the Greek goalie, but instead of finding the back of the net his haste allowed the keeper to recover. The striker didn't realise how much time he had. Scotland had more possession and more shots. So far, so good.

Then it wasn't good.

Greek manager Ivan Jovanović sent for the saviour. One of a few, to be fair. Kostantinos Karetsas became the youngest player of all time for his country and was an instant thorn in Scotland's right side. Greece scored but the linesman signalled the cross had swerved beyond the touchline before Christos Tzolis tapped it in. It was all a sign of what was to follow. Karetsas curled a shot just wide. Their big centre-back Konstantinos Mavropanos headed just wide. Tzolis hit the post from about three yards out.

Ten minutes to go; Greece were absolutely dominating. Three minutes to go; Greece penalty. He'd been awesome for 90 minutes. Greece's direct approach had been little match for him, but Hanley's hazardous leg tripped his man on the edge of the box. A definite foul. But definitely *just* outside the box. Phew.

> I think that was a game made for me. It's a strength of mine to defend the box under pressure. If you ask me to play 50 passes and take it past strikers then I might struggle but being under the cosh and defending the box suits my style of play. I had a hairy moment with the penalty shout but the VAR looked after me. We were under no illusions as to how good they were and how difficult it would be, so I took some pride in standing up to it and getting a result.

Porteous, making his first appearance since the opening game at the Euros, replaced a knackered Ralston and should probably have been sent off two minutes later for a tackle that belonged in an identity parade alongside his one in Munich. Tierney was on. Johnston was on. Scotland had a back six to see it out. Did they have enough fingers to cling on to the cliff edge? They did. Three bouncing wins against Croatia, Poland and Greece with three clean sheets in four going back to the Portugal draw.

Scotland hadn't faced as many shots in one game while keeping a clean sheet since that victory in the French capital. However, only one of Greece's 24 efforts was on target. Luckily they hadn't polished their shooting boots and the VAR momentarily lost his marbles to confirm our penalty.

Nights like these can serve to remind why Steve Clarke trusts Grant Hanley so much in certain situations. Ralston deserved some flowers too for winning eight out of eight one-on-one duels in the oily slipstream of constant questioning in lieu of his understudy role at Celtic Park. Souttar deserved a rose or two as well. He was an undisputed starter ahead of two lads Clarke picked to go to the Euros. The three of them made 32 clearances between them.

> You need to regularly adapt your game at international level. We defended so many crosses that night and I remember Greece being really, really good with a lot of top young players. Karetsas came on and beat Robbo quite quickly and I thought, 'Right, this boy must be good.' I was thinking, 'This is their generation.' Big Granty was unbelievable. There aren't many better than him when it comes to defending your box.

Lewis Ferguson had played on the left rather than centrally, but he was back in the team and pleased:

> I was just delighted to be involved again. I thought we were decent in the first half and you know what it'll be like in the second half, away from home. There's a storm coming. They were really good at suffocating us and we just defended for our lives and flung our bodies in front of the ball to get a result. It's never easy to

get results in these places never mind a clean sheet. It was about character and desire. I was having to double up with Robbo on Karetsas to shut off the space for him to come inside. I remember that being a really nice stadium with the fans being close to the pitch. It was getting really noisy when Greece were putting the pressure on.

The Scotland fans enjoyed each other's company for an hour after full time while the Greek authorities held them in their little pen in the corner of the stadium. Some of them would have to *begrudgingly* stay in Greece for a few more days on *The Man's* dollar as a fire at Heathrow airport caused an electrical outage and its temporary closure. Oh no!

'The game changed with the start Greece made to the second half,' said the head coach. 'We didn't progress up the pitch enough. That's something we have to do a little bit better.'

Greece were a side. Karetsas was a player. Gordon, McTominay and Clarke all mentioned him in their post-match comments. The boy himself was clear in his vision. 'That is how we have to play on Sunday in Scotland,' he said after nonchalantly mentioning he was nonplussed about facing Andy Robertson again. 'I think, if we play like that again, we will win.'

Well we'll see about that, young man, won't we …

Chapter 7
Nations League Play-Off Second Leg

WELL, WE did see about that.

The squad flew back from Greece while the Tartan Army were sinking their second post-match pints or hunting for some gyros. Kip on the plane preceded a middle-of-the-night touchdown and a lie-in on Friday morning before a 'recovery' session. There are very few to no physical demands placed on the players in between matches. A light session with a bit of team-shaping followed by some classwork was Saturday's offering.

In a sit-down with the new rights-holders, Clarke identified the Greeks 'disrupted our rhythm' but concluded our range of knowledge on them had widened. He alluded to the benefit of having Kieran Tierney on the pitch to help nullify Karetsas's growing threat in the second half.

On the pre-match discourse menu; to start, potentially re-deploying KT as one of three-centre backs. For your meaty main, the option – or necessity – of Christie playing in centre midfield.

The Bournemouth midfielder was a cog without which the Cherry machine could malfunction. Gone were the agile, floaty and gliding days of Ryan Christie as an attacking midfielder. Now 30 years old, he was thriving as a box-to-box central midfielder around England's top flight, excelling for a club ninth in the Premier League and in contention for European qualification. Unwittingly like Heath Ledger's Joker in *The Dark Knight*, Jamie

Carragher spent ten minutes on *Monday Night Football* enthusing about Christie's energetic importance to the Bournemouth cause in a victory over Newcastle. *And here we go!*

Except this time there was a detonation of clamour. Wholly understandable clamour.

Remember such hits as *Get Gauld in the squad! Doak must play! Start Ferguson in the middle!* Those suddenly became stale. *Play Christie where he plays for Bournemouth!*

While appearing on the *Hampden Roar* podcast about a month before the Greece tie, Christie explained that the change in responsibility surprised him towards the start of that season and Clarke had given him no indication he was preparing to move him from his usual left midfield role for his country.

> When I first went down to Bournemouth in the Championship I was still playing on the right-wing as an attacker. It wasn't until Iraola came in that I was seen as a deeper midfielder. As soon as he came in he asked the question. It wasn't completely alien to me. I'd played there during my youth with more of an eye on attacking than defending, so I've had to learn about that. He just turned to me one day in training during a pressing drill and moved me to number eight and asked, 'Do you think you could play there?' It was a new manager so I was just nodding my head and saying yes to absolutely everything! Playing there for Scotland hasn't crossed my mind too much. I've always said when it comes to Scotland that I'm happy to play anywhere. The manager knows that as well; I'm definitely not fussy when it comes to the national team. Wherever the gaffer wants to play me, I'm ready.

McLean and Gilmour had started seven consecutive games together in midfield during Scotland's reincarnation. The evidence proved

they were a good side with the pair in tandem. A berth for Christie –
and his importantly fresh legs – felt more likely in place of Ferguson
in the shape of a narrow wideman, but that was no guarantee. Clarke
had used Ryzo as a central option behind a striker in the box midfield
during the 3-4-2-1 era, usually with McTominay or McGinn next
to him. He had become accustomed to starting games in a deeper
position for Bournemouth but spent significant time on the edge of
the final third participating in Iraola's pressing ideology.

'I've got to decide the best way for this game at Hampden,
which might be different for the game in Greece,' said Clarke. 'We
want to play as well as we did in the first half in Athens. We want
to be on the front foot. We want to try and win the game here at
Hampden.' He was looking at his pegs rather than the holes.

Christie started but, as expected, not in centre midfield. Ferguson
was on the bench. Clarke's reasoning was that Christie offers more
in attack than Fergie. Apart from that, it was the same ten fighters
who went the full 12 rounds and won on points on Thursday. Clarke's
XI read: Gordon; Ralston, Souttar, Hanley, Robertson; Gilmour,
McLean; McGinn, McTominay, Christie; Adams.

'The good thing on the quick turnaround is we're playing the
same team, so it's very fresh, what happened on Thursday,' said the
decision maker.

McLean earned his 50th cap. Number 60 for McTominay.

The Scotland side emerged into Glasgow's springtime dusk.
They read 'LAWMAN' stretched across the north stand in tribute
to Scotland's joint-greatest goalscorer who died at the start of the
year. A minute's applause followed after Denis Law's great friend
Sir Alex Ferguson had stood at the side of the pitch and found the
muscle to hoist the weight of greatness; a dark-blue jersey with
'Law 10' on its back.

'I don't see it being gung-ho from any side,' said *Sportsound*'s
Willie Miller, trying to wipe off the tar coating his crystal ball. 'I
don't think either will throw caution to the wind because it's such
a tight scoreline.'

We had to take Clarke at his word for the front-foot pledges. His team had done it in Warsaw, Cologne and Amsterdam in the last year. It's also how Scotland started in Piraeus and it was indeed how they started at Hampden. McTominay and Robertson saw efforts flash wide while McGinn and Gilmour's crunching challenges drew fervour. The latter in particular was dictating much of the early flow with his short, sharp passing.

Having made six changes to the starting XI, this Greek side *clearly* weren't as capable as the ones left reeling on Thursday. Then, after 20 minutes, out of a Trojan Horse stationed in the Greek half exploded a youthful, exuberant gang of youths lighting fires and pinging slingshots across the grass. Scotland had been lulled. The visitors had had no option but the shock value. Their lived experience of launching balls into the box to see them eaten by Hanley was the clue Ivan Jovanović didn't need a microscope to spot. Scotland's defence and midfield quickly went from being in control of the ball to suffering whiplash watching it whizz past them. It was like whack-a-mole.

Karetsas had to start on the right. Slavia Prague's Christos Zafeiris and his namesake Mouzakitis of Olympiakos – aged 22 and 18 – were trusted in centre midfield. Among the other introductions, including Benfica's goal machine Vangelis Pavlidis, they clicked. Karetsas drove at a frightened rearguard and slipped the ball to the overlapping right-back Georgios Vagiannidis of Sporting Lisbon, whose cutback didn't require the breaking of stride to meet. Giannis Konstantelias – streaks ahead of Scotland's jogging and ball-watching midfielders – planted it in Gordon's bottom left-hand corner with about an eight-yard radius from near-enough the penalty spot. They didn't look back from there. Wee Karetsas became his country's youngest goalscorer five minutes before half-time with a finish like McGinn's against Israel in 2021. It stemmed from four quick passes through the Scottish lines.

Scotland had asked a few questions of Greece in the game's early stages. Now, they had no answer of their own and that relatively bright start was a distant memory. Greece somehow hadn't lost a competitive game when scoring the opening goal since a 2-1 defeat to Spain at Euro 2008. More than 120 matches ago. They won Euro 2004 by playing Clarke-ball. This was verging on Klopp's Liverpool.

Scotland were dazed at half-time. Tempers or anger never flared, but during a heated discussion Grant Hanley felt it necessary to remind the team they were one goal from levelling the tie. Fifteen seconds after the second whistle, Greece were three up. Many will have seen it on the TVs up at the kiosks rather than with their own eyes. Christie played a slightly loose pass infield and while our midfield were still trying to figure out where the ball had gone, Konstantelias was rolling it for Christos Tzolis to thump it past Gordon. Oh no. Greece's lightning speed of thought and ruthless finishing was sublime. McLean was the one stretching while Konstantelias raced onto it like Sonic the Hedgehog collecting rings.

It was all a bit mad. We're in the meeting room twice a day, we should know the way they'll play and what's coming. You don't get a lot of time on the training pitch at international level so for them to have the style they have, you can only be impressed. One hundred per cent, we could have done more but credit where it is due, they were much better than us over two games. Coming back from the first leg we knew we'd got away with one so we needed to be so much better. That's totally on us to take responsibility. We definitely didn't feel defeated but they adapted well to everything we did. We wanted to be on the front foot, be more aggressive and put pressure on the ball, but a lot of it was down to them. They adapted in-game very well and that left us in between with our press. They were ahead of us in those two games. It wasn't until afterwards I saw some of their players getting linked with moves for about £40m.

Boos rang round Hampden as Karetsas almost made it 4-0 and Souttar cleared one off the line. Used to the symphony in motion on England's south coast, the shoe was now on the other foot for Christie.

> I was so impressed by Greece's press. They don't have much structure, they're a very fluid team; their number ten will drift wide, the wingers come inside, they play on different sides. Playing against them is hard. How they play is unusual in international football unless it's one of the big guns. Normally at a goal kick it'll get rolled out and it's like, 'We'll meet you on the halfway line.' Not many teams want to give anything away or be caught out because there's not too much time to work on things and that's why 1-0 and 1-1 are very common scores at international level. Greece's press was to a T. We tried to prepare for it and wanted to dominate but it was hard to overcome. They actually had a similar 'jump' to us at Bournemouth; they shut off the full-backs with their body position, which forces the ball through the middle, but we like to get it wide and up to McGinn who can then back-in or maybe to Doak who can take it for a run. The Greek lads aren't household names so it's easy for the average punter to overlook how good they might be. Karetsas is very good. I spoke to KT about him after our game; you know what he's about to do. He's going to chop inside but it's too good to stop. You can't sell yourself. He's a game-changer.

Only one team had been playing with the 'expectation of success' since the opening goal. Scotland's passing and decision-making was frankly woeful. The support's clemency for Clarke was nourished during the Nations League but this had the capacity to unravel it. Not the defeat, no. Not the relegation, no. The manner of it all.

James Wilson made his debut and became the youngest Scottish international ever at 18 years and 17 days old. Tierney – on initially at left midfield after the wreckage had become a dive site – ventured into Greek territory with 20 minutes to go but found himself staring at a barren wasteland. Glasgow could have been powered for the night by the noise from 48,000 that greeted his subsequent long ball back to Gordon. Only two goals from extra time, but Scotland were done.

Grant Hanley was imperious in the first leg. 'Big Granty and Souttar needed a helmet and a few Anadin after that one,' McLean said during our video call. Ivan Jovanović knew he had to throw a curveball. Three strikes.

> They were interchanging, physically so quick, strong and sharp and tactically very difficult to mark. They were picking up pockets of space that are hard to get to as a centre-back, and for the full-backs as well because we didn't want to leave too much space wide. They rotate as well; for example, Tzolis will run in behind so then there's a pocket for one of their midfielders to come into because someone's had to follow Tzolis. Greece are one of the teams that have mastered that. Difficult moments and games like that are remembered. They fuel the fire. It's motivation to put things right.

'An embarrassing night' were among McGinn's accurate post-match words. 'No threat in behind, probably too easy to pick up. That will maybe give us a kick up the backside for the World Cup qualifiers.'

Steve Clarke had improved the Scotland national team. Of that, there was absolutely no question. Also evidential was his squad's ability to inexplicably veer into the central reservation ten minutes from the end of a five-hour drive. They normally emerged from the wreckage with only a banged head and a few scratches and the man behind the wheel would say there's no reason to doubt his boys. He said it was just a 'bump in the road' during his post-match duties. The problem was, there had been a fair number now.

Qualify for Euro 2020; lose to the Czech Republic at Hampden. Go on a six-match winning run to reach the World Cup play-offs; lose to Ukraine at Hampden. Win promotion from Nations League B and qualify automatically for Euro 2024; fail to have a shot on target in the decisive group game until stoppage time. Put an end to a year-long winless run and finish third to reach the Nations League play-off; you know what happened next.

The prefixing achievements were rightly met with accolades. As much as they were fully deserved, so was criticism in the aftermath of each calamity. Without sounding too demanding or entitled, we wanted to ask this Scotland team to meet expectation after they'd exceeded it. They had raised the standards.

As host of the *Hampden Roar* podcast, whenever I ask listeners to opine with their post-match thoughts, the thread of replies after a concerning evening is often double the length of one in light of an important victory. The span of the one resulting from this second leg against Greece might even have exceeded the length of this chapter.

Clarke was unusually reflective. 'Maybe I should have made more rotations. Maybe I could have done more to freshen up the team. I'll go away and look at myself.'

The likelihood is Clarke will take these thoughts to his grave. I wonder – and would have loved the opportunity to have a fair, constructive and enlightening conversation on these matters on top of the positive ones – who or what was on his mind in that regard. Tierney and the shape? McKenna on the left of a four? Ferguson or Christie in centre midfield? Conway or Hirst in attack? Where the heck we'd find a pacey alternative to Doak?

'Greece have set down a marker.' This was the cold, hard crux for Clarke. Scotland's relegation wasn't era defining, but the World Cup qualifiers later that year would contribute to its mould. We'd have to play Greece twice in the autumn and probably scavenge three or four points from a team that had just played us off the park with an XI that had an average age of 23 years old. The next generation for Scotland? Well, a few were introduced to first-team surroundings at this camp rather than being taken to the Pinatar Cup in Spain, where our under-21s were beaten 6-1 by Iceland's. Oh boy.

Lewis Ferguson and Grant Hanley recall their thoughts at the time echoed ours.

> Getting relegated to League B isn't the end of the world. You can accept that when you're against teams of a really high level and sometimes you have to hold your hands up and say you lost to a better team. I think the feeling of losing that game was worse because of the manner of it. The hangover from that was a worse feeling than an actual relegation.
>
> How well Greece beat us was more of a concern for me than being relegated. It's still a relatively new format that I think a lot of folk are getting to grips with. Let's be honest, it wasn't a play-off for a major tournament; it would have been totally different if it was. Being beaten at home in that manner was something we had to address.

To slightly ease the anxiety of contending with Greece, Portugal took care of Denmark in their Nations League quarter-final and the loser was confirmed as the top seed in Scotland's group. Hardly a jackpot, but certainly the bonus ball. Denmark are decent, but they are not Portugal. A potential two-way scuffle for a play-off place now looked like it could be a three-horse race for first.

If – *if* – Scotland could perform like they did in the Nations League, they'd be in it till the embers. For now, we were poking through the ashes of another bin fire.

Chapter 8

Summer Games

THE CURTAIN call of May. Three weeks to savour – four at a push – before the bleep tests. Can one adequately enjoy the only holiday they'll experience all year when the new campaign's pressures and expectations are just around the corner? Earning tens of thousands every week should allow for some fairly ample seclusion and relaxation to disengage the mind from what's been and what's to follow. Quality time with wives, children or friends and importantly, for the boys not topping up their tans in Palma, Naples or Bologna on a daily basis, some fucking sunshine. The brain needs as much rest as the body. I literally just spent 15 minutes on Skyscanner and booking.com after writing that sentence.

John McGinn had played 55 games that season. Andy Robertson, two fewer. Even somebody like Ché Adams who isn't involved in any European club competitions with Torino had played 42 times.

Playing international football is *the* privilege we've all dreamt of. The boys treasure their caps, and occasions like this are rightly seen by the peripherals and kids as a foot in the door. Contextually, for the lads who have nothing to prove, two games at the start of June with almost no promising consequences is the kind of assignment that has a place in their diaries rather than dreams. Iceland would come to Hampden and we'd go to Liechtenstein.

Expected to win both, it's a lose-lose situation. A pair of relatively comfortable victories by a couple of goals would certainly be welcomed, especially after March's shittery, and that's about it. Not beating Liechtenstein was unfathomable and would require addressing at Holyrood. Unless by a margin of four or five, beating Iceland in an end-of-season friendly would be met with a nod of the head and *job done* or perhaps in some quarters – Clarke's detractors – a shrug of the shoulders and *who cares?*

Ryan Christie was quite happy he'd miss these matches because of rehab after a groin operation.

> I'd never put on a friendly at the end of the season. It's the way it's going to be now but it shouldn't happen. Nobody says it because we enjoy being together and playing for Scotland but everybody wants a rest. A few weeks with family and in the sun to get in a good place to approach next season. There's no win out of it. Beat Iceland; it's expected. Don't beat them and it's a disaster.

Scotland are rubbish in friendlies; specifically rubbish in friendlies at Hampden. These two would be our last until March 2026 at the earliest, depending on how the World Cup qualifiers materialised. Scotland beat Czech Republic (Anya 10') and Denmark 1-0 (Richie 8') ten years before that. Since then we'd won three friendlies in total against Hungary, Luxembourg and Gibraltar.

Italy, France, Canada, the Netherlands (three times), Costa Rica, Peru, Mexico, Belgium, Portugal, Poland, Austria, Turkey, England, France, Northern Ireland and Finland is the comprehensive list of opponents of whom we hadn't got the better in that time frame.

The criteria here was to win and win well in both matches. Ideally seeing more than ten to 15 minutes of each of the would-be debutants.

There were seven of them in a squad blending experience and its opposite: Angus Gunn, *Robbie McCrorie, Ciaran Slicker, Josh Doig*, Grant Hanley, Jack Hendry, Max Johnston, Scott McKenna,

Nathan Patterson, Anthony Ralston, John Souttar, Kieran Tierney, *Connor Barron*, Lewis Ferguson, Billy GIlmour, *Andy Irving*, John McGinn, Scott McTominay, *Lennon Miller*, Che Adams, *Kieron Bowie*, Tommy Conway, James Wilson, George Hirst.

Scotland had the oldest squad at the Euros. This gathering contained a dozen players aged 25 or younger. While there were five potential outfield firstlings, there were a few more rookies like Hirst, Wilson, Conway and Johnston who had less than ten caps between them. There is credence in the debate about how fierce Clarke's loyalty is, but the stubbornness of those who decry him for exactly that trait have just as much of it in their bones. Seven uncapped players in the squad along with a handful of single-figure caps all fighting for a chance to impress, and a common response remained: *Hanley! Again!*

I have regularly supported Hanley on the *Hampden Roar* podcast and after a year of playing well for Scotland surrounding his lunge against Poland and limited game time at St Andrew's, I felt for the big man.

Gordon, Doak, Christie and Dykes were either injured or recovering. Citing familiarity with their aptitudes, Clarke left out Shankland, Nisbet, McLean, Porteous and Taylor, with the latter knocking the inside of the shop window to get the attention of passers-by. Greek side PAOK eventually picked him up. Clarke had been looking through the English Championship window from the pavement and sussed out Plymouth Argyle's Ryan Hardie. He watched him twice, but despite scoring 12 goals in a relegation season it wasn't enough. His summer move to Wrexham didn't bear fruit and he was subsequently loaned to League One's Huddersfield. The clamour for him and QPR centre-back Liam Morrison was lost in the ether by Halloween. File alongside Simon Murray of Dundee.

He was the flavour of May's last week after ending the season with 21 goals. Scotland needed a striker who could score goals. At 33 years old, we were told by domestic tribes that the menace could fix what was broken and had earned a shot in a time of need. A bit like Nicky Devlin during the Nations League. That shout was Bowie's, with the longevous look taken as part of a remedy to the fact McTominay and McGinn had scored 16 of Scotland's 33 goals in the last 18 months, with 'own goal' their third top scorer on four.

Clarke wasn't perturbed. Not publicly anyway. 'I'm a little bit selfish when it comes to my strikers because I make them play a certain way to link the team and bring the midfield players into the final third of the pitch,' he said. Ferguson was identified as one he hoped could contribute when given the chance, explaining Adams had grown 'desperate' to score since his sealer against Denmark in 2021. His other five goals had come against Gibraltar, Armenia, Moldova, Luxembourg and the Faroes.

Conway's credentials had spiked. Born in England, the 22-year-old said during his first call-up that he wanted to play for Scotland to make his grandfather proud as that's who'd often driven him to his training and games as a youth; there was no hanging around to gauge the contours of possibility for him. The Boro striker was the fifth highest scorer in the Championship that season and of that quintet had the best shot accuracy. He'd had a good year after leaving his hometown of Bristol.

Analysing the Scotland players' fortunes over the last nine months reflected interestingly. If we identify McTominay as having had a ten out of ten season by winning Player of the Year in Italy, relatively few experienced what I'd suggest as an *average* nine to ten months as a collective with their club. Adams finishing 11th with Torino, Conway tenth with Middlesbrough and Gunn 13th with Norwich fit snugly into that bracket, but more than just a couple of the players had significant joy in their day jobs. Only a few were suffering true disappointment come May.

Robertson won the Premier League for a second time. McTominay and Gilmour became Serie A champions and Ferguson lifted the Coppa Italia. Doig was promoted back to their top flight with Sassuolo. Johnston won the Austrian title with Sturm Graz. Ralston was a Scottish champion again with Celtic. Dykes and Hanley contributed to Birmingham City's record-breaking League One title, although were limited by injury and team selection. Bowie had returned to fitness and ended the season well as Hibs secured third in the Premiership.

At the other end of the spectrum, Slicker and Hirst were relegated from the Premier League with Ipswich, as was McKenna with La Liga's Las Palmas. Barron and Souttar were part of a Rangers team that finished second in Scotland.

So, five outfield newbies and some more freshmen among them. Let's see what they're all about ahead of the qualifiers!

'I think you know me quite well by now,' Clarke told BBC Scotland during the week. 'We don't really experiment too much. You're bringing these young players in to feel the level of the group, to understand where they need to get to, to be selected regularly. That's important.'

Iceland had lost six out of six against Scotland and just been relegated from Nations League B to C. This was our first meeting with them since a World Cup qualifier in 2009 when Ross McCormack and Steven Fletcher scored in a 2-1 win at Hampden. They rocketed from being a Pot 5 team to the Euro 2016 quarter-finals and a draw with Argentina at the World Cup in Russia, but had now started to slide back down the continental ladder with the country's football governing body (KSI) shrouded in a scandal about allegedly covering up sexual abuse.

In a favourite counterpoint of mine against this slothful argument, Iceland achieved those qualifications with a population smaller than Edinburgh. In fact, the 'population' thing in general winds me up. Halve the number immediately and filter it by age. Iceland has about 70,000 males between the ages of 16 to 40. Scotland has about 800,000.

Whatever the demographic, a shade more than 30,000 fancied it at Hampden on Friday, 6 June. The east stand was desolate. John McGinn's grandfather Jack – a former Scottish FA president –

had recently passed away and was honoured before kick-off with a minute's applause. With a match against what amounts to a county-select team on Monday this was Scotland's last tangible chance to iron out some creases before September's real stuff.

Clarke reminded us again that criticism doesn't bother him. His XI read: Gunn; Johnston, Hanley, Souttar, Tierney, Robertson; Gilmour, Ferguson, McGinn, McTominay; Hirst.

Either 3-4-2-1 or 5-4-1. The clue might have been the ten defenders in the squad. The lack of vibrancy in March without Doak's pace was glaring. We needed KT to make the evening's set-up work; we needed Doak for the other one. 'I think it's quite a sensible decision,' said the boss before the game. 'I've got an idea of where we went wrong against Greece, we've touched on it a bit this week.' Johnston and Hirst had earned their first starts and Tierney won his 50th cap. Gunn had a chance to re-establish himself in the team.

Off he went with an ankle injury in the seventh minute. Kilmarnock's Robby McCrorie remained unmoved on the bench having suffered an injury in the warm-up, unbeknown to us watching on. With no warning, Cieran Slicker was making his Scotland debut. He was retrieving the ball from his net a minute later.

His flimsy clearance was nodded back from whence it came by an Iceland midfielder and Andri Guðjohnsen – son of – whipped it across goal into Slicker's top right-hand corner. A phenomenal finish and the start of an agonising night for the 22-year-old. Slicker appeared on the *Beyond the Box* podcast in February 2026:

> I felt a bit flustered to be honest. I was thinking, 'I don't feel prepared for this.' I was the number three, so the other two are getting the bulk of the work at training. During the warm-up me and the other young goalie [Callan McKenna] are just doing volleys to each other while the other two properly warm-up. I could sit here and make excuses. I was nowhere near good

enough in that game. But there are things I'd have liked to have done differently if I knew I was playing. You can't mentally prepare yourself to play a game of that magnitude without … I dunno, if you don't know you're playing to prepare yourself in ten seconds – that's what it was. My first action was to clear the ball with my left foot, not ideal to work myself into the game with a left-footed clearance. I got decent contact but it's gone straight to their guy and he's headed it and he's put it top bins. The clearance should have been better.

Slicker was at the end of the second year of three he'd agreed to at Ipswich Town in 2023. A Manchester City youth grad, he'd played nine minutes all season. Two goalkeeping injuries occurring within 20 minutes added Gunn and McCrorie to a list containing Gordon, Clark and Kelly, which meant Steve Clark was encouragingly patting his sixth choice on the back as he trotted on to the Hampden turf. The manager had repeatedly emphasised his concern about how shallow the country's pool of keepers is, calling the long-term development of them an 'oversight' and alluding to 'complacency' during the oil-rich years when a Scotland manager could roll a dice and select David Marshall, Allan McGregor or Craig Gordon. He'd lamented the amount of first-team football being afforded to young keepers around the country.

Prior to Slicker's FA Cup cameo against Bristol City in January, he'd made two appearances the season before and three the season before that while on loan at Rochdale. None of them league fixtures. He had been served severely undercooked for this occasion at Hampden. Everyone knew who he was now.

Hirst was twice denied a goal by good goalkeeping during the match but missed an open net with a header from six yards before John Souttar put his noggin in harm's way to equalise from a corner. There weren't many smiles after the 25th-minute equaliser. There were absolutely no smiles on the stroke of half-time. Scotland conceded arguably their most comical goal of Clarke's reign.

An Icelandic corner was delivered. The ball took three touches – each off a separate Scotland player – and trickled into the net. Souttar headed it off McTominay, it deflected off Ferguson and Slicker dived over it. Gory, but entirely in keeping with the first-half performance. Icelandic manager Arnar Gunnlaugsson later admitted he instructed his players to target Slicker, but Scotland looked out of their depth over every blade of grass. Careless with the ball, hesitant in their decision-making and slow with their movement. Players who had achieved remarkable things throughout the season were staggering after their adrenaline dumps.

Lyndon Dykes was on punditry duty for BBC Scotland and felt comfortable enough to say 'we've been all over the place'.

> I've done a bit of punditry work now and it's difficult being involved when I'm still part of the team. I know things that I won't say publicly about the way we play or insider information. They're asking me questions, but I'm not gonna grill my team-mates and then go and be with them in the next camp. I'll always try and be positive about it but it can be an awkward one. I just stand there and let the others do the slagging.

Slicker was cajoled at half-time, with the experienced members of the team at least doing what's expected of them in that regard. On the pitch, they had been shocking. Scotland were pointlessly passing the ball around with no tempo. Iceland scored a third goal when Slicker swiped a strange paw at former Hibs defender Victor Pálsson's free header but only gave it a few extra beans en route to the back of the net. There were ironic cheers a few minutes later when he caught the ball. This had become a crying shame, as he continued explaining on the *Beyond the Box* podcast:

I just didn't feel myself in the game. There were things I did, some clearances that were poor, a decision to come out that I shouldn't have made and normally wouldn't make. I'm normally excited to make saves, I back myself, but in that game it was the complete opposite. It got to half-time and I'm thinking, 'I've fucked up.' I wanted the game to be over. It's my debut but it started off poorly and wasn't gonna be my day. The third goal was the worst of all, I think. That's a save I make 100 times out of 100 on the training pitch. I just felt so tense. I was thinking to myself, 'How have I not made that save? That's so simple.' I just remember looking at the time … I'm normally buzzing to be on the pitch but it was the opposite. We get to the end of the game and I know I've had a really bad day. The players were consoling me in the changing room, the experienced boys were really good, but they're just words, they don't mean too much cos I'm in my own head thinking, 'I've fucked it so badly, I don't know what happened.'

The atmosphere in Hampden wasn't toxic; the stadium consisted of a group of supporters who had become apathetic rather than apoplectic. A gentle hum of conversation vibrated around the bowl with the odd groan or frustrated shout when one Scotland player failed to find another. The boos at half-time and full time were as loud as the cheers that greeted Souttar's goal, despite barely anyone being left in the stadium by the conclusion. The players delve into the challenges of this later in the book while recalling a certain qualifying match against a bottom seed.

Lennon Miller made his debut and did alright. The only slight ray of light on a grey June evening.

I reflected on it after the game to let making my Scotland debut sink in. It is a special moment and will live with me forever, but my mindset before I came on was the same as it was every week at Motherwell … stamp my authority. I'm going on to change the game and make a difference. I feel differently to Ryan, understandably during the summer the boys want their holidays after a long season. I see where they are coming from but I was getting my first cap, it was a huge opportunity.

Hanley resonated with Slicker.

It was a really difficult game for Slicks but as a team we were terrible. The result wasn't just on him. I've been there and felt the pressure after Poland at home. I felt his feelings and everyone got round him to make sure he was alright. That's the biggest thing about this squad, how tightly-knit it is. It was a major disappointment after the Greece game. The players probably take circumstances into their thinking; it was a friendly at the end of the season with nothing on it and boys are tired, so I think they're some important lessons learned. Sometimes suffering a few negative results is a crash back to earth and extra motivation.

Slicker could not be a scapegoat. He was the evening's unfortunate protagonist but not at the centre of the whole story. From the resolution against Portugal, the persistence against Croatia and the entertainment against Poland, Scotland had regressed to dross. Was it relevant that this was just a friendly? Clarke had won two of his 12 in charge, and while the results aren't worth losing sleep over, the quality of our performances ahead of World Cup qualifying might be. I suppose we learn about our strengths and weaknesses in these games so the competitive ones aren't exercises in finding ourselves. If that's the whole point, sound the alarm. As

John McGinn said during our chat for *A Nation Again: The Inside Story of Scotland's Journey to the European Championship*, 'After that Kazakhstan game, if someone had told me we'd be at the next major tournament, I'd have laughed.'

'We need to get our hunger back,' said the injured striker with a mic. Where had it gone?

'I don't want to say too much,' said the captain. 'We need to digest this and speak in the changing room before we start doing interviews. I think we were too easily played through. Any chance they had, they scored. We weren't good enough on the ball; created chances but didn't take them. Nowhere near good enough.'

'We wanted to dominate and take the ball to them and we didn't do that tonight,' said Soapy.

Yes, panels only have a couple of minutes with players after matches for segments each player is not mandated to participate in. Yes, most of the pundits are friendly with and respect the footballers' code for the players, but probes for further context are rarely put on the table. 'Why didn't we do that tonight, John?'

Clarke took 45 minutes to brace for his pitch-side appearance. He refuted claims the performance was a result of the decision to change the shape – absolutely fair do's – but couldn't or wouldn't publicly pinpoint the evening's epicentre. 'I'll sit with Cieran over the next couple of days and have a little chat about it. I'll give him reassurance because he probably went in when it was too early. He wasn't quite ready for it. That wasn't his fault.'

James McFadden is one of the most passionate former internationals I've met through media work. He is a glass half full man but will remove dark blue specs when necessary. 'There has to be a concern. When you go into qualifying, these performances won't be tolerated.'

We were pages into Clarke's final chapter. The opportunity to build momentum for the autumn had been wasted and a no-win game in Liechtenstein had become a must-win. And we would win. We would beat the part-time team that had lost twice to

San Marino in the past year and in the previous five only beaten Hong Kong. Otherwise, the '75 per cent' likelihood of the head coach's departure after the World Cup journey would probably be shunted forwards by a few months and 25 per cent. Never mind a defeat; the thought of a repeat of Stephen McManus's 97th-minute winner at Hampden 15 years ago or the scrappy 1-0 in Vaduz (Craig Mackail-Smith, anyone?) in the same campaign was skin-crawling. Their coach Konrad Fünfstück exhaled with a chuckle when asked about his opponent's goalkeeping crisis.

Clarke wanted to take Slicker out the spotlight and not thrust Bournemouth teen McKenna under it. Needing a (seventh-choice) glovesman with more experience, Clarke sought one who had their feet up at home or was willing to give up their sun lounger. Celtic-bound Ross Doohan played 18 times for Aberdeen that season and answered the call from Clarke, ditching his family getaway in Turkey for a few days in the Alps' foothills and a Scotland debut. He'd enjoy many more holidays than he would caps.

The squad arrived mid-evening the day before the game after a delayed charter flight from Glasgow and an hour's drive over two borders from where they touched down in Friedrichshafen; a destination more commonly used for winter sports trips. Clarke emerged for the pre-match presser near 9.30pm, but with the one-hour time difference there was little stress for the hacks. They still had time to sample the same delights as those not on professional duty.

Apart from the ensuing thwacks to the bank balance, a Tartan Army trip to Vaduz is never a bad thing and certainly not in the height of summer. Business owners' pupils popped into Euro signs on what was a public holiday weekend, with market and shop doors thrust open and shelves healthily stocked with the good stuff. Nobody really cared about the game; this was a wee summer break with breathtaking surroundings. During his customary pre-match gig, Ted Christopher advised supporters that Liechtenstein's national anthem bears no lyrical relation to the one with which it shares an identical melody, 'God Save the King'. The eventual boos from three of the four small stands were satiric.

The skies were so clear and the water so pure, the bed of the River Rhine was visible as fans strolled along its banks for a kilometre towards the stadium, which kind of resembles McDiarmid Park but is a tad smaller and has the edge of the Alps towering over it. Among the pre-match gathering was an American travel vlogger looking for a quaint Alpine escape. He was swept into pre-match proceedings in a local square, force-fed beers and bought a ticket for the game. The stadium DJ understandably pandered with '500 Miles', 'Chelsea Dagger' and 'Yes Sir, I Can Boogie' leading his setlist. A local pipe band performed at half-time.

For a game that had to finish more than one- or two-nil and had 'no bearing' on Scotland's World Cup mission, in a 4-4-2 Clarke's XI read: Doohan; Ralston, Hendry, McKenna, Robertson; Ferguson, Gilmour, Miller, McGinn; Adams, Hirst.

Doohan debuted and barely touched the ball. When he did he was ironically cheered with a comedic angle rather than a cruel tone. Miller earned his first start and Hendry played his first game since the Euros. Tierney and McTominay hadn't travelled because of knocks.

I asked Ferguson if they felt as chilled out as Clarke hoped they would, safe in the knowledge Scotland would win this match.

> We just had to go there, be professional and win the game because of the disappointment beforehand. It wasn't like everybody was relaxed. We know if we turn up we're a miles better team and we'd win the game but it was about putting on a performance to win comfortably. Winning 1-0 or 2-0 would be seen negatively.

It was an evening spent in the sun watching Scotland pass the ball around for 90 minutes with the odd foray in behind, enjoying the influence of Lennon Miller and applauding Ché Adams for scoring a hat-trick; two clinical finishes and a bit of a near-post stoop right at the end. The first was his second goal in three years. Clarke didn't substitute him in the hope he'd complete his trio, which he did in the nick of time. Oh, and Hirst got off the mark with a back-post tap-in. 4-0.

The caveat of the opposition's level has to be noted alongside any *marvelling*, but Miller was brilliant. Three months after his ambition was shat on by his assistant manager and the media, he was the best player on the park. Doig (who excelled), Irving, Barron and Bowie made their debuts, Patterson played for the first time in 15 months and Conway got 25 minutes. Miller lasted the whole hog.

> It was a real chance for me to show what I could do. Making my debut was a confidence booster but singing the national anthem will live with me forever. There was a training session for the players that didn't start against Iceland and I was thinking, 'Only three days, it's a friendly, he might make all these changes.' I thought there was a real chance I would play and then on the day of the game the manager announced the team and I was starting next to Billy. There were definitely butterflies when he said it; doesn't matter if it's Liechtenstein, France, a qualifier or a friendly. There's that buzz for ten or 15 minutes, phoning my family and texting my mates. It's hard to describe the feeling. I performed well, which was nice. I'm pretty harsh on myself and I remember being critical with some of my passing, but my dad likes to keep me balanced. If I play 20 through balls and 18 of them come off, I'm thinking about the two that didn't. I've set high standards for myself and am always looking at what I can do better along with thinking about the good stuff. I really enjoyed playing

alongside Billy and it was nice to start against a lower-ranked nation. I had loads of the ball and could show what I was capable of.

It was an encouraging but easy night. Insufficient to forget Friday's misgivings or March's Greek tragedy, but satisfying. A whiff of Gibraltar pre-Euros loitered before the game but Adams's fourth-minute goal dispersed the scent. 'Our players had a little bit of anger in the performance at the start of the game,' acknowledged Clarke. 'They knew they'd let themselves down in the previous match.'

Doig, Patterson, Irving, Miller, Barron, Bowie and Conway were all on the park when the final whistle blew. Clarke proposed it was a glimpse into the future.

The season had ended. At long last. It would ridiculously begin again in about a month's time. The rollercoaster had been tumultuous as usual. From the great post-Euros depression, Scotland grew in the Nations League and mirrored the squad we'd come to recognise before resembling strangers off the street a few months later. Scotland fans walked back into Vaduz with the night still young, the sun setting over the ridges surrounding them. How brightly would it rise in September?

Chapter 9
Denmark (Away)

A VITAL World Cup qualifier in Copenhagen's Lego-like Parken Stadium at the start of September. Scotland had been here before, as recently as 2021, in fact, but we had no interest in returning if déjà vu held the puppet strings. Scotland were tormented by the Danes and fortunate to scurry off back home with just a 2-0 defeat and some question marks over Clarke's new contract. The passage of time couldn't care less about compassion; 53 years ago Scotland travelled to Copenhagen to begin the World Cup '74 qualifiers. They only went and left with a 4-1 win! (Clark; Buchan, Colquhoun, Forsyth, Brownlie; Macari 17', Bremner, Lorimer, Graham; Morgan 83', Bone 20'. Subs: Harper 80', Dalglish).

Mind you, if success or failure hung in the balance come mid-November, the Scandies wouldn't be drawing on inspiration from their last visit to Hampden in the most recent group's final game. Weirdly but totally accurately, the most recent World Cup qualifier they'd both played.

That fixture in the Danish capital was the sixth-last fixture of the group. So was this one, except it was also the first. Scotland's defeat left Clarke's side with five points from four games after earlier draws against Austria and Israel and a win against the Faroes. At the time, the suggestion Scotland would win six in a row to reach the play-offs was fanciful. The subsequent disintegration against Ukraine was spurring on the majority of the squad, knowing they wouldn't start a World Cup qualification campaign together again.

It was spurring on Clarke as he knew as well, this was it. Recent anguish topped up the misery he'd held on to for more than 30 years; included in Andy Roxburgh's provisional squad for Italia '90, Clarke was jettisoned for an apparent lack of playing time at Chelsea. The irony! He received one more cap to total six despite playing for Chelsea until 1998 and accruing more than 350 appearances. The old wives' tale is that it was harder to be dropped from than picked for Craig Brown's Scotland squad in the 90s.

That rejection probably defined his Scotland playing career. There was – fairly or unfairly – an inevitability that the next ten weeks would define his Scotland management tenure. Reaching two European Championships were dizzying highs in their moments, but their culminations, specifically in 2024, and fluctuating form between them meant Clarke's popularity descended as much as it ascended. The desperate winless run's recovery being abruptly terminated by Greece and Iceland was still fresh and proximate enough to the Euros for his approval rating to be sliding as Scotland took their place on 2026's starting blocks. A third- or fourth-place finish, or even a play-off defeat, would amplify the howls of unhappiness among the support to breaking point, and some would wish to wrestle the pen from his grip if the Scottish FA offered him a package too good to turn down.

Qualify, and he'd curtail the near 30-year wait for the World Cup, become the only person to take the country to three major tournaments and surely depart the gig as a national hero. What a juxtaposition. If there was an in between, a magnifying glass was required to see it.

'I feel the pressure,' he unusually admitted to Kelly Cates in a BBC feature. 'The whole country wants to get there and as the head coach that comes back on me.'

He felt it. The players knew it. Knew their time with a man held in their highest esteem was drawing to a close. Don't let the 75 per cent probability become 100 per cent in a flop's aftermath. Christie admits it was an elephant in the room:

The gaffer's future didn't really make its way into conversations but it added to the feeling we don't really speak about, which is the desperation to qualify for him as well as the country. He's spoken during his tenure about his dream to represent Scotland at a World Cup. The gap between the Ukraine game and the start of the campaign reminded us how rare they are and how quickly they can disappear. The Ukraine play-off gave us the feeling we couldn't let the next opportunity slip past us. The time passing is mental. I was naive in my early 20s that I'd just play forever. When you reach 30, you think about your opportunities quite deeply, about this being the last time. After the Hungary game, Clarke mentioned we had the World Cup box to tick and he believed we could do it.

This was the squad Clarke selected for the short flight to Copenhagen and the longer one to Belarus. Actually, no, wait. The second match was in the middle of Hungary's nowhere and behind closed doors. We'll come to that.

Zander Clark, Angus Gunn, Liam Kelly; Grant Hanley, Jack Hendry, Aaron Hickey, Dom Hyam, Max Johnston, Scott McKenna, Anthony Ralston, Andy Robertson, John Souttar, Kieran Tierney; Ryan Christie, Lewis Ferguson, Ben Gannon-Doak, Billy Gilmour, John McGinn, Kenny McLean, Scott McTominay, Lennon Miller; Ché Adams, Kieron Bowie, Lyndon Dykes, George Hirst.

Dykes, Hickey, Christie and Gannon-Doak were fit. Craig Gordon was not.

We were due to play Motherwell near the end of the season and I just woke up one morning in severe pain.

I had a disc injury in my neck. It gave me weakness down my right side into my hand, which is hardly ideal. If I was an outfielder I would have been able to play much sooner, but it took a bit longer to make sure I was strong enough to be able to protect my elbow and shoulder joints. If I don't have the bulk there then the joints become the next thing to get injured.

Clarke hinted this gang would be his campaign roster. Josh Doig (called in a few days later), Greg Taylor, James Wilson, Nathan Patterson and Ryan Porteous were omitted. Lawrence Shankland slightly surprisingly likewise. Tommy Conway didn't make it either.

'I feel a bit sorry for Tommy, but I've got Lyndon back fit,' he acknowledged. 'I just feel Lyndon's experience can give us a little bit more up front, certainly for these two away games. When I look at that squad, it's got a lot of good experience in it, players that know how to qualify for major tournaments. We need six top performances over a short space of time and I believe this group of players can deliver that.'

Clarke's inner circle had a returning member. John Carver's time with the national team was over at his behest and he took on the challenge of managing Lechia Gdańsk in the Polish top flight. Steven Naismith, who Clarke tried to sign twice (for West Brom and Kilmarnock), didn't have the desire to jump back into management after leaving Hearts the previous year but dived head first into this opportunity before a World Cup. He was one of Clarke's allies during qualifying for Qatar '22 and was back in the role he left to become Jambos boss.

Leicester City's set-piece coach signed up for the ride as well, filling the void left by Austin MacPhee's departure. Andrew Hughes knew McLean, Hanley and Gunn from a previous job at Norwich and was proud to be representing his dad's country.

About a third of the Scotland squad would be travelling to Glasgow from their new homes. Angus Gunn had left Norwich and signed for Nottingham Forest on a free transfer after spending the summer at the PFA's pre-season camp. He'd be Matz Sels's back-up, or at least he hoped he would. They spunked £10m on Brazilian John Victor at the end of August, and when he and Sels suffered injuries Forest went and got Stefan Ortega instead. Gunn was already publicly talking in the autumn about his contract being ripped up.

Hanley joined Hibs, Hyam signed up for the Wrexham 'fairy tale', Johnston swapped Graz for Derby, McKenna's continental adventure took him to Zagreb, Tierney went home, Miller became Motherwell's record sale when Udinese paid nearly £5m for him, and Gannon-Doak went from Liverpool to Bournemouth for five-times that. He was also no longer Ben Doak. The double-barrel preference was introduced during the Cherries' announcement, with Ben wanting both of his parents' surnames on his jersey. 'He has to play,' observed Clarke. 'He has to keep his standards high. He's the type of player we've maybe been missing a little bit and we certainly missed Ben when he was out injured.'

One transfer appeared to be a certainty for completion once the players had already gathered, but it crumbled. Dykes would be in Birmingham until New Year.

> Hibs did what was required from their side. I wasn't getting the minutes I wanted at Birmingham and this came up; I spoke to David Gray and was looking forward to it. Everything was agreed and I thought I was going, so, yeah, it was difficult because I had my eyes set on it. I needed to go somewhere and get a fair chance of playing.

Dykes wasn't the only one in the set-up scrambling for minutes. Ralston, Adams, Ferguson, Gunn, Miller and Gilmour were understudies and strangely so was Robertson. Milos Kerkez was Arne Slot's preferred left-back after his arrival from Bournemouth in exchange for about £40m. But hey, they'd all had pre-seasons – and at the start of September, this was no biggie. Hickey was being drip-fed by Brentford. After more than 650 days spent rehabbing, his literal availability was the priority rather than his number of starts. His eight minutes from the bench at the City Ground in mid-August were nectar. Christie had also come through a fair ordeal involving inflammation around his hip and groin and was content with his load management on the south coast.

> I had *osteitis pubis*. I'd been struggling with it all season and even sneezing was causing me a lot of pain. I eventually got an operation; a double-hernia, which is invasive and involved my groin adductors as well. It's a painstaking rehab, especially over the summer when I just wanted to be on a beach for a few weeks. It was really bad by the time it got towards the end of the season; I was having to lean on a wall to put socks on, couldn't roll over in bed, day to day life was just difficult. I'd wake up one week thinking it was improving, then I'd play a game and do well to break into a run during the week after it. Two weeks off, it calms down, then it comes back again. The op has relieved me of all my pain.

Young Miller wasn't expected to start in Copenhagen; Christie next to Gilmour in a 4-2-3-1 was the consensus. Tierney and Gannon-Doak's presences in the camp triggered some parenthesis on shape discussions, but most wanted BGD in the team. The 'one' in the line-up was who had spread clamour fever.

Bowie, 22, had started the season well for Hibs. He scored three in their first nine games of the season – including a double against Dundee – but it wasn't his ratio that propelled him to the lips of the Tartan Army and the *pundits*. Bowie looked like a cracking young player with promise, but the commotion was the result of his 40-yard screamer (NOT a volley!) against Partizan Belgrade in a Conference League qualifier, which was unlikely in isolation to earn him a starting spot in the group's hardest game but was a display of unpredictable striking brilliance. A footballing facet of which the Tartan Army had been starved.

They were quenched in Copenhagen. It pished down all day so, sounding similar to the start of a joke, fans spent the day of the game indoors on a block that provided Scottish, Irish and English pubs. Word spread about the Gasoline Grills dotted around the city, which had trails of dark blue jerseys queuing for what I'm told is one of the best burgers one can munch.

Wing-backs or wingers? That had been the question. When Tierney (and Ralston) left the camp with an injury, he squeezed the ambiguity into his suitcase. It would be a 4-2-3-1 for Scotland and Gannon-Doak would surely start. Fans spat out their Carlsberg when the team was dropped like it was hot because, well, it was hot.

Clarke's team for a World Cup qualifying opener in Copenhagen read: Gunn; Hickey, Souttar, Hanley, Robertson; McGinn, McTominay, Ferguson, Christie; Adams, Dykes.

4-4-2.

Reporters and commentators in the Danish capital had heard some whispers about this possibility, but few thought it could be true. Gilmour and Gannon-Doak on the bench! Clarke was forging the rod with which he'd be beaten, surely. There was stature and presence among this selection. The players had obviously known for a day or two and Dykes didn't mind it.

> It was a surprise to hear that's what we were going for. The last time I remember playing it was against the Czechs in the first game of the Euros. We try a lot of different things on the training ground and watch it back on the camera. Clarke wanted us to nullify what they were strong at; controlling games. It should allow

us to press more and when we attack it should give their defenders more difficulty in picking us up, rather than having two centre-backs staring at me. When we cleared the ball or got it back it gave us more time to get up the pitch.

'The last time we came here, Denmark put us under a lot of early pressure and we didn't really have an out ball, so hopefully with two up top we might be able to cause them an issue, get ourselves up the pitch, settle into the game and play,' said the boss.

Denmark had won 11 of their last 12 at home. They hadn't lost a qualifier here since the early knockings of the journey to Russia '18, when Montenegro bolted back to the Balkans with one goal and a clean sheet. A third World Cup in a row was the expectation. Their squad boasted players from Champions League level clubs and the Premier League; Barcelona, Napoli, Monaco, Marseille, Sporting Lisbon, Ajax, Porto, Eintracht Frankfurt and Manchester United, Newcastle, Brentford and Fulham. Celtic as well; Kasper Schmeichel.

Mika Biereth spent half a season on loan with Motherwell two years previously and caught up with Miller, Johnston and Kelly before the game. Since being recalled by Arsenal in January 2024, he'd been sold to Sturm Graz, on to Monaco for £13m and had become an international player. He banged in three hat-tricks in his first seven games for the Monegasque. Quite the rise! Can you just *imagine* the hype if he was Scottish? Copenhagen had recently been voted the happiest city in the world, but while the natives expressed some excitement about him, they generally downplayed expectations for the next couple of months.

Their boss Brian Reimer declared 'every team would like a Scott McTominay,' before adding that he thought Gilmour and his new Neapolitan neighbour could play for any club in the world. He'd left out Christian Eriksen as the playmaker hadn't found a new club yet after leaving Manchester United.

The Parken has an aura. As a shape, it's basically Ibrox without seats at a few of the corner bases. As the teams stood for the anthems a tifo filled the entire stand behind the goal to the left of your TV screen, resembling Japan's Rising Sun flag with red and white rays emanating from the goal's direction. After being hidden away in corners and top tiers inside the vast bowls visited during the Nations League's away days, Scotland fans were shoulder to shoulder yards from the pitch, like away fans at Tynecastle. Considering how big-boned Hampden and many of Europe's top stadiums are, they relished the proximity.

Denmark blitzed Scotland here in 2021 and Clarke reflected on that with his squad in the build-up. The Danes had two goals after 15 minutes, Robertson's gills were closing at right wing-back and the evening's 'out ball' of Ryan Fraser barely got a kick.

Ten minutes in now, Denmark had 85 per cent possession and Scotland had mustered 16 passes. Still level ten minutes later, McTominay wasted a huge chance to play in Adams for a one-on-one, instinctively trusting his own ability to score but seeing his shot from the box's edge blocked. As Clarke proffered, Scotland had settled. Greece were leading 3-0 and cruising against Belarus. The Tartan Army honoured former international Jimmy Bone after his death a few days before the match with an applause in the 20th minute – the minute in which he scored away to Denmark in 1972.

Lewis Ferguson was getting his chance in the middle of the park.

> It was quite old school with me and Scotty in the middle of the park. My role was to stay disciplined and keep things ticking over; shut off their spaces and not allow them to play. Scott was the one who could bomb on when we had the ball, but I had to read the game and be organised. Mikkel Damsgaard liked playing off my shoulder between me and the defence, so I was having

to watch the game in front of me but constantly listen to Grant and John behind me giving me instructions. Any discussions between me and the gaffer would have been tactical, not about any physicality. If someone was to ask me about my favourite position it would be a number eight, box-to-box midfielder but I'm comfortable being a defensive midfielder as well; I understand the role and discipline. If I'm told I'm playing there, my box-to-box instincts come out of my game and I don't need to hold back. When I first came over to Bologna I was more of an attacking midfielder but I've become more defensive in the last season or so since my injury.

At the first whistle and for some minutes afterwards, there was some understandable unhappiness seeing Gannon-Doak on the bench and Christie out wide. The former's impact for us and the latter's for Bournemouth had whetted appetites, but Hickey's first start in almost two years meant Clarke wanted a layer of protection before him in the form of McGinn. On the other side, of the options available, Christie was reliable in rolling his sleeves up ahead of Robertson.

I had to stop their full-back Kristensen coming forward and be honest with my tracking to help out Andy. When we go to places like this, the gaffer is so big on everybody doing their bit. There are no privileges. We thought they'd take the game to us to kick-off with three points but we dealt with it quite well. I liked the two up front approach. It was positive, the Danes wouldn't expect it and hopefully it'd give us a foothold. It was a typical international game, not like the Greece one at Hampden, can't give anything away at the start of the qualifiers. I'm sure from the outside, looking in, there were a few

The Scotland players begin to digest Hungary's winning goal to knock them out of Euro 2024

Grant Hanley knows his mistimed tackle will carry the consequence of a last-minute penalty to Poland in the Nations League opener

Scott McTominay celebrates his opening goal in Lisbon

This late own goal almost earned Scotland an important point in Zagreb, but Adams was offside in the build-up

Nicky Devlin only played for a few minutes against Portugal at Hampden but earned Scotland a point with this brilliant block

John McGinn lets it all out in front of the west stand after scoring the winner against Croatia

This was the only way Ben Gannon-Doak was being stopped by Gvardiol

Captain Andy Robertson thunders his stoppage-time header into the net and give Scotland the win in Warsaw...

...before embracing the carnage that awaited him towards the away dugout

Greece's golden boy Konstantinos Karetsas curls a beauty into the top corner as the visitors rip Scotland apart

Steve Clarke and Ivan Jovanovic watch on as Greece dominate at Hampden

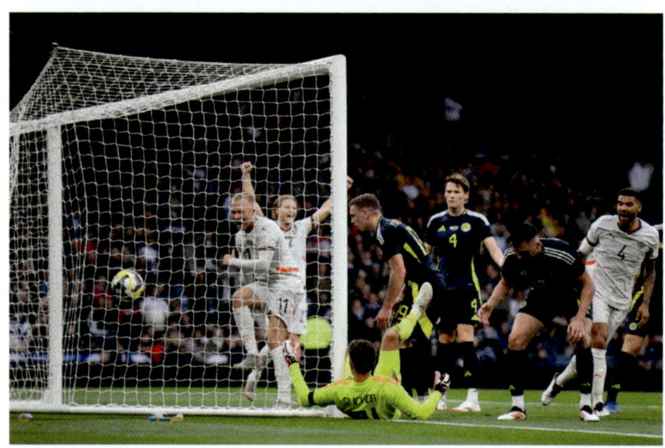

Iceland take the lead again after some calamitous Scottish defending

Lennon Miller impressed in Liechtenstein on his first start

The Tartan Army relished being close to the action in Denmark's Parken Stadium

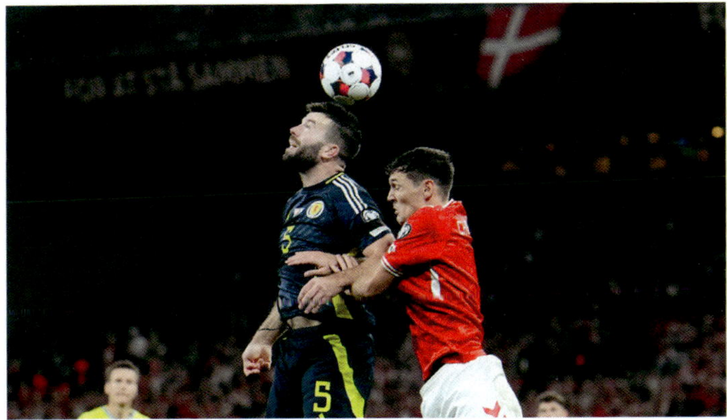

Grant Hanley was in imperious defensive form in Copenhagen as Scotland earned a 0-0 draw

Lewis Ferguson wasn't escaping Grant Hanley's clutches after putting Scotland into the lead at home against Greece...

Ché Adams scored
against Belarus
for his first truly
meaningful
Scotland goal
since his famous
sealer against
Denmark
in 2021

...a win sealed by Lyndon Dykes in stoppage time

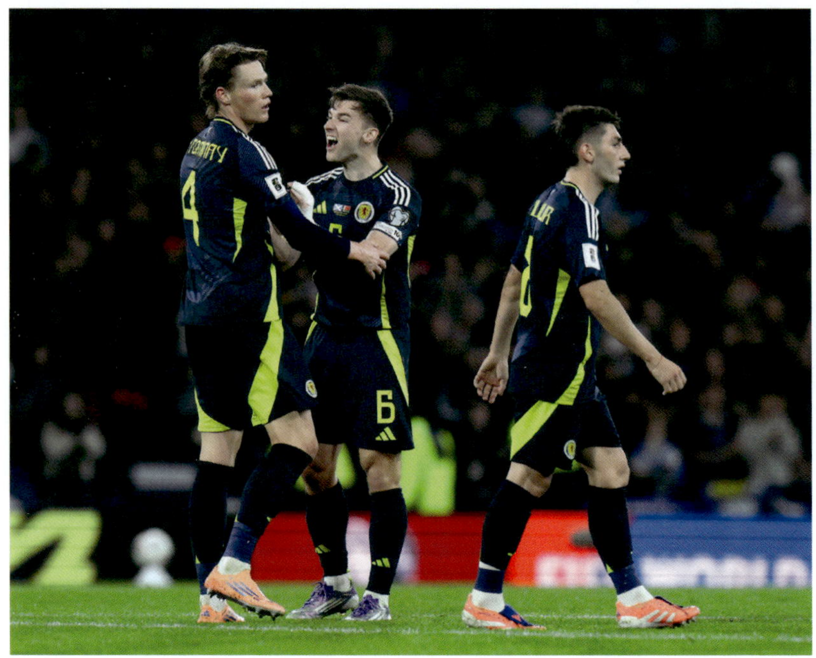

Scott McTominay wasn't in the mood to celebrate after scoring Scotland's second during a turgid performance at home to Belarus

Steve Clarke was furious with Scotland's display against the group's bottom seeds

Greece went 3-0 up in Athens and had seemingly consigned Scotland to the play-offs

Ryan Christie scored Scotland's second goal as they sought to complete an incredible comeback ahead of the final game against Denmark

The Tartan Army were full of belief as Scotland somehow maintained hopes of automatic qualification

In Hampden's biggest match for generations, Scott
McTominay scored Scotland's greatest ever goal

EE PROUDLY SPONSORS THE S
TO HAMPDEN PARK

Lawrence Shankland is welcomed by Ferguson after tapping Scotland into the lead again

Kieran Tierney has just scored the goal that will send Scotland to the World Cup

The most joyous scenes Hampden has witnessed in, perhaps forever?

USA! USA! USA!

questions about how we'd start qualifying because if we'd been pumped 3-0 by Denmark I'm sure the walls would have caved in pretty quickly.

A pattern I've noticed during my chats with squad members is that if one of them isn't selected, they accept Clarke's decision without probing the thought process. The majority of them have worked with him for long enough to get on with it. Enter Ben Gannon-Doak.

> I spoke to him the day after the game to ask why I wasn't picked. Not out of entitlement, but I want to play and want to know how to get into the team. He explained he wanted Aaron and Andy to have a bit more protection and stability down the flanks, and I completely understood that, so I wasn't worried or anything. I think any manager would be more concerned if players didn't want to play or if we didn't ask. If a manager ever gets annoyed I guess I'll just have to say sorry, but until that point I'm always going to ask what I need to do to play.

Christie and McGinn were pressing quite highly, and Adams was dropping deeper rather than a piece of string connecting him and Dykes. Robertson and Hickey's average position was narrower than the 18-yard box's confines. Force Denmark wide, clear the ball. This half-resembled the second half in Athens, but with a bit of extra juice from Scotland. Denmark mirrored Scotland in certain environments; loads of the ball but struggling to penetrate. Both sides' final ball wasn't great. Christie got caught in two minds with a back-post header and it bounced wide.

The whole team were working cohesively to plug gaps and get themselves in the way of the football. Hanley was imperious and deflected a Pierre-Emile Højbjerg shot just wide; the closest they had come.

On any other game, Hanley would probably have won Man of the Match. But counting context, Hickey was incredible. He started Scotland's classiest move of the match, winning a header on the edge of his own box and receiving a return pass from McGinn as he marauded towards halfway. He clipped it back infield to McGinn, who slotted in Adams. Scotland were scything through the Danes in rare fashion. Dykes was free in the middle! Adams found him. Dykes fluffed it.

> I wanted to hit it first time but I thought if I took a touch it would put me in a better position to score. It's easy to say after it that I should have shot first time, but I could have easily done that, missed the whole goal and then everyone would ask why I didn't take a touch! If the pass was teed up a bit softer then I'm thinking I'd have come onto it and whipped it. I could feel him [Kristensen] coming so had to get it onto my left to get the shot away, but he blocked it. It was the wrong decision. My numbers are pretty good for my minutes. Since the Norway goal they've been up and down. I didn't get a run in any friendlies against teams that we should be scoring against.

For my previous book, I remember asking Charlie Mulgrew about trying to fend off elite strikers and the challenges they each bring. He identified Romelu Lukaku as sometimes 'impossible' to stop because Lukaku would turn him if he got too close, but how could he possibly allow him a yard or two of space? Hanley was posed with one when Rasmus Højlund came off the bench as Denmark ran out of time.

> The size of him stood out; he was an absolute animal. I didn't realise how big and strong he was. Straight away I knew what I was up against so I prepared my mind for

dealing with him while the ball went wide. He's a big boy, likes to get a hold of you, similar I suppose to what Charlie said about Lukaku. My mindset with those types of players is to give them some space so they can't feel you but then bump them before they receive it so they can't nip it round the corner and maybe get there in front of him. Højlund is bigger and more powerful than me so I need to read his movements and get my body in at the right time to affect him. I'm not going to do anything like Lyndon did to Luke Shaw at the Euros, but it's the relentlessness for me. I'm going to hit you for 90 minutes and be consistent rather than go big once and hope you go away.

The durability of the Tartan Army's fabric has been proven over decades. They underwent a stress test in the closing stages as Denmark slugged to score a winner and deny Scotland of the point they deserved. Watching the national team in this form every time would be an exercise in masochism, but after the performances so far in 2025 the commitment, discipline, intensity and street wisdom were welcomed. Scotland's full-backs and midfielders were delivering surely tempting crosses, but nobody was willing to place a stake. McGinn was having a brilliant game, driving and roping in red shirts whenever he picked up the ball. He was the McGinn of old. Well, I say old; the McGinn of a couple of years ago.

After being one of Scotland's most consistent players in the Nations League, McLean found himself watching from the dugout again. A deep thinker, he observes and discusses the game's patterns with his kindred spirit Liam Kelly. What are Scotland doing well, and what do we need to do better? This isn't chat for the sake of it; it's a huge factor in why he always feels ready to come on. With ten minutes to go, he entered the fray in his traditional *closer* capacity.

I'm very proud of that role and feel fortunate the manager puts his trust in me to do that. We have something to protect; I can come on and help us achieve that. We knew we were close to a good point in Copenhagen. The manager knows I'm tactically aware in a lot of situations, and with about 700 games he knows what I'm going to do. We had a few breakaways that we could have made more of, but would have taken a point before the game.

Max Johnston replaced Hickey with 20 minutes to play. One minute later, referee Daniel Siebert was advised to take a slow-motion look at a replay of the incident for which he'd booked the Derby full-back; a handball about 50 yards from goal, but crucially with nobody between him and Angus Gunn as Mika Biereth ambushed him. Johnston's legs 'turned to jelly'. The yellow stood. Biereth had shoved Johnston off balance. The right call. The boy he'd replaced was being showered with compliments he wouldn't be aware of until he spoke to his family.

Starting against Denmark was a big turning point for me. I'd come off the bench for Brentford a few times but was waiting on a start. I was thinking about the September break and felt buzzing. It was a massive thing for me and gave me real confidence going back to Brentford. That game was one of my aims in my journey back. I felt like I'd hit the ground running.

Hirst and Gannon-Doak also came on for Dykes and Adams as Clarke explored the opportunity of a sucker punch while Denmark wildly windmilled. Wee BGD's impact was felt within two minutes as he somehow rescued Robertson's long ball before it crossed the byline and rifled a shot that fizzed into the side netting. His energy was infectious.

Højbjerg headed a six-yard header into Gunn's arms in the final minute – an enormous waste – and the home side were booed towards the tunnel. The Scots looked knackered. The evening's resolve deserved independent credit, but the matches that preceded this opening qualifier had to be considered as well. The organisation, confidence and determination absent at Hampden earlier in the year were abundant in the Parken. Perhaps a win was there for the taking, as pundits mused. Could Gannon-Doak have been introduced earlier than the 83rd minute, or Bowie introduced at all as a chaos agent? The Danes did look a bit vulnerable towards their own goal, but if they had more space in which to attack and found a late goal then the head coach would have *gotten it*. At the end of the day, Scotland stifled Denmark very, very well. Football fans are quick to criticise – sometimes in advance – so it's only fair to give credit when it is due. Clarke and his boys were due it.

While identifying Hanley as the night's outstanding figure, McGinn said, 'We suffered a lot in the first 15 minutes. The effort from everyone was superb and we managed to keep a clean sheet, which is brilliant. It was about staying in the game. Tonight we looked like a Steve Clarke team.'

Dykes was McGinn's echo, referencing the 'character' among the squad. Wearing his club trackie and chilling in a hotel room on our Zoom call, he reflected:

> That was a good point. We were happy with how we played. The Parken is a good stadium to play in, the crowd is very up for it. A good vibes stadium. I remember a few years ago I came off the bench and struggled. The 0-0 game was a big ask for Ché and I both attackingly and defensively, but I think the two up top threw Denmark off the scent a bit because we hadn't done it for a while. It helped because when we cleared the ball or got it back, it gave us more time

to get up the pitch. When one of us comes short, the other has gone long, so it gave a balance.

Loveable broadcaster Roddy Forsyth spoke on the *Hampden Roar* podcast the next day and said he'd swapped a couple of text messages with the head coach after the game.

'It was sweaty but we got our decisions right and got the result we came for,' was Clarke's reply.

'It's only one point. We have to keep our feet on the ground,' he told BBC Scotland a wee while after full time, sniffing potential hype from a mile away. 'A good start. A very disciplined performance, which we needed it to be.'

It was easy to forget that not only had Scotland plundered an esteemed point of their own, they'd hindered Denmark's pursuit of a perfect start. The top seeds had dropped points already. Greece battered Belarus 5-1. Our hosts and us both seemed more concerned with them rather than each other during post-match conversations during the walk back to the metro and into the city centre, where Allaster McKallaster skipped between parties with his microphone.

Scotland regularly have cement setting around their ankles when a World Cup qualifying campaign begins. They broke free from one win in four to reach the play-offs before Qatar '22, but leaving themselves with an unscalable mountain was a tradition. Winning one from four at the start of the Russia '18 campaign – with a draw at home to Lithuania – was too much to overcome. Two draws at home to Serbia and Macedonia before losing in Cardiff ended aspirations for Brazil in 2014; we didn't win any of our opening six qualifiers. Macedonia also wrote off our vehicle on the long trip to South Africa for the 2010 showpiece by beating us in the first game, and we drew at home to Norway a couple of matches later (yep, *that* miss) before the Netherlands thumped us. Again, one win in four. We narrowly missed out on the play-offs on three of those occasions, but we designed the blueprints for disappointment with the flimsiest foundations.

A draw in Copenhagen with Belarus in an empty stadium to follow. Then two home games. If we had one tally in the win column at the end of that run, giving up would feel like the kind option for our sanities.

Although 2025 had been distressing for Scotland supporters, in the last 12 months we had beaten Poland, Greece and Croatia, drawn with Portugal at Hampden and now Denmark in the Parken. Something didn't add up. I've already referenced the more recent tradition that had developed for Scotland since Clarke took the job: rebounding from regrets. Scotland irrefutably found form after Euro 2020, the World Cup 2022 play-offs, the trip to Dublin that followed and Euro 2024. Greece put us in our place at Hampden in March, and playing them twice in two months was daunting after such a setback.

Fans had gone to Denmark more in hope than expectation, but the ball was rolling. Shouldn't we feel quite optimistic?

Chapter 10
Belarus (Away)

AS A commentator, especially on the national team games, I hold stats close to my heart. So here's one in cold, hard form.

Since failing to qualify for the 2002 World Cup, Scotland went *20* years without collecting maximum points from matches against the bottom two seeds in a qualifying campaign. Beating Faroe Islands and Moldova in the ultimately fruitless attempt to reach the World Cup in 2022 was the first time we'd achieved such a *feat* since Broon's days. We didn't manage it in the pursuit of a place at Euro 2024, but we'd already qualified when Lawrence Shankland scored a late equaliser in Tbilisi.

This was a personality trait of Steve Clarke's Scotland side. Generally, they dispatched of fodder with few fucks. Rarely – or never – four, five or six zip, but stress was sparse. In reverse chronology since wee Berti's term, Scotland had paid for dropping points against Kazakhstan, Lithuania, Georgia, Wales, Macedonia, Lithuania, Macedonia, Georgia, Belarus, Moldova, Lithuania and the Faroe Islands.

Belarus. Zoinks!

Technically, we were one of the bottom two seeds in this group, but realistically Belarus stood alone in that regard – and right now they stood between Scotland and a brilliant start to Group C. They would stand between Scotland and four points in Zalaegerszeg, Hungary?

UEFA sanctions have restricted Belarus since their government – led by Putin bum-licker Alexander Lukashenko – helped facilitate Russia's invasion of Ukraine. Ergo, no matches in a UEFA competition can be played in the country and the games they do play on neutral ground must not have any supporters there to stave off the plausibility of protests or activist violence. Latvia, Lithuania and Poland are all only across one boundary so you, like me, might think it odd UEFA planned the game 900 miles and four borders away in Zalaegerszeg, a small city around the size of Inverness plotted near Hungary's western edge. As Michael Grant reported in *The Times*, the Hungarian Football Federation's President – and convenient billionaire – Sándor Csányi is on UEFA's executive council and fulfils the same role for Aleksander Čeferin as Lukashenko does for Putin. The odd bone is thrown for these trusty lapdogs. Like the Champions League Final in 2026.

A flight to Minsk or Budapest from Scotland are each around three hours long and Belarus were on their way back from Greece anyway. At the end of the day, no fans would be at the game so did it really matter for us?

Belarus were understandably a bit fed up. 'When you rent a home, it is not your home. We always have troubles. We spend almost no time in Belarus. We want to play with our supporters,' said their boss Carlos Alós.

Scotland flew in to the tiny Hévíz-Balaton airport, which is around three-quarters of an hour from Zalaegerszeg and surrounded by fields and derelict, three-storey apartment blocks that belong on a *Call of Duty* map. They drove on tight, winding roads through tiny villages with a petrol station and convenience shop. This would be Belarus' fourth match in the relatively small ZTE Arena; an all-seater with a capacity of 11,200 and the vibe of a council leisure centre without the (gorgeous) smell of chlorine. They'd drawn against Bulgaria, Northern Ireland and Luxembourg recently and beaten Kosovo and Andorra in other stadiums but lost 12 of their last 13 World Cup qualifying fixtures regardless of the location. Scotland had lost only one of their last 17 World Cup qualifiers with 11 wins yet were absent in Qatar and Russia. Make it make sense!

We saw in March how dangerous the Greeks are – *we* could have ended up conceding five – so judging the Belarussians on that result alone would probably be naive.

Make no mistake though, Scotland should win this football match. Two of their players were in the Kairat side that knocked Celtic out of the Champions League qualifying play-off, Dinamo Minsk were heavily populated as were smaller clubs in Russia, Poland and Slovenia. A repeat of Gordon Strachan's hubris in 2015, starting Hutton, Martin and Robertson in a back three against Gibraltar, was more improbable than Scotland actually losing that game at Hampden, but a narrative developed – as usual – that this was a good *opportunity* to play a few of the more inexperienced boys in the team. One might ask, had we learned anything, ever?

Although, there was merit in a debate. Any of the players who came in would be in Belarus' *star* bracket. Johnston, Bowie, Miller and Gannon-Doak were the pre-match storyline's protagonists. Their involvement shouldn't stifle Scotland in the slightest. In fact, it could invigorate the team, but the suggestion of rests or experiments contains a complacent scent. The number of goals and minutes for fringe players was definitely a preoccupation for some thinking with an assumption of problem-free points gathering.

'We'll take the win if we can get it, however it comes,' said the manager, tossing the Tartan Army's script in the bin. 'If it's by one goal, if it's by two goals, whatever. First of all, we need to make sure we get the win.'

Must-win, it was.

Comparing us to a serial killer, Neil McCann said on *Sportsound* that Scotland must be 'a bit unhinged in how we attack, but also calculated'.

The only maniac in Scotland's ranks was Gannon-Doak. I mean that in an affectionate way, of course. Surely there was no excuse for benching the wee man this evening, with the pace in his legs causing him third-degree burns. Clarke is a man who swears over the bible of pragmatism and preached a verse to the media on necessary rotation after trudging for 90 minutes through the mud on the Baltic Sea's shores. He'd gone from bemoaning the peripheral options available to revealing his delight at who he saw when he turned to his bench.

A couple dozen Scotland fans rocked-up in Hungary in total knowledge they'd be watching the game in a local bar. They greeted the players outside the ZTE Arena – sadly none of the squad members acknowledged or greeted them back – and hung their saltires around the perimeter fencing before proceeding to their watering hole for the night. A few remained to catch glimpses through the corner gaps. The players understandably drew comparisons with the Covid era when I asked them about this game. They could travel, enjoy their pre-match meals and change as one, but the eerie empty stadium was a curious throwback to a time when Scotland did very well, stringing together six games without loss and sealing qualification in Belgrade for the Euros.

The evening was balmy following an afternoon of 20°C sunshine and Scott McTominay signed an autograph for a local suit inside the stadium. The atmosphere around the ground and city was as if a game wasn't happening and the locals didn't care that it was. Some of the players were able to wander around the town without needing any invisibility cloaks. They stopped for some photos with fans who had travelled, but with the low density weren't required to stop every two seconds. The lads sauntered around the pitch before the game in what looked like a pair of navy blue pyjamas, doing that strangely socially accepted thing footballers do by having conversations with their earphones still in. They can't have been chatting about the pre-match message from above: *Get in and get out with three points. Do not mess up your good work the other night.* The players were certain in their recollections.

'Clarke was 100 per cent on must-win,' said Lyndon Dykes. 'If we want to top the group, we have to beat Belarus home and away.'

Do not add Zalaegerszeg to the list beneath Astana, Tbilisi and Skopje.

In a 4-2-3-1 shape and wearing the minty away kit, Clarke's XI was: Gunn; Johnston, Souttar, McKenna, Robertson; Gilmour, Ferguson; McGinn, McTominay, Gannon-Doak; Adams.

Hickey was recovering from Friday's exertions, Gilmour was brought in for creation and Gannon-Doak for, well, do I need to say it? He was also put on the left to give Johnston more protection in the form of McGinn. Christie was on a yellow card and saved for the Greece game. McKenna started to give the defence a 'left-footed balance', which meant Hanley was on the bench.

> Horses for courses, I know the way it goes. I'm experienced enough to understand that. I'm at the stage now where I'm getting towards the end and every cap is precious, but I'm long enough in the tooth to know the reasons and be comfortable with that. When you see the lads in the squad and the quality around the place, it explains itself. I always put the shoe on the other foot and think about Scotty who hasn't played in games I've started, and he must think, 'How is this old fucker still in the team?' For every game I've played there's been someone else disappointed, and vice versa. My views have changed as I've got older. I'm grateful for every cap I get with guys like Ryan Porteous, Jack Hendry and Scott McKenna in the squad as well as others like Liam Lindsay that have been in the squad at times.' These are top centre-halves and the manager is still putting his trust in me. I think because of the injuries I've been through as well, going through a period of three years without being in a squad, then my recent injury, there have been times I've thought I wouldn't play for Scotland again, so I view it all with an open mind.

Flower of Scotland's crescendo was met with a 'Come on Scotland!' from outwith the confines. It was reasonable to expect the ball to be under Scotland's control and numbers showed they had it for 80 per cent of the game. That doesn't necessarily translate. Scotland were alright in the early stages but too pedestrian. Belarus had 13 per cent possession midway through the first half but had had more shots. Greece were 4-0 up by this point. The hosts made a change to five at the back against us to try and prevent a repeat of such horrors. They should probably have taken the lead when Johnston had a bit of a brain freeze and Belarus' Max Ebong ran through one-on-one. He hesitated to pull the trigger and Gunn saved. 'You cannot switch off!' Everyone heard Robertson. A little scare and reminder that while patience was important, we didn't have forever. Johnston was getting it *tight* throughout the half. 'Fucking get back!' 'Get fucking up!' Anything notable derived from Gannon-Doak's drive.

> I quite enjoyed that game, saw plenty of the ball. I need to play a bit differently on the left and be more controlled, but I enjoyed it. I prefer playing on the right because I can go both ways. I can on the left as well but it takes a bit of adjustment and getting the ball a couple of times. I have to keep it simple before I can try a few things. I enjoyed myself that night. I don't get the chance to play next to Robbo often, so when I do I feel secure with his experience and guidance for where to be off the ball. That really helps my defensive side. I was disappointed we didn't cut them open well enough and score some more goals but the whole theme was just do it, just win. If we play well then brilliant but if we don't, just win.

Passes were traded from side to side, into the channel and back again or into a dead end. Clarke exhibited some irritation with the lack of creation. 'Get fucking into them!' Robertson would occasionally roar. McTominay prodded one just wide, Gilmour flew a few tame ones on target, one of them palmed onto the post, but Scotland's threat was minimal. A few teasing not tantalising balls were thrown into Belarus' area while they sat deeply, but the only signs of ignition came from our teenager as he burst down the wing or chopped inside. It was becoming a frustrating watch. Christie's eyes narrowed on the bench at times:

> It was a really strange night. I couldn't even tell you where we played it. I remember being on the bench about 20 minutes in thinking, 'We need to score quickly here. If we want to qualify, we need to win this game.' Scoring just before half-time settled a few nerves.

Let's get to that then, in the 43rd minute. I've noted the impact Gannon-Doak was having, but it was two of the old guard who combined to set up Ché Adams. He anticipated McTominay's knock-down from one of McGinn's teasing balls and stretched sufficiently to poke the ball in. Gannon-Doak clenched his fists and yelled a very Scottish 'Yaasss!' Gilmour ran to share a high-five with McGinn. 'Go on, Ché!' shouted Clarke. Adams released a bit of anger as he punched the air. His first *meaningful* goal for Scotland since sending Hampden into raptures with the sealer against Denmark in 2021, and into double figures as a national team goalscorer.

He continued his habit of scoring against minnows but this was a difference-maker, regardless of the opposition. McTominay's hot form had cooled – he had one in eight, a penalty – while McGinn had scored two from open play in two years, so any goal scored by a striker in a competitive game was a welcome one. This was the first time one had done so since Shankland in Tbilisi in November 2023. There are 14 games under that umbrella, so Adams was part of a group regularly insulted by stakeholders as simply not good enough. I'm too young to know from experience, but I gather it was the same in the 80s and 90s when our paucity of options included Sturrock, Brazil, Archibald, Jordan and Nicholas or McCoist, McAvennie, Robertson and Johnston.

Scotland were leading, but you know what it's like. McTominay couldn't beat the keeper with quite a simple header – think Lisbon, again – and Belarus had a few half-chances. The empty stadium fogged the thin line being tread. Vladislav Kalinin should have been sent off for nearly breaking Ferguson's ankle. 'Hawl you! Fucking send him off!' bellowed McKenna towards the ref. This was a red card offence 50 years ago as well as in today's diluted world. He admitted after the game he had no regrets for the retribution dealt out only a few minutes after Gannon-Doak had flown into a challenge like a border collie on to a tennis ball. He was still our main threat and, truthfully, the only source of excitement if not efficiency. McTominay was operating in second gear.

Not only did Adams give us the lead, he provided the match's outstanding moment of quality to take the game beyond Belarus. Gilmour was at the heart of the whole thing; happy on the half-turn on the inside left, he strode towards Belarus' area and slid it to Adams. Billy continued his run into the box and Adams took out his sand wedge to scoop it over the jagged home line and onto Gilmour's head. He nodded it into McTominay's path, but Zakhar Volkov got there first and sent it into his own goal. With 65 played, that was the game done. Ferguson knew it.

> The game in Denmark took a lot out of us. It was only 2-0 but I don't think you can underestimate how dangerous a team Belarus can be. They never had any chances to get into the game. These can be really tricky places to go, in the middle of nowhere, with nobody in the stadium, so the energy and drive can only come from us. I thought our professionalism was really good.

Right, Steve, let's see a few of the young boys for 20 minutes now.

Christie and Hickey were the first changes ten minutes after the second goal, Dykes and Mclean with ten to play, and Miller in stoppage time.

It felt like a perfect opportunity wasted to play Miller, Bowie and/or Doig in a (semi)competitive environment, specifically for Bowie and the potential for him to hit the ground running with Scotland's two main midfield sources of goals drying up. A couple of minutes for Miller felt underwhelming as well in the circumstances. McLean was more than happy to receive another cap and isn't precious about the clamour for his competition.

> I wouldn't say I'm aware of fans wanting it, but they should want to see more of Lennon. I'm also pushing for him and desperate to do well. I'll always try and help him and do what I can, but the manager makes the decisions. He won't do what he thinks the fans want him to do at 3-0 or 4-0. Lennon has lots of caps ahead of him; I've trained about ten times with him and trust me, he will get loads of caps. I haven't seen his ability in many young players; the way he receives the ball, passes it and has awareness of his situations. The way he receives the ball is something I look at in a young player – I think I can identify that quite quickly – and a few minutes into his first session he was receiving the ball knowing exactly where his attackers and the defenders were. It was amazing to see and I know he will be the future of this country. I want to help him become the player I know he will be.

Oh, the privilege of winning a World Cup qualifier away from home and reflecting on the minutes afforded to the kids. Nothing was surprising about the way this fixture transpired. The Scots fulfilled Clarke's wishes to the letter; get in, get out with three points. AC/

DC's 'Hells Bells' reverberated off the empty, dusty seats at full time, which wasn't reflective of Scotland's acoustic performance; they had total control but never looked like dropping points or running away with it. 'Professional' was the evening's word. If rock 'n' roll was your priority, switching over to Greece v Denmark would have served you more appropriately. Who saw Denmark's head-banging 3-0 win coming? The group was wide open with us and them on four and the Greeks on three.

'We could have had more, but a job well done,' said our captain, reminding us Belarus' change of shape meant Scotland had to adapt their plans.

'It's a good start but it's only a start. Clean sheets are what we have to build our campaign on,' said the head coach.

Well, we had two of them with two home games to come in a month where the team would have the backing of 50,000 Scots rather than a handful hanging around the confines. And you know the score … if we want to qualify for a World Cup, we must win our home games. Full steam ahead!

Chapter 11

Greece (Home)

Somewhat typically in Scotland, the build-up to a game that would shape the World Cup qualifying campaign was dominated by a manager's future. Steve Clarke's '75 per cent' admission hadn't changed but the timing was floating without anchor; November, March or maybe the following summer? What was the point of speculating about who would be next and when, especially when the team had started qualification strongly and had a tangible reward for which to strive? A reward at the end of a 20-year tunnel. Let's just keep our eyes on the road here, please?

The Scottish media slowed down to stare at the wreckage on the hard shoulder. Oh dear, a write-off. No question.

Of course, I'm being sardonic. Clarke wasn't the manager at the centre of the conversations. The catastrophic start to Rangers' season and Russell Martin's job security was the hot topic around town. Celtic's civil war bore endless back-page fruit as well and their fans' ironic schadenfreude is another story. Glasgow was outdoing itself. The hacks were patting their bellies with an 'Oh boy!' after the almost daily three-course meals being served up between the pair. Hearts' terrific start commanded attention too. A Scotland squad full of the same names as a few weeks previously doesn't write headlines; Craig Gordon was involved again and a couple of fringe players were left out as the squad was trimmed by a couple.

Former Scotland international Martin was wrestling for control at Ibrox as September became October. The tyres blew out four days before Scotland's match against Greece. He emerged from the royal blue debris with a few bruises, a chunky pay-off and Lucy Pinder waiting for a cuddle.

Clarke's semi-regular reminders that he doesn't really pay attention to what the papers are writing probably wouldn't stand up in court circumstantially. He can be partial to a bit of passive aggression in response to a narrative he sees as unjustified, and while he didn't consciously bring the topic to the table, he did concede he felt it was 'strange' that a game of such significance wasn't being given the build-up it warranted. I'd have thought that's the way Clarke would've manipulated it if he had the choice. Christie has experience of both bowls as a former Celtic player:

> I didn't really think about that at the time, but it's good that the gaffer mentioned it. As a squad, we rarely look at the media narrative. We have to just focus on the game. When you do press after a game it's hard to avoid it, but beforehand we like to keep ourselves in a bubble. We did speak among ourselves about the situation in the Scottish league, but that was about it. I'm glad I have Ben at Bournemouth now because until that I had nobody to speak to about Scottish football. I could have mentioned what was happening with Hearts and the lads would say, 'Who're they?' One of the nice things about meeting up with the boys is chatting about Scottish football. I still keep an eye on Inverness. It's only when you step away you realise how mad it is. It's a really strange aspect of life; the better you are for Celtic, the worse your life is because you can't do as much away from football. It's a huge sacrifice if you want to be successful. Bournemouth is the total opposite. I could walk through the town centre in my full kit and nobody would stop me. It starts at 3pm on a Saturday and ends a few hours later.

Given the Scotland team stayed at Glasgow's Blythswood Hotel on the same nights as a global popstar, there was the tiresome hunt for a gimmick from a man who has never been anything but tired of gimmicks. Like panning for gold in a sewer. Clarke even provided the needless yet obligatory 'no disrespect to Katy' before clarifying he is of a 'different generation' to Miss Perry and wouldn't be able to name one of her many numbers. Gary Cotterill must have been bereft at not being sent north by Sky Sports News for that press conference.

Anyway, the squad had barely changed. That doesn't mean there weren't any subjects to sweep over.

Despite now being the deputy at Hearts to new signing Alexander Schwolow, Craig Gordon was back after recovering from a neck injury – closer to his 43rd birthday than his 42nd, six months after Clarke convinced him not to retire and three months after the head coach publicly aired his concerns about the future of Scottish goalkeeping. Angus Gunn was the moment's first choice, but we'd seen the mess made in June by a lack of experience.

> The initial discussion was around the time of the play-off against Greece and he told me to give it one more year. There was no chat in the summer, just that one. We only had six months to know if we'd be at a World Cup at the end of the season, so why would I not give myself the opportunity to be part of it? I spoke to a specialist about my neck and got a rough timeline for recovery. I took my time to make sure the injury wasn't going to be too long-term and would be something I could come back from before I committed to an extra year. Hearts were looking for an answer and I agreed a one-year deal. Potentially being part of a World Cup squad was a huge part of it for me. I felt I had a part to play and could still do it at the top level. They could have gone down the Jon McCracken or Scott Bain route but all of a sudden

> I was back in the conversation. It came out the blue a
> little bit, I didn't totally expect it having not played but
> that was the opportunity and it was up to me to take it.

Clarke didn't deviate from his earlier stance because, well, a stork hadn't dropped a 24-year-old, 6ft 3in goalkeeper with a few seasons of first-team experience on the steps of Hampden. With Gunn third choice at Forest, Kelly on Rangers' bench and Clark on loan in England's League One with Doncaster Rovers, none of the keepers Clarke regularly called up were in appropriate nick. This problem could be kicked to the kerb … for now. 'I think the issue comes between November and March,' he said with his fingers publicly crossed that the January transfer window would offer a solution for Gunn or another.

It was unlikely Gordon would play nine more games to match Jim Leighton's haul of 90, but there would be one broken record by mid-October. Clarke would supersede Craig Brown as the man to take charge of more Scotland games than anyone else – 72. 'I haven't really thought about it, to be honest,' said the impending history-maker. That *would* stand up in court.

If Ben Gannon-Doak didn't start against Greece, the Tartan Army would demand Clarke be taken there charged with a crime against football. He surely, *suuuurely* would, but the teenager was unfortunately quite physically fragile. He'd already suffered two muscular injuries restricting him for months on end, and while fit for this break we had learned his uniquity was truly that. McGinn, Christie, Gauld, Morgan and a few others can also do a job out wide; none of them can carry it out with the ruthless efficiency of Gannon-Doak. Who else could? Oliver Burke?

Not to the same extent, no. But he is fast. Very fast. Scotland have no *very fast* players regularly picked apart from BGD. Could Burke be the other very fast option in case our only very fast player pulls out before the game or pulls up during it? 'That could work,' thought significant factions of the support, having watched a team for a few years whose most painful trait was a lack of pace. Ryan Fraser, James Forrest and Ikechi Anya are the three players over the last decade who have had matches to strike, and all three of them sporadically showed their ability. Burke's not a goalscorer and any suggestion of it is simply a fallacy, but scoring a hat-trick against Eintracht Frankfurt between the international breaks hardly does the cause any harm. Derek Rae had his loudspeaker in hand and led the clamour. Clarke – eternally grateful for Burke's last-minute winner in his bow against Cyprus – had his earmuffs on and shut the blinds. 'I got a lot of text messages when Oli hit that hat-trick,' he revealed. 'He's sort of drifted a little bit over the last five years. If he can find a home and play well week in, week out, then that will be good for us.'

Did you find the clamour for his reinstatement easy to ignore? 'Yes, to be honest!'

His exclusion was no surprise, but Shankland's was. He'd scored seven goals in ten games for Hearts – including a match-winning double against Rangers – had experience with Scotland and had scored competitive goals for Scotland; superior to Bowie and Hirst on both counts as well as the club form.

> If you were in the previous squad Clarke tends to give you a call to let you know but if otherwise you don't expect to hear anything. He phoned Del [McInnes] before the October break to say he'd thought about me for this one. I knew I'd started the season well and was closer to it than I was at the end of last season, but it's not something I get too caught up in. I just try and get myself in the next one and there are that many camps these days I was confident that if my form continued I'd be involved in November. I'm never one to say someone like Bowie shouldn't be in before me. He'd been scoring a few goals and was in form so fair play to him. You just need to focus on yourself because if you do well, you'll give yourself the opportunity.

'I think about all these players,' said Clarke when asked about the aforementioned duo. 'Because I tend to pick the same players more often than not, people think I don't look outside or at other options. I'm always looking at other options because you never know when you're going to get injuries or suspensions. I just felt the players I had in the last camp did well and they've done well for their clubs in between, so I didn't see too much reason to change.' Leaving Shankland out was an eyebrow-raiser and worthy of questioning, but there could be little arguing Clarke's overall point. If the decision not to call up Burke was the second-greatest gripe, we were doing okay.

And we *were* doing okay. We had four points from two games, with three of the remaining four at Hampden, a stadium in which we hadn't lost a qualifying game since back-to-back matches against Russia and Belgium in Clarke's third and fourth games in charge. We hadn't lost a World Cup qualifier in Mount Florida since Germany won 3-2 more than ten years ago. Beat Greece and Belarus and Scotland would be clutching ten points after four games. We had reason to believe but the nation's optimism cannot escape the clutches of ingrained scepticism, particularly with the memory of March's *doing* still fresh. This was too good to be true.

Ah yes, wait a minute, Greece. What the hell to make of a side that eviscerated us in March, but then lost by the same scoreline to a Danish side that didn't lay siege to our goal a few days before they went to Athens?

Well, there was a rumour about the prodigious Konstantinos Karetsas. Unwell, apparently, and to be rested for their trip to Copenhagen a few days after their one to Glasgow. He played 62 minutes for Genk at the weekend, but their press didn't reckon there was too much smoke billowing around the mirrors. Greece would still pose a serious threat without him. Club Brugge's Christos Tzolis was just as impressive as the kid in March, while players like Olympiakos' Georgios Masouras, Sporting Lisbon's

Fotis Ioannidis, PAOK's Giannis Konstantelias and Como's Anastasios Douvikas could all feasibly start and tie Scotland in the same knot.

The Greek media thought a breeze of arrogance had rippled through the squad after their pumping of Belarus; a result that arrived in the port after putting four past Bulgaria and Slovakia in the summer and, of course, three in our net in March. That waft could be fatal. Now, they couldn't really afford to lose at Hampden.

That was a bit of a contradiction to Scotland according to chief executive Ian Maxwell, who used words like 'smell' and 'touch' when asked about qualification prospects following the promising start. Who gives a fuck about *one game at a time*?

Scotland really did have to view it through that clichéd scope. Lose to Greece and the travellator's gradient would steepen. Greece walloped us on their last trip to Hampden, but we now had Gannon-Doak and Hickey available. They wouldn't have got in the way of the Greeks that night, but they would positively affect our chances on 9 October.

Scotland's home qualifying games against the seeds directly above and sometimes below them tend to be fraught fixtures decided by the odd goal or drawn. Considering ones outwith the Covid era over the last ten to 15 years, recall those tense games against Israel, Slovakia, Slovenia, Poland, Republic of Ireland and Czech Republic. The last team in this bracket we probably *blew away* was Ukraine in 2007, or maybe more recently the game in the rain against Georgia. The games are usually sell-outs if not close to, and this was heading the way of the former.

The clocks were close to going back. The hordes gathered on this dark and dry evening after a pleasant Thursday afternoon. Clarke's XI read: Gunn; Hickey, Souttar, Hanley, Robertson; Ferguson, Christie; McGinn, McTominay, Gannon-Doak; Adams.

That's a strong XI. No Gilmour, but Ryan Christie in central midfield! Rejoice!

I didn't have a clue until a few days before the game. We did some team-shaping, I got put in the middle and I thought, 'Okay, this is happening.' It's less of a tweak to my game. I wanted to stake my claim because centre midfield is what I know now and I've been happy with my performances in the Premier League over the last year. I want to show coming back to Scotland why I'm playing at such a high standard and for them to realise that too. I was desperate to try and play well in centre midfield.

McLean knew it was coming.

It was a matter of time until Ryan got put in the middle. The manager trusted him where he usually got played and it was working for us as a team so it's hard to break that up, but when you're playing at such a high level consistently I think he knew he had to put him in there. He's been incredible for Bournemouth and it was absolutely the right call.

Former Scottish FA President Rod Petrie was remembered before the game after his untimely death aged 69 following a battle with cancer. The whistle blew and Scotland immediately sought Gannon-Doak. His heavy touch took the ball out of play. They looked for him again, and quickly again, and again before the number of minutes played required counting with two hands. On the left, as explained in the previous chapter, he requires longer to feel and find his way into the night. He is a backer of one's self, but the chalk snorted by his boots on the right flank gives him an extra few miles per hour. The Greeks were prepared for his deployment. They were prepared for anything Scotland tried. Vice versa does not apply. Scotland had been welcomed out for their warm-up by Simple Minds' 'Alive & Kicking'. The irony.

Six months after the fact, Greece picked up from where they left off. Sleek, stylish, streamlined; ten outfield players shared one brain. It momentarily malfunctioned when Tzolis fired the ball across the corridor and Vangelis Pavlidis forgot to kick it into an open goal from three yards. Hampden groaned and made sure they had their brollies with them; that was a thunderclap. And so began another lesson. Even now, with the highlights on, I am equally in awe and horror watching Greece.

Greece treated the football the way a football would love to be treated. Collecting loose blades as it sifted across the turf from instep to instep, up and down, between the lines and back again. Scotland didn't trust it as far as Angus Gunn could throw it. The Scotland fans' trust thinned before long, too. Sexy Greek possession – with a purpose – and Scotland flirting with them through loose possession earned boos not more than 20 minutes into the date. Greece had more than 70 per cent of the ball but, crucially, looked like going the whole way. And this was without Karetsas – benched because of that illness – and March's Man of the Match, Konstantelias; benched, just cos.

Scotland were incredibly uncomfortable. Nobody knew who to prioritise or where to go. We couldn't get near Greece or anywhere near their box. By the 30th minute, McTominay – our talisman who finished 18th in the Ballon d'Or ranking – had touched the ball five times. Ferguson recalls the troubles:

> We'd worked on trying to stop their good players getting on the ball, but we were caught in between with our pressing and off the ball work. We never got it right, which was disappointing because we'd already experienced them at Hampden. Their number six [Dimitrios Kourbelis] was a good player, small but technically very good. Their movement and execution of passes were brilliant. Off the ball they're a really good team in terms of putting pressure on you and not allowing time or space.

Christie's big night wasn't playing out as he'd imagined.

> It was a different challenge for me than in the spring.
> Seeing their press from centre midfield was impressive.
> I was probably more defensively-minded than Fergie;
> on the left where their attacking midfielder [Anastasios
> Bakasetas] was a harmful pocket in March, so the idea
> was to close that gap. I've been playing that position
> down south and love it so it wasn't unnatural, but
> we're pretty gung-ho with our press whether it's
> against Manchester City or whoever. Naturally at
> international level it happens less. Most of the time
> it's about keeping a structure and restricting space to
> force teams to break us down.

It's tactic talk that does little for me other than underline *Greece good, us bad*. Bakasetas was conducting the middle third not a beat out of time while we struggled to count to four. Clarke kept his dry demeanour when slowly pivoting towards his dugout on occasion to exchange words with Naismith. Ivan Jovanović – like a little cartoon mushroom that'd wished to be human – had the paperback of a fiery character, but that's not how his managerial personality read as he stood calmly and surely satisfied by everything his team were doing besides their finishing.

Scotland had their hands in the cookie jar by getting into the dressing room at 0-0. Denmark had already scored four against Belarus. We simply had to be better. Had to show energy and an intent to win the game or risk finding ourselves at base camp. The atmosphere in the changing room reflected one that would've been understandable had Scotland been 3-0 down. Once emotion had diffused to logic, they remembered they hadn't conceded. *We don't need to win this game 3-0, we just need to win it.*

Masouras and Pavlidis missed huge chances at the start of the second half. Nothing had changed. It looked like we had nine men. Hickey went off clutching his hamstring and later said, 'It was just a tweak but the same one. I didn't want to risk anything.' Gilmour came on with 25 minutes to go to try and help us keep the ball. The response from the stands to Gannon-Doak's departure was, eh, an unhappy one. He shook his head as he walked around behind the goal – not at the decision, but his performance.

> It was terrible to be on the park while they were doing that to us. We were horrendous that night, to put it bluntly, and they were unbelievable. Our press was off, our timing was off, every time we tried to get to them they'd bop it round us. We just didn't play well, especially me. I was on the left again and it was frustrating. I didn't get a lot of the ball.

Greece continued on their merry way and scored a matter of minutes later. Kostas Tsimikas potted it into the corner after another fine move down the inside right, during which three Scotland players simultaneously pointed at Tzolis while he moseyed beyond our defence. That Mediterranean roar you'll have heard watching Serie A and La Liga echoed around Hampden. The brollies were opened. They could maybe shield the atrocity as well as the impending deluge. Half an hour to go. McLean's anxious thoughts were taking over in the dugout: 'I don't feel nerves when I'm playing, but I get very nervy on the bench because I'm not in control.'

I'll paraphrase here, but a few of the players explained to me that Tsimikas's goal was essentially the launch code for a rocket up their arse. 'It was now or never,' remembered Ferguson.

It was *now*.

The boys are all pretty vague about the specifics of dressing-room conversations. I'm not sure it's deliberate; there are so many they must smoothly merge without conscious thought. Moods are often well recalled, but unless something significant is said or occurs, they struggle to discern. Whatever was said between Clarke and the players at half-time on top of the substance-over-style-just-win-it vibes hadn't exactly worked a treat. Scotland had been shite since the break and were now losing. Whatever Clarke wanted to see, he wasn't seeing. Now 1-0 down, he must have summoned the ghost of Ronnie Briggs to impart wisdom from the technical area.

From kick-off, Greece were given a task they'd barely had to consider since quarter to eight: defend. Ferguson's cross was bundled behind and Christie – operating at left midfield since Gilmour came on – was given the ball to deliver by a limbering Lyndon Dykes. Not his finest cross. Nor was Ralston's, who collected Christie's overhit one and scooped it back in. Hanley helped it on, a Greek head nodded it down and Christie had teleported to snuggle it through a few bodies and in. What the fuck?

> That was supposed to be a worked-on corner! I was supposed to find Robbo on the penalty spot. I was about to hit it and saw him give me the signal that the plan isn't on anymore, but I thought fuck it and aimed for him anyway. I overhit it all the way to Tony and the crowd goes mental because I've not put it in the box. Rightfully so! He lumps it in … stramash … goal. It's funny looking back that the opposite of the plan happened and we still scored. I think that's my second most important goal for us behind Serbia. I'd started my international career with scoring a lot so I think the gaffer expects it from me. I always want to be a threat and help my country as a direct result of that. I was delighted to do it in a big game. It's funny how it works; I was desperate to play centre midfield to get control of a game, get moved back out left and score a goal!

A VAR check was necessary. Hanley would have been offside had a striding Greek defender's knee not been at a right angle. That was the antithesis of what the Greeks stood for. Being on the same pitch as such a heinous attacking phase of play must have left them feeling like Harry Potter when Voldemort is around the corner. Hampden had a pulse now. Greece made some subs and arguably became stronger by firing Ioannidis, Konstantelias and Karetsas from their cannon.

The visitors' weak backbone – scrutinised by their national media – could be stress-tested now. Scotland had been shaken up. Christie and Ferguson's legs found an extra half-yard in midfield. Ryan was booked and would miss Belarus a few days later.

It had been on my mind before the game but it genuinely wasn't tactical. One of their players skipped away from me down the line and the manager shouted, 'Take him down,' so I smashed him. It worked out well, I suppose. I didn't want to go into the Belarus or Greece games with a booking hanging over me.

- Sidenote: That is arguably the worst rule in football. How can a player who receives two bookings over a six-game stretch be punished with a one-match suspension, the same repercussion for being literally sent off in a match? A booking in the first minute of the opening game and the 90th minute of the fifth game would suspend a player for a potential decider on MD6. Mental.
- Second sidenote: While I'm whining, I'd also change penalty kicks. No rebounds allowed. If a keeper parries the taker's effort, or it hits the frame and comes back out, the ball is dead. The 'reward' for being fouled in the box (which is normally disproportionate anyway) should be ONE shot at goal. If the keeper stops you or you miss the target, tough.

Scotland weren't dominating but they were no longer being dominated. Ferguson won a free kick on the left junction of Greece's box when Tsimikas clotheslined him. Perfect for Robertson to float one.

For whatever reason, Greece allowed themselves to be outnumbered at the back post. The cross bounced off Souttar and Ferguson almost ripped the net from its hinges from six yards out. His first goal for Scotland. The beauty was in the eye of the beholder.

> That felt so good. Scoring for Scotland was something I'd dreamt of as a kid; for it to come at that time made it a bit sweeter. I'd been hoping for it for a long time and was just so happy seeing it hit the back of the net. A dream come true. I started trying to run away but just felt Granty's big arms coming round me, no chance I was getting away from him.

Set-piece coach Andrew Hughes high-fived Clarke and Briggs. Realising the key was lost for eternity, the players battered down the door. Dykes, who was getting ready to come on along with Tierney as Clarke opted to see it out with five at the back, was keen to elaborate on dead balls when I asked how much can really be planned with so many moving variables.

> There's a lot of thought in them. They're probably a lot more structured than you think. Everyone has certain positions to be, places to run and roles to carry out. Say we have four corners or set plays that the coach wants us to do, we'll go through them all the day before the game and there are signals given to the taker to let him know what the situation is. It depends on the team we're playing and how they like to set up, what we can exploit and how we can execute it. The taker has a massive say;

we're not robots and football isn't perfect, they might not hit the right area. But if you look at my goals against Ukraine in the Nations League game, Austin MacPhee thought they were weak in the front zone and I scored two goals from Ryan Fraser's crosses there. It worked to a T for what we were asked to deliver. Everyone has roles like being a decoy or blocking – we need strong players to be able to do that. That's really important if the opposition are marking one-on-one because then someone will be able to run free. We have to be switched on and know our roles. If we aren't in the right positions, we'll get a bollocking in the meeting because it could cost us a goal or a game.

I'm not concrete on the i's being dotted and t's crossed in cursive in this instance with a few ricochets and a lash, but Scotland had set up to make Greece's life difficult and they couldn't handle it. There was an exclamation mark, no matter what.

Greece couldn't lose this match. They thought, 'Hang on, Scotland couldn't live with us earlier,' and so started sliding smoothly up the park again. Scotland had set up camp on the edge of their 18. A comment on BBC Scotland's live update feed read: 'Sitting in a bar in Rhodes. The locals can't believe what's happening.'

The same could be said for pubs up and down Scotland.

They might have covered their eyes when Karetsas approached Tierney with a few step-overs and then rubbed them when Gunn leapt at full stretch to tip his top-bag-bound curler wide of his right post. Phew. Scotland had played awfully, but that paled in comparison to three foraged points.

I put to you there is no better goal to score in football than a *sealer*. Putting a few more feathers in a cushion with barely any time left to alleviate the pressure felt from frantically protecting a one-goal advantage. It's essentially the full-time whistle.

Souttar clipped one down the right for Dykes, but he couldn't bring it out of the sky and his touch nudged the ball towards the byline for a goal kick. Not on keeper Tzolakis's watch; that ball would be kept in play as he pounced on it like a selfless soldier spotting a live grenade. It squirmed from underneath him and suddenly Dykes had an empty goal. Hampden exploded with ecstasy.

I feel compelled to include this stellar summation from Daniel Gray, the fantastic writer and editor of *Nutmeg* magazine: 'Tzolakis came to fetch the ball on the byline but instead pawed at it like a cat with a dead mouse. Lyndon Dykes did the rest and suddenly 45,000 people knew what it was like to get away with murder.'

So did Dykes, mind you! His effort from around five yards and a tight angle hit the roof of the net before its back. The angle was so deceiving McLean was shouting from the bench for him to square it to an arriving McTominay, from whom Dykes collected congratulations and ran towards the west stand with his arms stretched to their limits, much like his smile. Double digits for him now as well.

> I didn't mean to put it that high! It gave me a heart attack but I'll take it. It was nice to get to ten, I'd been stuck on nine for a while. Those ones are funny; every day if I had that opportunity in training it'd be very natural but in a game like that, playing for your country, straight away I'm thinking, 'Fucking hell, don't miss this.' It's hard to compose yourself there. It's not like we were attacking and I was bearing down on goal, one-on-one, getting ready to shoot. It just popped up to me and I'd no idea how it'd happened. It felt so quiet, then when I was running away I was just thinking, 'Thank fuck for that.' Those goals are great. When it's just one between us everyone is on edge and you're vulnerable but that second means everyone can breathe. I was scratching my head after the game thinking, 'How the hell did we

win that?' Greece were very strong and they should have scored more, but football is a funny game. There was a feeling that we got away with it, but winning when you don't play well is important because we won't always be at 100 per cent.

Put Simple Minds back on. It was almost inexplicable, but Scotland's World Cup dream was indeed alive and kicking. It had been a different game for Hanley in comparison to Copenhagen.

If we didn't have the togetherness and hadn't been through everything together, we wouldn't be willing to suffer and hurt for each other, and I don't think we'd have got that result. I would always take a positive from it; we played a right good side, dug in, didn't play well for large periods but hung in there and got what we needed.

Hanley and Souttar had cemented themselves as our first-choice duo. Here's Hanley's partner:

I think we earned it rather than got away with it. We back ourselves to stick together and hope something goes our way up the other end. We got away with one early doors when the ball went under Pavlidis's foot, but those things happen sometimes.

If Christie's goal hadn't rocked Greece so rapidly after Tsimikas's opener – literally from kick-off – I'm not sure Scotland find their way back into that.

That felt like lift-off. I don't think we've had to dig as deeply as that for a win as a squad. There was a feeling we were getting away with it. It just happens at Hampden; we get a goal and the feeling completely changes, the Greeks run out of legs and we use our strength at a set play. At 2-1 it wasn't over, but we were fortunate. I was lucky to be in centre midfield with Fergie. I think he's a brilliant player and has truly earned his spot. I used to hate playing against him when he was at Aberdeen. He'd mark me at throw-ins or be next to me at goal kicks and be nipping me and standing on my toes. In terms of results, it was going as smoothly as it could. Greece were probably angry and they had Denmark next so we hoped one of them would be deleted from the run in.

On the night Clarke equalled Craig Brown's record, this match was the perfect sample size to illustrate his reign as a whole. Some good, some bad, at times hideous but ultimately euphoric.

'Football is a 90-minute game,' he said after the match. No arguments. We'd scored with all of our shots on target; two set-piece second phases and an open-goal gift from their keeper. 'Maybe 3-1 flatters us, but we did enough to win. When they scored the goal, the shackles came off a bit and from there we finished the game strongly. The Scottish public should love to have this team. They never know when they're beat.'

'We were given a footballing lesson, but we gave a lesson on winning,' were Willie Miller's wise words on the radio, somewhat echoed by Robertson: 'If you want to complain about the performance, be my guest, crack on. We're delighted with the three points. A game is 90 minutes, not 60.'

For those 60, Scotland offered zilch. Christie was ineffectual in the middle with Ferguson unable to take control either. McTominay and McGinn were anonymous, the full-backs didn't cross the halfway line and Adams was fed with crumbs, not scraps. Scotland were impotent, and it was worthy of comment among the thrill of the win.

It wasn't young Gannon-Doak's night either. Probably his most irritating so far since his arrival on the scene.

> I was next to Connor Barron and George Hirst on the bench, feeling so frustrated, but as soon as Fergie scored that just disappeared. I didn't care how bad I or anyone else had been. I was just buzzing. Each goal we scored, I just thought, 'How are we doing this?' We knew fans would be frustrated but we had to block out the negativity.

Scotland were on seven points and joint-top with Denmark, who had just put six in Belarus' net. If they beat Greece in Copenhagen on Sunday while we took care of the Belarussians, a play-off spot was in the back pocket. If Scotland made it to the Americas, a smile would accompany any retrospect of this night at Hampden. 'Remember when Greece had two-thirds of the ball and 15 shots?'

We'd have a laugh at the sheer cheek of us. No guilt while cheersing the 6am pints at Edinburgh airport.

If we didn't make it, we'd argue this *performance* was a sign of things to come, rather than the *result*.

The players returned to their rotten digs at the Blythswood, had some food and chilled out in the cinema room to catch up on *Celebrity Traitors*; Liam Kelly is usually in charge of the remote. Most of the players find it difficult to go to sleep quickly while the adrenaline's ashes drift through the bloodstream. Sufficiently self-aware, they siphon themselves off from the noise. There is no gathering for *Sportscene*. There is no need to be told what they already knew. They knew they wouldn't get away with that again.

Chapter 12
Belarus (Home)

THE TIME frame was well worn; first World Cup in 28 years. If Scotland wanted certainty on their 2026 participation by mid-November, winning the group was non-negotiable. Mentioned sporadically on the journey through time is the last time the national team managed to do that: 1981. Scotland, Northern Ireland, Sweden, Portugal, Israel. In that order. A trivial defeat to Portugal in the final game wrecked the unbeaten record. Boo-hoo.

Nearly 45 years later (*I know*), after just more than a month and only three games, Scotland suddenly had a frightful opportunity to bypass the play-offs with bottom seeds Belarus on their way to Glasgow; affairs hadn't been as promising since the final game before France '98 when Scotland beat Latvia to ensure Sweden couldn't catch us but Austria beat Belarus to ensure Scotland couldn't catch them.

If Scotland and Denmark won on Sunday, 12 October, Greece wouldn't be able to catch either of them. Most fans I remember speaking with at this time agreed Scotland were more likely to win the group rather than finish second and stumble or sail through an unpredictable play-off draw. A single-legged semi then final against the troublesome likes of Ukraine, Turkey, Poland, Italy, Czech Republic, Albania and Wales would be the catch for finishing behind Denmark. Both games could be away from home if the draw wasn't feeling generous.

Oh dear, my sincere apologies. *Game at a time.*

Clarke and Robertson made valid points while Belarus were on their way to Glasgow airport. The bottom line was Scotland won a football match played over 90 minutes and its stoppages. That should not airbrush the performance from history or censor fans from sharing their observations of it. Three colossal fixtures were ahead; a repeat on Sunday of the display against Greece would be akin to describing a rearrangement of the deck chairs as strategy. It would be like testing gravity in Athens in a month's time just to make sure it was still working.

Scotland had – surprisingly – 33 per cent possession against Greece and 26 against the Danes but took four points from those games. Pragmatism before poetry, fair enough, but it didn't feel sustainable in pursuit of the goal. Talk of using set pieces to plaster a bullet wound would be outrageous, we were joint-top of the group, but Scotland have players to control the flow of a football match (I refer you back to the friendly against the Netherlands in 2024) and had only managed it against Liechtenstein and Belarus so far that year. Ferguson, Christie, McLean, McTominay, McGinn and Miller are far from flapping fish out of water following such directives but with a fin scything through middle third's surface is Gilmour.

A glance at fixtures he hasn't started for Scotland since he became an instant regular tells us when the going gets physical, Billy sometimes gets benched; Ukraine (away), Norway (away), Spain (away), Germany (neutral, but away), Denmark (away), Greece (home). Many of us (maybe you, maybe I) reckon he is evidentially Scotland's best ball-handler and won't be moved from the hill declaring the team should be built around him. He had significantly contributed to our successful Nations League group stage after the Euros by starting all six games against League A opponents and even more in Napoli's title-winning campaign. He'd helped turn the tide on Thursday with his willingness to receive the ball and play forward. 'I don't think anyone likes being on the bench so, no, it wasn't great,' acknowledged Gilmour. 'But it's a squad game and

I can't be moaning around and blaming stuff. When I come off the bench I want to try and prove to him that he shouldn't leave me out.'

Clarke prioritised central midfield energy against Greece but Christie was now suspended, remember? Oh, and so was Ferguson; booked in the 97th minute when the game was *finito*. He pleaded the fifth when I asked if that was a coincidence. With Scotland unlikely to be chasing shadows on Sunday and those two confined to the stand, Gilmour's inclusion was certain and should be advantageous. Reinforcements were hauled in with Connor Barron and Josh Mulligan joining the squad. Mulligan had been terrific at Hibs so far since joining on a free transfer after leaving Dundee, exhibiting drive and running power from central midfield or right wing-back.

Like Greece, Belarus were fresh opponents for Scotland to consider, and if our aspirations were legitimate then they could not be involved in a repetition of history. They'd already scribbled their name before Georgia and Lithuania on the list of pesky opponents that Scotland had fallen short against during qualification campaigns. Scotland eventually finished five points behind second-placed Norway in World Cup 2002 qualifying, which started for us with a home draw and defeat against Slovenia and Norway. A draw in Moldova followed that and Berti Vogts was finished. Walter Smith helped revitalise the campaign as we drew with Italy and won in Norway and the grip on hope tightened but, crucially, we dropped two points in Minsk and took one further step back at Hampden against those opponents. Five points chucked against the fifth seeds and two against the bottom ones. Deary me. Norway did what they had to do anyway.

Winning would give Denmark almost no margin for error. If they slipped up while we won, we'd be on ten and either two or three points ahead of them. The best scenario they'd have in that case would be coming to Hampden on MD6 with it all hanging in the balance.

This was Clarke's record-breaking game in charge. His qualifying win rate stood proudly at 58 per cent. Lose this, and what brilliantly came before might be caveated by one fixture. He conceded a speck of pride at his longevity and referred to what his squad had achieved with him. 'We've managed to do it twice but we want to do it again because we're all greedy.'

I'm not sure I can agree with Clarke on that one. In fact, I don't. The hunger to qualify for the World Cup from a group devoid of a powerhouse isn't borne from gluttony. That's the consequence of raised expectations and standards. Also, as far as World Cup qualification went, Scotland were frankly malnourished. Were we now the spoiled, bratty 20-somethings who post a self-absorbing video online to complain about a new squeeze introducing them to a lifestyle they couldn't maintain after a few dates? I don't think so, and Clarke's reading of supporter ambition as voracity seemed odd. Although, I hear his humour is as dry as Mahatma Gandhi's flip-flops, so maybe his tone has gone over my head.

Without name-dropping, he referred to the wrong turns taken against the filth during our wilderness years and underlined his exemplary record in those scenarios. Reporters will do well to extract a *must-win* from Clarke in black and white, but he said as much the day before the game. 'If you want to qualify, these are the games you have to win. It's very important we get the points off Belarus. They'll come here, they'll be organised, they'll be difficult to break down, and until you break them down it's a long night.'

Greece scored five, and Denmark six. Struggling to break them down would probably be more of a reflection on us than them.

Thursday's shift was comparable to March's runaround, after which Clarke confessed he regretted not making more changes before the second leg. His XI for the visit of Belarus included five – some enforced – changes: Gunn; Ralston, Hendry, McKenna, Robertson; Gilmour, McLean; Gannon-Doak, McTominay, McGinn; Adams.

Ralston deputising, a breather for Souttar, McKenna for progression and the two central midfielders replacing the suspended ones. 'I stayed around and had free food with my mates for four days.' Who wouldn't, Ryan?

McLean is a man hell-bent on carrying his share of the load. As a starter or a sub, in training and during downtime, if there's something that'll benefit the national team, he wants to be part of it. He valued the trust Clarke had in him and his run of starts during the Nations League last year, but a returning Ferguson and versatile Christie – as well as fan clamour for Miller – weren't causing rumination in the way they might have a couple of years previously.

Struggling to force his way off the bench, never mind into Clarke's preferred selection, during the few years after the pandemic and now into his 30s, McLean wrestled with the meaning of this life. He missed the Euros with a knee injury and started the game immediately after it when Denmark gubbed us 2-0. From there, he wasn't sure what to make of it all.

Clarke and I did have a serious chat one time. He initiated it. We were away to the Faroes in the second game of a camp. I didn't come on in the first one, which was the 3-2 game against Israel when McTominay scored. He named his team in the afternoon before lunch, then we had a few hours to ourselves. He chapped my door and said, 'I know how disappointed you are with the situation, but there is a lot more in you.' I hoped he couldn't sense my disappointment because I don't want to be seen as moping. I want to be a good team-mate, but he probably knew what I was thinking. Am I needed? What is my place? He gave me reassurance that I'd be important to him going forward. I didn't come on that night in the Faroes either, and I'm not saying I'd ever have chucked it, but before he came to speak to me I was thinking, 'If he doesn't trust me to play against the Faroes, does he still trust me to do a job at all?' It showed his man-management skills and he was able to read the situation before I'd figured it out. Everyone wants to start but he knows me well enough to know that when we're setting up the team-shaping and I'm part of the 'opposition', I'll do everything I can to help the lads by giving them problems and solutions at the same time. Circumstances have put guys like Lewis and Ryan ahead of me. Who am I to be saying I should be in the team instead of them? It's about being a good team-mate and that's something I'd always want people to say about me.

A more encouraging performance was necessary after pulling the rug from under Greece's feet. About 0.01 per cent of the Tartan Army would swap another act of three-point thievery for a charitable donation to Belarus' points column after holding them in our palm, but that's not to say we'd be content with slamming another get-out-of-jail-free card on the table with an evil laugh.

A calm, mild evening above Hampden absorbed another spine-tingling anthem, as we continued with the rugby's superior example of an acapella verse after a first led by pipes. A number of the selected XI looked to their left and right while adding words of encouragement into the anthem's slipstream. *Let's win this. Let's dominate this.*

Belarus won three corners in the first ten minutes and skimmed the bar with a header from the third. The home support were affronted; Belarus weren't interested in laying out a welcome mat in front of their 18-yard box this time. After 15 minutes, they'd been in Scotland's box just as much as the entirety of the fixture in Hungary. Scotland were hesitant again, unsure of who to mark, where to run or pass the ball.

Ralston held the ball, level with the penalty spot. Now 15 minutes in, exasperated groans were already trundling across the running track as the Celtic right-back squinted his eyes for some dark-blue movement among Belarus' minty-green. Gannon-Doak emerged and thus began a tidy sequence of 15 passes resulting in Gilmour's cross being headed away. Hendry, making his first competitive appearance since the Euros, toddled on to the loose ball and rattled it towards Adams whose first touch, second and thunderous strike to

the keeper's bottom left-hand corner were sublime. Argh, offside…
Wait, onside! Footage proved a straggler at right-back kept Adams
on. Yes! Five goals in five games for Adams.

That was needed. A disheartening start had been nullified.
Hopefully that bursts the dam.

It was a woeful half of football.

Overhit crosses and aimless balls into channels trickled into
irrelevancy. The Belarussian bus wasn't marooned on their 18's
edge; Scotland had space in which to work and proved yet again
they could pass the ball to each other, but Belarus were zipping it
around with purpose to their play. What method was there in this
Scottish madness? Their pondering was a mystery. Hampden was
a mortuary. Clarke's usual touchline manner meant it was tough
to assess whether he was quietly satisfied or somewhere between
simmering and boiling.

Gannon-Doak had their left-back doing the Dashing White
Sargeant but his inability to make the most of positions he'd
carved from the boring stone was maddening. Greece quickly
stomped on the template of *get ball to Ben, Ben run, Ben shoot or
cross*, but back in right midfield he was repeatedly showing the
Belarus left-back a clean pair of heels. Clarke spoke to him about
his decision-making on their way to the tunnel and post-match
referred to a lack of action at club level hindering his improvement
in that regard.

The head coach had a quiet word with Gannon-Doak, but he
was ready to unload within the dressing room's four walls. It had
been appalling. Christie and Ferguson were standing in the indoor
warm-up area adjacent to the room, and the door was open …

'Ohhh!' he was shouting. It's the most animated I've
ever seen him. He's normally very cool but that was
full on. He was trying to remind us that if we didn't
qualify because of this game, it would haunt us forever.
No going through the motions.

Christie was blameless, but McLean's fingerprints were one of ten sets all over this.

> A few things got kicked around. Conversations were happening among us before we walked into the changing room and then he arrived, angry with the situation. There was a lot of frustration from him because that wasn't the team he wants to see on the pitch; no aggression. We were at home and allowed Belarus to be comfortable in possession in a game that meant so much to us. He doesn't like it when we're passive and wanted a major reaction. It was a heated half-time.

BGD was less forthcoming with the picture he chose to paint. It was as if he felt a chill in the air.

> Yes, he was visibly angry. The decibels were raised a bit. It wasn't funny at the time and it's only funny now because we've qualified. I don't want to say any more.

'Half-time, deservedly so, was the wildest I've seen him in 72 games,' said McGinn when it was all over.

At least we were winning already. Clarke's anger steeped among the team and they started the second half more encouragingly with McGinn, Gilmour and Gannon-Doak peppering the goal. A penalty to Scotland wouldn't have been exorbitant after Adams was sort of rugby tackled round the ankles, but a VAR check showed he handled the ball in the previous phase and so that foul was immaterial. Boos swirled Hampden. A second goal felt as far from certain as could be.

Oh, you thought the boos a minute ago for the referee were bad?

Belarus scored on the hour. McTominay was dispossessed on the halfway line; he'd picked up a not-so-subtle habit since signing for Napoli of falling over very easily for someone who is 'built like the bionic man', according to a friend who used to work for the Scottish FA. The resulting ball across the box evaded Ralston, Hendry and McKenna before Evgeni Malashevich of Dinamo Minsk punished a ball-watching Robertson to blend in and score.

'Oh my God,' blurted out Faddy on comms.

Ralston and McGinn immediately remonstrated and the VAR advice was for referee Marian Barbu to come and assess the severity of the trip on McTominay. I must admit, from my place in Row L of B8, I was convinced this would be ruled out. It looked soft on TV replays, but Evgeni Yablonski stepped across McTom and took out his shin while doing so. Case closed. Although the jury was rightly out on our defending. Belarus warranted parity but they wouldn't get it right now. They were full of fire and burning with belief. Scotland had confused a time bomb with a recliner and bolted upright as the ticking began. But nothing really changed. Belarus continued to pass us off the park.

Hampden was not an enjoyable place to host. As a fan, I've contemplated for years about the roles we and the players have in dictating the atmosphere at the national stadium. Scotland were having an off night. An off night again in a decisive World Cup qualifier. An off night in which we were leading the game. Win this and we step into tantalising territory. Before the game, Clarke said: 'It's up to us to make sure that we create enough chances in the game to get the crowd excited. The crowd need to back the players, the players need to give the crowd something to shout about and that's what we'll try to achieve.'

Who is the chicken and who is the egg?

The team needed the supporters in the here and now. During discussions with players for my book on our Euro 2020 qualification and the impact of playing in empty stadiums, it became clear that playing in a full Hampden during high-stakes games with expectation bearing down can be severely compressing. *The 55th minute can have the illusion of the 90th.*

As Alex McLeish's assistant in 2019, James McFadden put a few of the players in their place while they departed the Stadio di Serravalle in San Marino following a gruesome 2-0 win that could have been the Belarus game's biological father. Everything was toxic in the aftermath of the 3-0 defeat in Kazakhstan and a two-goal win in central Italy just would not cut it.

'That's terrible, we've won and they're booing us,' Faddy remembered a few of the players inferring, before he reminded them many had been in Kazakhstan, spent shitloads of money and were entitled to express how they felt and what they thought of the performance.

Anxiety stems from and thrives under a lack of control. Unleashing exasperation is much easier than manufacturing encouragement but there is no question in my mind that – while understandable – it hampers the side. Everyone is entitled to their own expression and while there is no right or wrong, there is probably a wise and unwise. Christie was in the stand biting his lip as we limped through the second half.

> Things seem to happen for us at Hampden when we have that feeling of togetherness as a country. I've wrestled with the argument of how fans should approach it. It's easy for me to say they should be supporting us 100 per cent, through thick and thin, yet when I was watching Bournemouth against Manchester United on the tele the other night [he was injured], I was screaming at the boys, so I get it. Fans want to see us have a go from the first minute and be all over teams like Belarus, and we weren't, so they're rightfully frustrated. I'm not sure where I fall overall on the argument.

Clarke covered all bases with his pre-match wishes. We all want the same thing, so if Scotland aren't performing to what we think is their potential, is it incumbent on us to remind them we are with them all the way rather than articulate our outrage with jeers and swearies? We could help them but ultimately – and this isn't

exclusive to *us* or Hampden – supporters are usually a mir
what they're seeing on the pitch. The reflection was not
McLean's thought about it too:

> Every fan is reactive, that's normal. At the start of the
> game they're always behind us but if we're passive or
> not aggressive enough, that feeds into the stands. In
> a game of that magnitude they are seeing we need to
> do more and it becomes frustrating. We can feel the
> anxiety and they're reacting to what we're doing; even
> winning a corner or putting a tackle in can help the
> energy. I'd say the onus is more on us as players to give
> them something to get behind and then we need to
> take that on and continue it. If we are losing tackles
> and headers and conceding chances there's only going
> to be disappointment. It's hard not to feel that way as
> a fan, I'm one myself, but there are times we need to
> be picked up as well.

It's a toughie. In the first ten to 15 minutes of a game, I'd argue
load is largely with us. After that, opposition dependent, person
I think it levels out to around 60/40 (fans/players).

Faint murmurs of 'Sccoottttland, Sccoottttland…' floa
around Hampden as Scotland attacked from their corner's secc
phase. Doak whacked a ball across goal and Adams sort
shouldered it in, but he was offside. The chasm between the av
game and this one was extraordinary but surely, like in Hungar
second goal would finish this.

McGinn's endeavour down the left put Belarus on the back fc
and McTominay pounced on Robertson's eventual cross to wr
the ball into the keeper's bottom left-hand corner. Professior
lipreaders weren't on standby to decipher Scott's thoughts as
gave any hint of a celebration a berth as wide as Hampden. F
looked abhorred. *Fook me.*

McGinn collected the ball and thundered it back to the halfway line. Scotland had eight added minutes for the good of their goal difference.

Dykes came on for stoppage time after queasily watching the previous 89 minutes:

> It does get twitchy. The worst part is not being able to affect what's happening. It's more stressful on the bench than the park. We're just thinking, 'Please hold out, score another, do something.' We needed six points from our games against them.

Belarus had been the side that looked like scoring (again) and didn't give up. Scotland somehow survived another attack before they scored with their 22nd effort on goal. Gleb Kuchko, on his trip to Scotland from the Polish second tier, spun Robertson with ease and rolled the ball under Gunn in front of a now half-empty east stand. They'd pulled the trigger almost double the amount of times as Scotland. We were begging for the final whistle against Belarus.

It was met with confliction. How were we supposed to respond to what had just happened? A fusion of claps and boos jarringly meshed, but not as abrasively as the decision to unleash 'Freed From Desire' through the PA system while the players meandered around the pitch in full view but unable to look the fans in the eye, like a loveable golden retriever who ripped up a cushion while his owners were at work. Scotland were top of their group yet disappeared up the tunnel to little acclaim with no public displays of pride. Clarke reminded a quiet dressing room of his disappointment and anger without putting his laces through any stray objects this time.

Matters must have been confusing for the players as well. They don't want to play badly, yet they had in back-to-back games and still achieved maximum points during a tiny qualification campaign.

McTominay lauded the *spirit* of his team-mates but demanded he and they show more quality. Robertson didn't feel like Scotland

had just won a vital qualifier and criticised his team's ability on the ball and organisation off it. Adams identified concentration and decision-making, not excusing the full-time boos but agreeing with them. Accepting criticism would have to be taken on the chin, McGinn aired a distressing detail in that he felt the team weren't *gelling* and said the team were capable of more entertaining football.

These are all respectable admissions from key players, but we rarely get the chance to delve into deeper meanings, especially when broadcasters are restricted to a couple of questions. How can a team that had shown what they were capable of in the previous two qualification campaigns – and recent Nations League – look like they hadn't met each other until the anthems? *Why was the performance nowhere near where it needed to be, Andy?*

Even on the majority of our Zoom calls, the players seem quite unsure or hesitant on what to put their fingers. My instinct is it would perhaps involve calling out one another or the tactics, which I understand is a no-no when there is a common cause to fight for.

The way the staff see the team's chances of scoring being maximised will be illustrated in the final chapter, but for a layman, Scotland want to hit the byline within the box's confines and find an arrival. I asked McLean during our call if it was a fair observation that Scotland are prone to running out of ideas when they cross the middle third into the final one.

> I'd say that's fair. We work on it a lot; where we think we can hurt the opposition and how we can get into the correct zones to be the biggest threat we can. Across that campaign, Hanley and Souttar were two of our best players and that's the foundation to build from, so the next stage is how can we do more at the other end. The gaffer and his staff are constantly looking at ways to get the best out of us. We want to be more free-flowing and expansive but it is tough when you see each other every so often for a couple of sessions.

'People can get excited. We can get excited,' McGinn added with a nod to the group table. If Denmark beat Greece over the next few hours Scotland's play-off place would be settled. That's exactly what happened; Scotland had a play-off for the World Cup. But trepidation was weighing more heavily than anticipation. How could we expect to finish top of the group or progress through two play-off ties in this form?

Clarke backs his players until he is blue in the face. On the night he broke a record, he wasn't a broken record. This was one of the worst performances of his 72 games in charge, but we had taken one step closer to heaven. We were told we should (and do) *love* them for the way they refused to crumble against Greece on Thursday. Prefixing the evening's reflection with 'performances don't get you qualification', Clarke was scratching his head on BBC Scotland, confused and irritated at his team bowing to Belarus' press and consenting to their 90-minute dictation. He even admitted that if Belarus' equaliser had stood, he didn't fancy his boys to go and get a second.

'Tonight I was really, really disappointed in my team. I don't think we got anywhere near the levels we can reach. We didn't control the game without the ball and we weren't good enough with it. Tonight, Belarus came and had a go, I would expect our players to be able to handle that pressure, get on the ball and dictate the tempo. We didn't do that. They dictated it all night.'

It was gloomy and glorious all at once, the sun puncturing a few holes in amongst the dark grey. The league table never lies? Scotland were neck and neck with Denmark, and if pipped could deploy the play-off parachute through the clouds, yet we were playing brutally. 'When it comes to the crunch, we'll be ready,' assured the head coach.

This was Scotland all over; uncompromisingly uncomfortable. If we wanted the rainbow, we'd have to put up with the rain. As David Brent reminded us, "Do you know who said that? Dolly Parton. And people say she's just a big pair of tits."

Chapter 13
Greece (Away)

POSITIVELY PROUD and passionate; certainly a little short-tempered, definitely self-deprecating; fully faithful.

Adding more adjectives to the long and never lost list of ways to describe Scotland fans is not an arduous task. Opposition supporters and their national associations are rarely coy with their compliments after our visits. This is in no small part accelerated by the consistently commendable efforts of the Tartan Army Sunshine Appeal but also the congeniality and humour of the wider squadron.

There have been ebbs and flow with fortune and promise over barren and teasing years, but extracting from the quartet above, I'd argue the non-negotiable label is faithful. There has been doubt before and there will be again but the heart always overpowers the head. Always resuscitates us after hope thought it had finished us off.

Heading to Athens in the terrifying knowledge that a point gained would take us to within three of salvation, the Tartan Army weren't the only faithfuls on the shores of the Mediterranean.

For a few days in their disgustingly luxurious five-star hotel in the Turkish town of Belek, all but four members of the Scotland squad were faithful too. Between golf, the spa facilities, the games room, their private beach and actually training, the Scotland squad were meeting for round tables of deception, manipulation and a fucking laugh. After becoming attached to a party game called 'Wolf' during international camps, on which the tele series is based, Andy Robertson-Winkleman curated a real-life schedule for *The Traitors: Scotland Edition* to unfold.

Aaron Hickey, John Souttar and Ché Adams were tapped on the shoulder by the captain; costume and seductive stroll not included. Conspiracies and theories were shared and heard in between times and the trio would stealthily inform Robbo who was to be murdered before they returned to the round table, as well as overnight, at the Regnum Carya resort (seriously, Google it). 'It actually got quite heated at times,' said Hanley with a smile.

'He's corrupt. Robbo's giving them to his mates! I saw him give the shields out!' McGinn exclaimed with a smirk as the players warmed up before one of their sessions.

Faithfuls were wrongly banished one by one – Gordon was the first to go and Christie wasn't far behind him – but Hickey was fortuitously eliminated. As part of the game, Robertson split the boys into groups for a quiz. Although they were in those groups, they competed individually and answered national team-based questions relating to goals and games from the land before their times as well as testing their knowledge on the current squad and recent happenings. The worst quizzers in each group – four boys in total – were at risk of banishment because of their poor knowledge; one had to be picked and punted. Hickey was the majority choice. When he revealed his status as a traitor, the gang were *buzzing*.

Tierney was recruited. Hanley mistakenly suspected McLean after the midfielder assertively accused him, but the *quiet* Adams's cover was blown while Tierney and Souttar went undetected together towards the end until Souttar – the underdog – ran out of steam and got voted out by the two eventual winners. KT was in the final three, lying through his teeth to Ralston and Gannon-Doak. 'I fucking knew KT was a traitor,' remembers McLean. 'Tony really didn't want to vote against his Celtic buddy.'

Ultimately, *Raldo* and *Doaky* smelled a rat and the two faithfuls celebrated their victory. Heads over hearts, unlike us.

The perception I have listening to the Scotland players talk about their time together is that they struggle to sufficiently explain how strong and meaningful their bond is. Their free time is spent more than satisfactorily with a coffee and blether, they won't succumb to boredom in the company of a team-mate or two, although some friendships are naturally stronger than others based on childhoods and day jobs. It may not surprise you to hear Hanley and McLean are close friends, like Souttar, Robertson and Gauld, like Christie and Armstrong or Ferguson and Gilmour, who've never drifted since their days in the Scotland youths and regularly FaceTime in Italy. One could pick all these names out a tombola along with the others in the squad to create a table plan for lunchtime with no resistance. McLean is a very popular and central figure in the group's harmony.

> I'm 34 years old now and have never been part of a squad like this. I genuinely wouldn't mind being stuck in a lift with any of them. I'm close with Kelly, McGinn, Robbo and Souttar – we've got a little group chat going on. I'm close with Granty too; we've been playing together for so long and our wives are close as well, so our families go on holiday together. I use Robbo for his house in Portugal more than anything!

There is a poker club with a £50 buy-in (beware McLean and Dykes), the wolf gang, a coffee-club and a *COD* school (Xbox game *Call of Duty* for the ill-informed, not a seafood culinary class). A season or two ago, a four-day major golf tournament was set up on Christie's Xbox and players were given tee times each day to come in and complete their 18 holes with their playing partners.

As team-mates or otherwise, a lot of the lads around the 30 mark have known of each other for donkeys. Christie reminisced:

> I remember McGinn being a 3ft bulldozer in the middle of the park for St Mirren when we were young

teenagers. It's really weird thinking about the journey we've been on since playing against each other at youth level, in the Premiership back home and now in England while playing so many games together for Scotland. That makes it special. It's mad that back then we had no idea we'd be going to the World Cup together one day. I remember playing against St Mirren while I was coming through into the first team at Caley Thistle. I saw John warming up and thought, 'Fuck sake, that's that guy. I'm sick of playing against him!' Then we got called up for Scotland youths together, I realised he's actually alright and ten years later we are good mates and playing for our country. We love meeting up at camps because we spend so much of our career weaving in and out of each other's paths.

We know the squad's spine – tactically and socially – rarely fractures. Some come, some go. Some like Oli Burke, David Turnbull and Ryan Fraser have seemingly gone for good. Boys like Barron, Bowie, Miller, Mulligan, Conway, Johnston and Doig have recently come along and stand good chances of sticking around. But if you think of a Scotland squad over the last five years, the chances are it'll include Dykes, McTominay, McGinn, Robertson, McLean, Gilmour, Hendry, Adams, Christie, Hanley and McKenna. Twelve of the Euro 2020 squad were preparing for the final two group games for the World Cup five years later. Some like Armstrong and Forrest had faded from contention, but time escapes no man. Except Craig Gordon.

Angus Gunn had 'opened up his knee ligaments' during Nottingham Forest training. What rotten luck for a third-choice keeper. Gordon was back. Again.

Scott Bain, Craig Gordon, Liam Kelly; Josh Doig, Grant Hanley, Jack Hendry, Aaron Hickey, Ross

McCrorie, Scott McKenna, Anthony Ralston, Andy Robertson, John Souttar, Kieran Tierney; Ryan Christie, Lewis Ferguson, Ben Gannon-Doak, Billy Gilmour, John McGinn, Kenny McLean, Scott McTominay, Lennon Miller; Ché Adams, Lyndon Dykes, George Hirst, Lawrence Shankland.

If Gordon played in Piraeus, it'd be his first game of the season. Kelly was a domestic cup keeper for Rangers and Bain was playing every week and doing well for newly-promoted Falkirk, revealing he thinks he should have left Celtic sooner than the window just gone. There would be a 'debate' among the media – even on the *Hampden Roar* podcast I expressed a bit of genuine doubt about Gordon's starting credentials – and although Clarke said he would assess the three lads, only one outcome felt probable; the man set for his 82nd cap who kept a clean sheet in the same stadium eight months ago starting again. Gunn had started games after sitting in the City Ground's stand, and denying Gordon on grounds of rustiness would only have served contradiction. He was ready for it.

The Turkey training camp was a good four days. We worked on a lot and spent a lot of time out on the pitch. I never looked at a single thing [media-related]. Never watched anything, never read anything. I shut myself off to concentrate; I was aware I'd be the topic of conversation. The rest of the team had been so settled that I knew the keepers would be what people spoke about and I didn't want to hear any of it, whether it was positive or negative. All I wanted to do was focus on my job. There is a good rapport among the keepers, always has been. Even when I got left out of the Euros squad, the first thing we did was go for a coffee and I wished them the best for the tournament. No matter who is playing, only one of us can but everyone wants the best for Scotland. We have meetings where we discuss the opposition and everyone voices their opinion to try and help the keeper who is playing. If they've played against an attacker before, for example, you never know what piece of information could end up being the difference.

Any consternation around Gordon wasn't a reflection on the squad, who were not privately discussing Craigy's minutes or wondering what sort of state he'd be in for two of the country's biggest games in nearly 20 years. Ask a centre-back – say, Grant Hanley – how they feel about having Gordon behind them and they might say something like this:

> He is clearly one of the best goalies I've ever played with, but it is his drive and hunger to keep playing as well. He has an absolutely phenomenal work rate and desire. We did think he was retired at one point after his send-off against Finland, but the manager was saying, 'Craigy assures me he will be back.' He really believed he would be, it wasn't tongue-in-cheek at all.

It had been a year since Shankland played for Scotland. He replaced Bowie in the squad after the Hibs striker's form coasted into the run-off area while he cruised to the top of the table with Hearts. 'If you need someone in the squad for goals, Lawrence is your man,' said Clarke, slightly undermining himself given the slim opportunities he'd allowed Shankland over the last couple of years. Shanks fulfilled this responsibility to the letter in Tbilisi two years ago, preventing defeat in stoppage time after coming off the bench in the 87th minute. His standing in the squad was hard for us to comprehend at times; this born goalscorer wouldn't change overnight. 'I have a good relationship with most of my players,' said Clarke at his squad announcement. 'We are always very honest with each other.'

Shankland, who is so laid-back on our call he should be horizontal, is as precious as a hunk of quartz.

> Football moves on quickly. I saw the opportunity for us to qualify and I was eager to be involved. I didn't get a heads-up about it, but I knew I was in form so if the gaffer was thinking about me for the last one I thought there was a good chance I'd be in this one. I think the manager has shown in quite a few games he'll fling me on when we need a goal and that's how he sees me. It's quite clear to me. I'm not saying he's told me I'll always be on the bench but I know my role in the squad as a goalscorer. It's my main strength and I'm one of the best in the team at it. It's a compliment, I don't really see it as a bad place for me.

'If this wasn't for me, I'd be playing golf somewhere or doing a bit of fishing,' Clarke said after being asked if he was still feeling the pressure. 'I wasn't spooked by it,' he added, referring to the Belarus game. One should be forgiven for assuming he was still practising the latter oftentimes with some of his answers during pressers. He wasn't casting with his general observations at Hampden last month, lambasting his players' ability to handle Belarus adopting the serve and volley. After the dust settled, he reflected on a bit of panic in the ranks because of the game's high stakes. Being under the weight of expectation at Hampden doesn't help, but after the two performances we'd witnessed that somehow, *somehow*, yielded maximum points, how could we possibly expect Scotland to take at least one in Piraeus followed by three against Denmark? We just could. The heart never lies.

'It is real. Everyone understands where we are,' said Steven Naismith, dismissing the notion of the unspeakable jinx.

A couple of grumbles would follow one of Clarke's squad announcements brimming with the talent of Spain's, but across the board – Gunn aside – this wasn't far from full strength at worst. Hickey had recovered, Fergie and Christie had served their suspensions and Tierney was in one piece. Not bad!

Gilmour texted Clarke to reassure him the injury that prompted his substitution during Napoli's draw with Como a week ago was no big deal and he'd be sound for the two games. He was declared unfit for the Greece game by Scotland's medical staff and didn't travel to Turkey. Miller and McCrorie were ruled out of both; Barron and Irving were drafted in. The players should have been able to guess the team from the week's shaping exercises.

With a week of the sun on their skin and wholesome as all hell, Scotland skipped across the Aegean Sea to face the team whose manager was convinced his boys were better than ours. And you know what, fair enough. For two and a half of the three games we'd played against each other, we looked inferior in every aspect apart from scoring set pieces and heading the ball away from our own box. Ivan Jovanović would be without three key players; centre-back Dinos Mavropanos, attacking midfielder Giannis Konstantelias (*pler*) and striker Fotis Ioannidis.

Vangelis Pavlidis had 14 goals in 22 games for Benfica, wee Karetsas would shake the stadium upside-down to find an 18th birthday present, and Tzolis was targeting revenge for the 'embarrassment' we caused in October by contributing to their reality that fell so, so far short of what the Greeks expected after matching England for points in their Nations League group and wiping the floor with us in March. Hanley heard it first-hand while catching up with his former Norwich team-mates Tzolis and Dimi Giannoulis; it was seen as a *disaster* they hadn't qualified, never mind having two dead rubbers to round off the group. The Greek media knew they had a captivating yet complicated crop. Marvels with brittle-bone disease.

It was fashion week in Athens. A few of our players might look like they belong on one, but Scotland had fought with gravity to keep their poise on the catwalk so far. There was nothing trendy about their style at Hampden. Scotland don't generally score many goals. They conceded two from the 37 shots they allowed on their goal in October. The balance of probability didn't add up.

The fans I've spoken to recollect a vibe nervier than the norm in the build-up to kick-off. One could settle the jitters in the Piraeus pubs down by the port offering five-litre jugs of beer. Every eventuality regarding our fortune was calculated with the aid of a very simple equation; Denmark would beat Belarus, of course. They already had, 6-0 away. In the Parken, the conclusion was foregone.

Because they would, it meant we had to avoid defeat in Greece. A draw meant we'd be two points behind Denmark. Because they'd beaten Belarus by half a dozen and put three past Greece twice, a Danish win in tandem with a Scottish defeat in the penultimate games would cause an insurmountable chasm of three points and about a million goals with one game to play.

Bottom line: do not lose in Greece, and no matter how the Danish pastry crumbles we'd have a decider on Tuesday in which a win would take us to America. Greece had already crumbled more easily than their national cheese and their natives weren't overly arsed about this one; only 18,000 people were in the stadium with 2,500 of them in the away end.

In a 4-2-3-1 shape and wearing the (much, much, much improved) new home kit, Clarke's XI read: Gordon; Hickey, Souttar, Hanley, Robertson; Ferguson, Christie; Gannon-Doak, McTominay, McGinn; Adams.

Gordon's first competitive appearance since May. The ten outfielders starting also started against the Greeks a month ago. Our oldest starting team in a World Cup qualifier since 2004.

In case you hadn't noticed, Scotland had been churning out results while performing questionably, so I'd forgive you like I did myself when I did a double take at the fact Scotland could create history in Athens by making their current run of away games the longest they'd ever been on without conceding a goal. How the …?

Ah, right enough: Greece (1-0), Liechtenstein (4-0), Denmark (0-0) and Belarus (2-0).

That was wrecked after seven minutes in the Karaiskakis. Souttar misread a long ball's flight, Gordon brilliantly parried Pavlidis's shot and Hanley was beaten to the rebound by an evasive Bakasetas, who scored. Sunday league stuff all round.

> I remember it coming past me and turning quickly, but I didn't want to dangle a toe so I stood my ground, but he touched it past me and finished it.

Fear of giving away a penalty hindered Hanley, but Souttar accepts culpability for this one:

> I remember it coming between Andy and I. I didn't go for it, it bounced over me and they scored. I knew it was my fault. I'd played against Pavlidis in the Europa League the season before. He's very clever with great technique. He's not the quickest but takes you into areas you don't want to go into. You can't afford to switch off.

Déjà vu for me and you and the team too. This was no illusion. There was nothing to suggest Scotland had taken anything on board from the lessons Greece dealt throughout the year. Ten, 15, 20 minutes gone; they were free-wheeling again but managed to score 53 minutes quicker than they did at Hampden. Scotland were putting no pressure on the ball and had no care when they possessed it. We reached Greece's third of the pitch for the third time in the 25th minute when Robertson chased an overhit ball that went out for a goal kick. Gordon tipped a header around the post two minutes later, one of a few top saves he made in the period. They'd had seven efforts on goal by the halfway mark of the half. We'd had none. A second was coming. Karetsas was prancing. Denmark led Belarus. Shit.

I was commentating on this game for UEFA's World Feed, so if you watched the match in an English-speaking country outside of the UK then the chances are you were listening to me – unless the channel (such as ESPN, BEIN Sports, Optus, etc.) paid to put their own production on the broadcast. All the English-speaking commentaries for the UEFA qualifiers are done within the intestines of IMG at Stockley Park on London's western edge. Our observations are made while watching on a 32in screen flanked by a couple of office-sized monitors. One shows technical and logistical information I don't begin to understand, while the other switches between the line-ups and all the usual in-play stats; crucially, letting me know which players have received a yellow card. Reliance on the match director cannot be understated. You'll sometimes hear commentators working *off-tube* leave their own boot in on the director for their flamboyance, e.g. showing one too many replays or a slow-motion montage and returning to the action just as a player gets a shot away.

Lewis Ferguson was harshly booked in the tenth minute for a slightly late arrival. He made the tackle, we saw the referee brandish his yellow and the on-screen graphics (your screen as well as my little helper) confirmed his tightrope. After 30 minutes, he just about caught Pavlidis in the face as the Benfica forward looked to advance over the halfway line. Here came the referee… Oh no. Another yellow. I explained as much on the broadcast. A goal behind and a man down.

Ferguson started walking, but not towards the dugouts. *Has he just been booked twice and not been sent off?* Fans watching on BBC Scotland and around the world all pondered the same thing. Suddenly, the info on my peripheral screen flickered and the yellow rectangle that had been next to Ferguson's name was now next to McGinn's. A new, solitary yellow appeared next to Ferguson's name as I tried to figure out what was going on.

Ferguson was obviously oblivious and knew there hadn't been a miscarriage of justice.

> I was speaking to one of my mates after the game and he asked if I'd been booked twice. I was racking my brain … 'No?' He sent me a video, saying, 'You need to watch this, you were defo booked twice.' But I had no idea what he was on about. In the first ten minutes I made a soft foul that John McGinn definitely didn't think was a foul, and his words got him a yellow. On the TV screen it looked like I was closer to the ref, as if I had got the card, but I was totally oblivious. It didn't cross my mind at all that I was in real trouble when I made the second foul. I saw John get the first yellow.

During our conversations – maybe because this is ultimately a torture tale with a happy ending – I got the impression the boys didn't really like discussing Greece's dominance or what didn't go well in Athens. They continued to control the tempo as the minutes wore on for us, absolutely unfettered by any ounce of pressure but again finishing quite poorly or unable to beat Gordon. We got lucky at Hampden. We wouldn't again, would we? Ben Gannon-Doak's mitigation was succinct:

> There were a lot of nerves early in the game and we didn't want to take any risks.

Hearing the half-time whistle while within a goal of Greece was the target. Just get inside at *one*. There is a ticket to America needing punched here, lads. Or a barcode needing scanned, realistically.

Stoppage time. Bang! McTominay shakes the crossbar from the D, Adams puts a tightly angled header into the side of an open net and Gannon-Doak shoots straight at the keeper in a one-on-one. All three chances created through incisive, speedy play within three minutes of each other. Half-time within one, but somehow not level!

> The five minutes before half-time changed our perspective a lot. The gaffer was telling us, 'There it is, that's what I want from you.' All we needed was five minutes to regain our confidence in our attacking football.

Ryan Christie there, who was playing centre midfield and in the second half was positioned closer to the Greek defence. The break had arrived at a frustrating moment for Scotland, but they emerged similarly unshackled, chasing an equaliser and putting pressure on Greece towards the home goal. A three-minute whirlwind for Karetsas towards the hour took the game further from Scotland's grasp as they clawed for parity. The kid played a hospital ball into his own half and had his mind read by Christie, who pounced and then read the lunging defender's mind to skip towards the Greek 18-yard box. His next touch – far too heavy for his liking – forced him to prod it towards Adams as the keeper closed him down. His 12-yard shot towards what was a gaping goal a second ago was blocked by Karetsas, who had delivered a lesson in desire to get between Adams and the goal after being responsible for the transition. Watching the highlights, his recovery is remarkable. It was typical of Scotland lately; gifted a plate of delicious chicken wings, no teeth with which to tuck in. Karetsas leapt and punched the air when Greece cleared, as if he had scored a goal.

Three minutes later, he did. Gannon-Doak was tackled as he tried to negotiate a crossing angle and Greece worked the ball towards their sub Andrews Tetteh, who breezed past Hanley on the halfway line and barrelled down the inside-left. Karetsas arrived for Tetteh's measured cutback and caressed it into Gordon's near corner. A terrific finish. Scotland's two centre-halves were pretty much in the right-back position when Greece manoeuvred their path to halfway. 'I didn't cover myself in glory,' recalls Hanley. They then hit the post from a corner's header. Dykes, Shankland and Hirst had all been sent to warm up a few minutes ago as Scotland began to bloom, but here came the herbicide.

By that I mean Greece's third goal, scored five minutes after Karetsas's. Tzolis from 25 yards into the top corner whilst still rising. What a strike. He had an excellent first half, but replays showed Gordon could probably have got stronger wrists on it. A taste of our own medicine, if you will, after starting the second half so encouragingly. And it definitely wasn't Calpol.

I said on commentary, 'Scotland will have to settle for the play-offs.' Liam McLeod transmitted a similar message on the national broadcaster, which a couple of senior players didn't like in hindsight. But we were behind by three in Athens, and Denmark were in charge against Belarus. Steve Clarke quickly made a few tweaks with the 'play-offs in mind'.

> We went out confidently for the second half and were quite shocked at how it had become 3-0. We had nothing to lose, let's go and get back in the game. It shouldn't take us going down and feeling like we have nothing to lose before we start to play. When we do that from the beginning, everyone can see we're a bloody good side and it's about doing it consistently. We've got an unbelievable squad, it's about time we showed it.

Not the words of an experienced leader, but now 20-year-old Gannon-Doak.

Some travelling fans had seen enough and decided they'd rather spend the next half an hour in a bar. Cue mayhem.

Belarus equalised via Valery Gromyko in the 62nd minute. As it stood, things would now go to the final game, but there was still half an hour for Denmark to score again.

As briefly mentioned earlier, the Greek media accused their team of complacency after beating Belarus on MD1. Now pumping us, that soft centre started to reveal itself again. Tsimikas was caught out by Gannon-Doak, who raced past him to meet McGinn's fizzing cross and rattle it into the roof. Ripping the ball from Koulierakis's grip, he raced back to the centre circle. 'It felt great for about a minute. I wanted to win,' Gannon-Doak said. Ferguson had thought, 'This isn't meant to be,' two minutes ago but looked at the clock and now knew there was time. The fans who had left early heard the roar as they entered the surrounding streets.

Over to Copenhagen; 65th minute. Nikita Demchenko; 2-1 Belarus. Denmark now needed to score twice or there'd be a *final* on Tuesday regardless of proceedings in Piraeus. Kitman Jim McAllister was providing the live updates to Dykes and the rest of the subs:

> There was a surge on the bench when it happened. I was eager to get on and make an impact. When Christie scored I remember thinking it had given the fans a big lift. Everything changed at that point. I was desperate to get on.

Andy Robertson sent in a *cross*. The perfect cross. If I could design a cross, it would be this cross. This beautiful cross that had a bit of everything. Pace, curl, dip and direction. Christie had his eyes on it the whole way and boshed it in with his head. He gestured for the Tartan Army to crank it up a notch. Where had this come from? All that in the space of five minutes.

> I'm thinking, 'This is on.' I said to McGinn as we got back to our half, 'They're gone, by the way, we can get another here.' It felt like a great performance in the second half. Even when they went 3-0 up, I had a look at how long was left and thought it wasn't over.

The lads on the pitch now think they are one goal from keeping a grip on fate. Clarke retracted the in-game tweaks he'd made.

The subs were just as interested in what was happening at the other end of the continent. The intel wasn't passed on to the pitch from there, but the encouragement from the dugout was effusive. If Belarus held on and we equalised, a draw would seal the deal on Tuesday. We've never come from three down to equalise in our history. McLean knew he probably wouldn't be coming on as Scotland chased the game:

> When they scored their third I was thinking, 'Right, it's the play-offs.' When we realised it was 2-1 to Belarus after we'd scored a couple, we couldn't believe our luck. It was very exciting when we were on the front foot. Info from the other game was being passed along the bench every 30 seconds. It was an emotional rollercoaster.

Nobody on the park knew what was going on, or if they did they won't admit it. Christie thinks it would have 'upset the rhythm' of the second-half display if news filtered through. Some fans near the hoardings shouted updates, but whether they were heard or not, I don't know. 'For all I knew, Denmark were 5-0 up and we needed to get at least a draw,' said Gannon-Doak. Hickey and Hanley's jaws dropped when they got the gossip after being subbed, with the right-back being protected from a yellow card that would rule him out of the Denmark game. Dykes and Shankland were thrown on with ten minutes to go, and when McGinn asked for an update Lawrence told him he hadn't the foggiest. We ended the game with three centre-forwards on the park when Hirst came on five minutes later. Hey! Scotland needed a goal, and Clarke had put on Shankland!

> When Christie scored, the thinking was: 'Let's get a draw here and then we're alright regardless of what happens in Denmark.' It was a bit gung-ho to get an equaliser. It was a very, very long five minutes when I found out Denmark had equalised.

Scotland played with the anticipation of success. Among all the joy and disappointment we've experienced following the national team in our lives, this half an hour serves as the most bonkers scenario I can recall. Another goal, and we'd go top. Gannon-Doak robbed a Greek defender, squared it for Adams who didn't get a shot away and Christie had his shot saved. Gannon-Doak was thriving. As the clock approached 80 minutes, he plucked out a cross on the byline and as usual McTominay timed his arrival to the second. His volley from ten yards was miraculously saved by Vlachodimos's left foot. Robertson dropped to his knees. Christie stood with his hands over his face. Scotland kept pushing with the anticipation of success. Denmark equalised at almost the exact same moment. Sliding doors. Denmark needed one more goal to qualify. A goal for us would nullify their actions. Greece were shown a red card; Bakasetas's second yellow was for barging into Lewis Ferguson as they challenged for a header. Harsh.

Stoppage time. We'd seen the McGinn we knew and loved in the second half. He muscled his way into the box and hit the byline before rolling it across the face. Hirst or Shankland were about to tap it in, but Vlachodimos threw out a leg and deflected it away from their path. One more chance before the end. Craig Gordon began to make his way forward for a Scotland corner.

> I was going to go up for an equaliser and the bench were shouting on at me not to go forward. I was thinking, 'Why? We need a draw here, someone needs to put the ball in the net.' Someone shouted that Denmark were drawing. I couldn't believe it. That was the first time I knew what was going on, and I probably prefer it that way. We assumed we'd have to do it ourselves so the thought didn't enter my head until the final minute.

The corner came to nothing. The whistle blew. Scotland had somehow not drawn the game after somehow not being 4-0 down after half an hour. Almost everyone in the away end was refreshing whatever app they were using. Four minutes remained in Copenhagen. The lads were down but not out. Not out, yet.

'If this goes our way, boys, we can't celebrate. Thank the fans, get inside,' said the captain as they congregated on the pitch to gather around Jim McAllister's phone, like the Manchester United squad hoping someone in Danish red wasn't about to have his Aguero moment. Cameras were peering over their shoulders, potentially perversely catching the heartbreak.

'A horrendous wait,' recalls BGD.

'I was convinced Denmark were going to score,' remembers McLean.

They didn't. Belarus had pulled off something amazing. Something unconsidered in all pre-match hypotheses.

> Robbo had told us not to celebrate but when the Scotland fans were going mental we had a smile on our faces. It was hard not to feel excited about the opportunity that had presented itself. It was our fault in Greece but not our fault Denmark fucked up. We took what we were given. We saw Belarus were a decent team and they showed that I suppose.
>
> The play-offs only came into my head during the Denmark game. The Greece game felt so strange that I didn't think it was over at any point. After we'd finished huddling round Jim, I was keen to go and tell everyone that Belarus are no mugs!

Ryan Christie following on from McLean, there. Despite savaging his squad in the moment in October, Clarke couldn't resist either: 'I think it proves that the last game at Hampden when we got booed off the pitch, maybe the three points were better than people thought.' He added: 'We need to believe in ourselves more.' That much was true. Akin to his confronting of the BBC's Chris

McLaughlin for specifics on how many people had told him they were angry with the performances at the Euros, media folks would have been justified in requesting Clarke give clear examples when he replied 'plenty of them' after being asked if he'd been part of a night as dramatic as this one.

The changing room was a confusing place for a minute or two. After all the luck gratefully welcomed in October, it was only right it ran out. It had, then it hadn't. Performing for 30 minutes wasn't enough on our terms and Danish shortcomings gave us another grin from Miss Luck. Hickey sat between Robertson and Souttar thinking we'd got away with it. Clarke told the players their directness, energy, bravery and creation was everything that had brought them success over the last five years, and told the press that dealing with long balls had been the evening's problem. A little bit of affirmation was necessary, and there was no room for rumination. Gordon remembers the be all and end all:

> There was a momentum shift with how it ended up. The boys that were on the bench were going round the changing room lifting everyone, saying, 'One more chance, let's go, we can do this.' The manager spoke and said we shouldn't really feel very positive but we do, so let's use it while we have the chance. There was only room for positivity. The context was important; a bit of momentum to remind ourselves we could play like that. The final 20 to 30 minutes was much better from us – that gave everyone a lift and we could try and carry it forward into Denmark. We would have snatched the hand off for one night at Hampden and a lot of boys knew this was career-defining.

The squad stayed overnight in Greece and flew home in the morning to give the players a better night's sleep. They took off after their play-off first leg in Athens on the night of the game and it didn't exactly set up the players proficiently, plus it removed the possibility of being stranded at the airport during the night while waiting for a delayed flight – like Naismith experienced after the defeat in Georgia in 2015 when the SFA decided against having an aircraft ready and waiting for their arrival. That result ultimately cost Scotland a play-off place for Euro 2016. This was a different dimension.

'This opportunity … we can't let it go,' said McGinn. The opportunity that an unhealthy chunk of the players probably wouldn't see again. The opportunity that Steve Clarke had said will essentially be his last to grasp. The opportunity to qualify for the World Cup.

Chapter 14
Denmark (Home)

I CAN'T bring myself to detail the box office smash of the summer, the price of a three-bed semi, the top of the pops or the pricks in power. It was ages ago. Eight members of the squad weren't born. Here we were in 2026, and Scotland stood in front of a vortex to transport them to a land to which we'd yearned to follow them for almost three decades. 2026; as close to 1998 as 1998 is to 1970. That sums up the desolation well enough.

Scotland had been to one World Cup play-off in that time, and it was a one-legged semi-final, thanks to FIFA and UEFA's lust for making relatively simple processes more complicated. We had competed well in three European Championship play-off ties since our appearance in '96, taking England to the wire, beating the Netherlands in our first leg at Hampden and overcoming Serbia on penalties, but in my opinion being one match – one winner-takes-all match – from a World Cup supersedes a Euros play-off. Recalling critical qualification games in the final international break of campaigns from down the recent years conjures memories of Slovenia '17, Poland '15, Spain '11 and Italy '07. Obviously none went our way. Italy was huge at the time and qualification from that group would arguably be eternally noted as the national team's greatest achievement. James McFadden still thinks about his missed chance at 1-1. The era is reflected upon with fondness of the journey, not regret at failing to reach the destination, which was a Euros ten years after our last major tournament. Huge at the time and rightly so, but not this.

This was a World Cup nearly 20 years on from that campaign, and the importance of this game against Denmark, on 18 November 2026, was perhaps not only Scotland's most important qualifier since playing Latvia at Celtic Park on the final day of World Cup '98 qualifying, but maybe – given the context – our most important qualifying match of all time. We hadn't qualified for anything at a full-time whistle inside Hampden since 1989, in an era when qualifying for World Cups wasn't laced with generational trauma. When would Scotland next be in a situation replicating the one they had before them? A home game against a strong team, but not an elite team. Win this match and the wait is over. No play-offs, no relying on other results to complement ours. Win one more match and the wait is over.

Scotland arrived home from Greece the day after the game and partook in the usual meetings before family visiting hours and some recovery stuff. God, it sounds like a slog; some stretching, massages, chillaxing in the Blythswood's spa facilities. Basically, nothing that involves running, as far as I'm aware. Team-shaping, set pieces and walk-throughs are for the next day. McLean explains:

> A lot of that is 11 v 11 and playing out certain scenarios. Also phases of play, crosses for strikers and full-backs, different bits for the centre midfielders. We'll split up and look at some tactical stuff for each position but mainly it's 11 on 11. Naisy and Alan come in and take bits, Clarke knows how to spread the load. Previously he was in control of everything but now they do a lot of the attacking stuff with Clarke's message through them. It's about finer details because he has a lot of trust in us.

Billy Gilmour didn't make it to consideration. He eventually spent four months out after an operation to sort *osteitis pubis*, the same condition on which Ryan Christie had an operation the previous summer and that had plagued Kieran Tierney for years, causing him issues getting out of bed in the morning before heading to Celtic training wondering if he'd have to retire. Basically, the joint that connects the hip to the thigh becomes inflamed due to repetitive overuse. Lennon Miller, not a clone but probably the nearest thing to Gilmour – was unfit as well, remember. Ferguson and Christie together in midfield felt likely. McKenna for Hanley and Dykes for Adams were the two changes speculated.

Rumours of a virus spreading through the Danish camp weren't fake news, but San Diego winger Anders Dreyer was the only one eventually unable to make the short trip over the North Sea. Rasmus Højlund was fine after being rested and training on his own, while Fulham's Joachim Andersen, Sporting Lisbon's Morten Hjulmand (both having been under threat of suspension) and Porto's Victor Froholdt were all expected to play after some time off on Saturday. That went well. This should have been an end-of-year field trip for them. They had 35 shots against Belarus, their most in a game for 19 years, but scored only twice. Now they had to contend with an emotionally-charged stadium at which they didn't have a great record even at half capacity.

Denmark's last three visits to Hampden stretching nearly 15 years had resulted in defeat. Embarrassingly for them as well, two were of the seemingly unwinnable-for-us friendly nature. The other one rivals Spain at Hampden in 2023 for the defining Hampden night of the Steve Clarke era, but his record in games balancing expectation and pressure with high stakes was quite hard to assess. Wins against Serbia and Israel were earned through different kinds of excellent performances; the ones against Norway and Greece were like stealing cash from the ATM after the old dear had put in her pin number. They were all won, and Clarke could point to them when questioned. Performing abjectly against Ukraine and for many, many minutes of the tournaments for which we qualified were on the other side of the list. He was warned by dissenters when he accepted the job that he was about to hook himself up to a poisoned chalice through a drip, but by the time the ten o'clock news titles rolled on Tuesday he might have reached three out of four tournaments, become the only manager to take us to three finals and ended the wait for a World Cup. Yet his 'big game' credentials were – some would say fairly or otherwise – under the spotlight.

'We'll need the crowd. We'll need them more in the difficult moments than the easy ones,' said the manager, which was a sentiment repeated unprompted by Robertson, asking fans to get in their seats early and 'make it an incredible atmosphere for the lads, because we'll react off that'.

Perhaps there was a little rancour for how we responded at times during the Greece and Belarus games. Robertson said, 'We hope the fans get behind us no matter what. There might be setbacks and frustrations. It's up to us to try and perform and it's up to them to try to help us as well.'

Alluding to Scotland's seeding, Clarke emphasised his side had already achieved something by making sure the final game was a decider. Contextually, I'm not sure about that, or Robertson's assertion the squad would have 'bitten your hand off for a play-off spot' when the group was drawn. Clarke was black-and-white about the view that Scotland had a second bite at the cherry because of Danish incompetence. 'I think it's the first opportunity if I read the group right? We've got ten points, Denmark have got 11.' Can't argue with that.

As expected, Clarke wasn't keen to publicly expand on his tactical blueprint for the evening. Why would he? Despite the thrilling and effective nature of the final 30 minutes in Athens, Clarke rejected the idea his side would attack from the start – 'It's better if I don't tell you what I'm going to do.' Even if that's what he had drawn up, there's little to no benefit in giving a pre-match peek behind the curtain to reporters. We can speculate among ourselves, it's all part of the fun. *Our* own Plan A? Hope, followed by a Plan B of denial.

Players are regularly inundated with ticket requests for the games nobody wants to miss. Their WhatsApps and Instagrams become a stream of good luck messages from team-mates, friends and family, former coaches, staff at their clubs and even school teachers. The guys haven't been shy with their love for one another and some of the players' ability to switch off from the task at hand once they arrive back at their hotel from a training session. You know Lyndon Dykes by now, don't you? Vibrant, boisterous, confident.

> There were some nerves and a bit of tension the night before. The majority of the squad have been there for a long time, got loads of caps and been through all the ups and downs. The major thing has always been making it to the World Cup. We'd done the Euros. It was the World Cup now. You could tell there was a sense of underlying pressure but with the luck we had with Belarus, I felt we could go and make history. Make sure we make it hard for Denmark; be solid, be strong, be Scottish. I wanted to start that game. I felt that if I did I'd help us win with what I can bring. I was disappointed not to start in Greece. I was desperate to start.

There is no binary match prep operation on gameday. It was a special morning in the Ferguson family; Lewis FaceTimed home to say happy birthday to his daughter and watch her opening her presents. He doesn't like to set an alarm, whereas Hickey prefers not to sleep in. He and Gannon-Doak don't mind solitude with their phones (Gen-Z, innit), while McLean and Souttar prefer to socialise. Christie gets *bullied* into taking his Xbox by Dykes. Gordon wanted space and time to make sense of it all:

> I tried to take the emotion out of it. First of all, I needed to recover and make sure I was ready three days after my first game of the season. That took a bit of doing. I

was busy in the Greece game so to get myself physically ready was one thing, but mentally I conjured up the past disappointments I'd had and campaigns that hadn't gone well, to try and use the experiences to make me as ready as possible. Lessons learned from things like Harry Kane's equaliser. That's one I was thinking about as well as the Italy game in 2007 – those nearly moments. They were things that I desperately wanted to put right. To have this one moment in my career to look back on and say we'd done it. Nothing will be bigger than getting to a World Cup for a Scotland team. I didn't socialise much on game day. I was getting in the zone by myself, thinking about what I needed to do in the game and getting any last-minute massages to make sure I'm in the best possible condition. I got some sleep during the day as well and blocked everything else out. Everything was on the line and I had to accept that and process it so it was all out my system and I could fully focus on the game when it was time to go to the pre-match meeting with the players. Every player dealt with things mentally, realising how big the game was and what a chance we had. Leading up to the game was pretty emotional knowing this was my last chance; if this goes wrong, it's my last game for Scotland.

Omelettes, yoghurts, fruit salads, scrambled eggs; the buffet is an obviously healthy one for the boys who make their way down during the morning. Some head back to bed for more sleep afterwards, some get a coffee and take a walk in the fenced area outside the Blythswood like rare zoo animals while pedestrians peer through, shout encouragement and ask for photographs. Christie is one of the ones who enjoys a morning stroll after breakfast:

Serbia felt different because we were natural underdogs, we felt we'd been written off. The Ukraine game was bizarre; it was in the summer and the political climate around it was bizarre as well, it shouldn't have been played then. A game like that must be played in-season. This was the first time I'd felt the pressure of expectation in one of these qualifying games. If we had been told at the start of the group we'd need a win in the final game against Denmark, we'd have taken it. We did wonder if Denmark would be fragile after the Belarus game, but we are good as a group to be able to have a laugh and chat shite for a day or two and not think about the game too much. I had loads of people messaging me saying they were going to the game – 'What a night it'll be!' – almost pre-empting we'll do it. We needed to keep the head and realise Denmark were in almost the exact same situation as us.

The team was privately revealed in the early afternoon as usual. This was Clarke's XI for Scotland's biggest qualification game of the millennium: Gordon; Hickey, Souttar, McKenna, Robertson; Ferguson, Christie; Gannon-Doak, McTominay, McGinn; Dykes.

For once, we'd been able to accurately predict a Clarke selection. Hickey had been passed fit for Athens after recovering from the slight hamstring pull suffered in the corresponding fixture, but playing two games in such quick succession was a red flag for Brentford after his 18 months recovering from the repeated tears and operations on the same leg. Aaron had to stand up for himself.

In some people's heads it was the best thing for me not to play in that game, but in my head I needed to play in it. I'll do everything I can to play. The player normally makes the final decision on fitness but you have to listen to both sides and think about the bigger picture. I spoke to the manager and he goes off what I'm saying, but it's his decision to pick the team. It was during the shape the day before the game I had a good idea I'd be starting. It was actually quite a crazy few days between Greece and Denmark, but once I knew I was going to be involved I was buzzing, to know I'd walk out at Hampden in a game like that is an experience of a lifetime.

Shankland wasn't surprised or dejected at being on the bench again.

With Dyksey not getting much of a game down the road with Birmingham, I thought he wouldn't last much longer than 60 to 70 minutes. In a pressure game with high intensity, it was gonna be hard for him. I had an idea that if we needed a goal Clarke would go with two strikers at about 60 minutes. Mentally, I was preparing for that role, that I'd more than likely get about half an hour.

The players' free time is straddled by the early-afternoon team announcement and tactical meeting. Away matches don't restrict the players as much as there are quiet areas they can find to stretch their legs, but in Glasgow's city centre, on a day like this? Impossible, unless they wanted to double up with an excessively long trenchcoat, trilby and shades. Another walk around the Blythswood cage killed some time for the majority of them among encouraging shouts and pumping car horns, but after that a lot of the boys took the opportunity to spend an hour or two in their rooms. Andy Robertson showed bravery after the match to reveal he had spent the day grieving for his friend and Liverpool team-mate Diogo Jota, that he was 'in a bit of trouble in his room' and had to mask his anguish from the squad. Shankland managed to catch some shut-eye, perhaps helped by his calm presence of mind. Christie was paddling in a different pool.

I was hoping I'd continue in centre midfield. I was struggling with my knee a bit after the Greece game but I thought with the magnitude of the match it'd get me through. When it's confirmed you're starting, the nerves start to kick in. The bigger games for Scotland are the ones that get me and this was right up there. I like to nap in the afternoon before a night game but I stared at the ceiling for a few hours. At pre-match [their meal], all the lads said it was the same for them. It's probably better to just hang around with the boys because we just chat nonsense rather than think about the game. I'd rather not ramp myself up too early at two in the afternoon, burn off nervous energy and then be exhausted by the time the game comes around.

Dykes continued with his big-game tradition: the skinhead. It has become a cog in the whole break's machine to the extent team-mates question why he hasn't whipped out the razor as the team bus's departure time edges closer. The ritual started before Belgrade on the day of the Euro 2020 play-off final, with Lyndon hoping it would intimidate the Serbians. He produced one of the most effective performances ever produced by a Scottish centre-forward. Instant heritage. This time it was done with time to spare.

The boys like me to do it. If I haven't done it, they'll complain. I shaved it because I was starting and it makes me feel really up for the game; strong and ready to go out and put my head on the line. We got a barber at the hotel the day before and I got it down to the skin. I've done it quite a lot but the two that stick out are probably Serbia and Norway, away. It's a bit of fun as well, done in good spirits, but it does help me feel ready for the game.

Pre-match consists of what you're probably expecting; some chicken and fish, various pasta options, fresh vegetables 'n that.

Lewis Ferguson's pre-match meal of four pancakes with syrup, bananas, blueberries and strawberries is a surprising one.

Gannon-Doak came down to join the lads at a table. He is unique among the squad with one of his rituals, and a recent one at that.

> I don't usually get nervous for games but I was for that one. With the late kick-off we had the full day to sit and stew over it; could be easy for your arse to collapse. I stuck to my routine. It's not a strict one but I'll find the time to do it: have a nap and read my Bible. It calms me right down. I've had a tough time with injuries and ever since I've learned about faith, when these challenges arise I handle it so much better because I don't feel like I'm doing it alone and it's all part of the plan. There's no need to be scared going into a game because God has put me there to try and make people happy.

Most of the players were careful and eager not to betray Clarke's confidence in revealing too many specific contents of his rousing speech before they boarded the team bus. It contained references to the journey they had been on as a squad, how much he wanted to represent his country at a World Cup and take them with him, and how much he thought they deserved to be there. He pointed to the Ukraine game, circled it and told the players this was the missing chapter in their success story.

> A very good speech; powerful, emotional. Everyone left the meeting thinking, 'Fucking hell, that was amazing.'

That's how Clarke's words impacted Ferguson. How about Gordon and Christie?

> He struck a great balance between using things that hadn't gone well and things that could still happen for us.

It really resonated with the players that we're all in this together. We came out really ready to fight for each other.

It was a bit of a *Braveheart* speech. Playing a team for the second time, you sort of know the tactical stuff and what to expect. There are those elements, but in big games like that there are only so many tactical things that come into play. He had a chat with us that was amazing. He doesn't speak in-depth too often so when he does we know it's really meaningful. Everybody was ready to go to war after that meeting.

Dykes elaborated a bit further:

He had a lot of passionate words before we left the hotel. He told a story about who has been in the squad from the start with him, the number of players who have been through it all and what we've achieved. He spoke about a few personal things and his feelings about us. It was a really good speech. Everyone felt it. It will always stay with me. Some parts were more personal, which we'll keep to ourselves, but it was a major point before we left. We could feel how much he believed in us and how much he wanted to take us to the World Cup.

The bus journey to Mount Florida was relatively quiet, but resident DJ Kieran Tierney had control of the music as usual. 'We weren't really talking about it, but we could feel it,' remembers McLean.

This November night was grisly. Not quite to the extent of 18 years and two days previously in November '07 when a monsoon plagued Hampden during the infamous decider against Italy, but light rain was struggling to make up its mind and the temperature was cold, expected to be below freezing by full time. Supporters on their way to and from the Clockwork, the Florida Park and Minnesota Fats roared encouragement at the team bus as it slowly turned off Carmunnock Road and past Lesser Hampden before disappearing beneath Hampden's surrounding concrete.

The Danes arrived in town with the mathematical advantage. They did not need to win this game of football. This silly game of football that would dictate our nation's personality for weeks rather than days. What frivolity! It meant everything. Thomas Kristensen was the voice of TV2 in Denmark, their Liam McLeod.

> I think our fans were a bit nervous. If the Danish team could have that mental breakdown for five minutes against Belarus, what could happen against Scotland? If we played that game again against Belarus, we would score five or six goals each time. At 1-0, everything was clicking and we were on our way to America, yet five minutes later we were losing 2-1, Scotland had scored twice and Belarus missed a big sitter for 3-1. My co-commentator and I looked at each other like, 'What the fuck is happening here?' I really didn't think it would end up in the last game. I thought we'd have already qualified by the time we got to Hampden.

The odd Dannebrog – *blood cloth* – draped shoulders among the horde of saltires, mostly filtering towards Hampden's west stand. A piper's presence is standard. Hats, scarves and flags were sold with the usual surreal vocal emphasis on the first two items. Food trucks took their £6 from those who'd come straight from work or craved something greasy after five pints. Hampden was busier ahead of schedule.

Robertson had asked the Tartan Army to be in their seats well ahead of time, and while there were many more than normal blocking out red and blue, there isn't the cultural element often seen in places like South America or Germany where fans will congregate and chant for an hour or more before the first whistle. At around 7.15pm, with half an hour to go before kick-off, the stadium was around a third full.

'We want this more than them,' encouraged McTominay as the players emerged wearing that awful warm-up top with the yellow trim. By the time they trotted inside for their final prep, about three-quarters of the 50,000 were ready and '500 Miles' – I know it's not the track's official name – was gathering quite the choral support.

I remember Stephen O'Donnell telling a story for my previous book about continually passing the ball out of play during a possession box and losing his ability to take a first touch before kick-off in Belgrade. Christie doesn't remember anyone having a *nuke*, as they call it in the industry, before centre on this occasion, but he can relate.

> Similar to Sods, a Scottish cup semi-final against Celtic was my first game at Hampden for Inverness. In the warm-up, I couldn't control the ball and thought I was in for an absolute disaster. It comes with experience. Now we kind of enter an automatic focus mode. The place erupted when we came out for the warm-up. I felt reassured; I'd rather be us than them. We're different in warm-ups … a few sprints and I'm ready, I just want it to start. Some like to take it more slowly, some rat around and kick folk! Scott McKenna is one of them, volleying his own team-mates in a warm-up. Mental!

Clarke explained to BBC Scotland that he expected the Danes' desire was a physical 90 minutes and his own was to start the game well. We'd seen Scotland reap the rewards of following that template over the last two seasons against Poland, Switzerland, Cyprus, Georgia and Spain. 'We have to make sure when we have the chance to play, we play. We have to be progressive and create chances.'

One of the decisions taken to aid progression was the selection of Scott McKenna at left centre half. That was at Hanley's expense, with Souttar next to Scotty. The Hibs centre-back had spent the afternoon feeling quite relaxed and didn't feel the need to go for a nap after digesting Clarke's decision to opt for McKenna. He felt he hadn't had a great game in Athens but was naturally disappointed while understanding the manager's logic. His evening was about to slip its leash.

> I was disappointed not to be starting and probably felt sorry for myself for a wee while. Coming on at half-time in the first game of the Euros stands out similarly; I'd been starting for a little while, playing most games and then got put on the bench, so coming on at half-time against Germany was good prep mentally for what happened before the Denmark game. I'd got past the disappointment of the Greece game to making sure I was ready to come on. You're never 100 per cent full and firing during a warm-up if you're not starting. Fifteen minutes before kick-off, Naisy shouted me over. I thought he needed some help with headers for the centre-halves, but he pulled me and said John was struggling. I said, 'You're kidding,' but I could tell when I looked at Soapy's face he had a problem. I did about four or five headers, a couple of sprints and headed up the tunnel to get ready for the game.

The butterflies erupted from their cocoons. His family in the south stand, and the vast majority of us surrounding it, didn't know he'd be emerging from the tunnel as a starter until we witnessed it. Granty had changed out of his warm-up gear and was now dressed for the occasion, trying to remain calm among a dressing room of players who'd had all afternoon to prepare for the adrenaline rush about to course through their veins. The lads didn't made a big deal of his introduction in fear of exacerbating any nerves. The team were minutes from arriving in the tunnel and embarking on the final stretch. Hanley glanced down; shin-guards, boots, but no socks.

I had my small socks on and strapped my shinnies over them but had put my boots straight on after that – nerves, 100 per cent. It was actually a wee kick up the arse to get my head straight. I was about to play in a huge game, and I'm at my best when I'm calm and fully conscious of my decision-making. Nobody saw it thankfully. I got away with it. That will always live with me. As funny as it is now, it cleared my head at the time.

Souttar had jogged inside to get a once-over from the physio but, despite what Hickey asserts earlier in the chapter, the decision was taken out of his hands.

I just took a step back and felt my calf. There would be so much adrenaline in the game you think you might be alright, but I was going through the last bit of defensive shape and knew I was in trouble. I tried to keep going but once I was inside the gaffer made the decision there and then. I was out for five weeks.

'Seven Nation Army' blared around Hampden, seizing heartbeats into its bassy rhythm. The Scotland team stood in the gaping Hampden tunnel as fireworks soared from the roof and turf. 'Alright, boys, let's go!' McTominay raised his voice again. They were greeted by a truly visceral Hampden Roar. Then, the anthem, with its beautiful, captivating acapella second verse. The players looked to their lefts and rights after its crescendo and knew their time had to be now. Our time had to be now. It certainly had to be Gordon's.

The anthem is the loudest I can remember. It was brilliant, a real moment of thinking, 'Listen to that, we have to do this.' It was huge for us to feel that backing before the game began. They were so behind us.

The strength of the wind in the sails couldn't do anything but propel a full-tilt Scotland. They'd played their best football of the year during the final half an hour in Athens, Clarke's pre-match speech had them *ready for war* and almost 50,000 raucous supporters were in their corner. Adhering to Clarke's – and all our – wishes, Scotland attacked Denmark; unusually towards the west stand in the first half. This was a proper, old-fashioned Hampden cauldron. Young Ben Gannon-Doak must have been in awe!

> Folk think I'm a weirdo, but I don't hear anything because I'm concentrating … I don't hear the crowd, I barely hear my team-mates … anything. Especially when the ball is near me, I block it all out. I'm that concentrated, and I need to be because if I'm not a defender might get in behind me then I'm getting whipped. I need to be absolutely locked in, so I don't take in the atmosphere.

Spurred on by his own manic mannerisms rather than the frenzy flanking him, Gannon-Doak took it for a run, as he is prone to do. Never mind the blocked cross, we'll come again. Christie tried … blocked again, but our number 11 chased Mikkel Damsgaard towards the corner flag and disrupted his plans to clear it. Gannon-Doak collected it as Hampden surged with expectation. His step-over fooled Pierre-Emile Højbjerg and he crossed with his weaker left foot. Fifty thousand people gasped as Scott McTominay defied gravity, hung in the Hampden night and like nothing we'd ever seen in dark blue, thundered the ball into Kasper Schmeichel's bottom right-hand corner with a perfect overhead kick – 8ft and 3in at his apex.

Archie against the Dutch or Faddy against the French? That has been the conversation for 20 years. Hah!

The Scottish support responded in a way I don't think we'd seen since Leigh Griffiths scored his second against England. The blur of bouncing bodies around the stadium complementing the unfettered boom were a sight and sound to behold. McTominay held his team-mates at arms' length as he almost nonchalantly trotted towards the dugout. 'Where's my mum?' he enquired on arrival, staring towards the comfy seats and blowing a kiss towards his family while Naismith patted him on the chest. The rest of the lads met to celebrate within the park's confines. McTominay stands alone in this goal's lore, but BGD played his part:

> It was all in the pass! That's my claim to fame. I can put my name on that goal forever! I wasn't actually even aiming for him, it was just a ball into a decent area. I looked up, saw a few shirts and thought to just put it in and maybe something will happen. Scott pulled a bit of magic out the bag. It's the best goal I've seen in a game I've played in, no doubt, just outrageous less than five minutes in. I remember running across to join the celebrations and making eye contact with Grant Hanley thinking, 'Oh my God!'

Ferguson thrust his arms at 90-degree angles and caught McTominay's drift, Hanley's protective instincts quickly took over after the initial thrill, Hickey decided he wouldn't catch McTominay and absorbed the moment with the fans, Christie had kept the attack going and turned to face the west stand with his arms outstretched.

> An absolutely mental start to the game with everything else around it. The anthem, how emotional that was and the feeling it gave us. We naturally wanted to start quickly to get the fans on side, then Scotty goes and does that. I remember just as Doaky put the ball in, seeing Scotty set himself and thinking, 'Don't be fucking ridiculous.' Then he pulls it off ... of course he pulled it off. Nobody else could. He's a player of

a different calibre. I just turned around to the crowd thinking, 'What have I just witnessed?'

If McTominay had taken a fresh-air swipe, the ball might have landed at Dykes's feet as he loitered.

I had the best view in the house! It was mental. I couldn't believe it actually went in. It just oozes the confidence he has. Since he went to Napoli it's like he can't do anything wrong. When it went in I was just thinking, 'What the fuck has just happened?!' If it was a tap-in we'd have all still been buzzing but the goal itself gave it a whole different feeling. We quickly realised we still had about 85 minutes to go. The pulses of everyone must have been through the roof.

Gordon was locked in at the other end of the pitch, responding like we'd just stuck a fourth past the Faroes in a friendly.

Watch the first three goals, I don't celebrate any of them. Scott scored one of the best goals Hampden has ever seen, I just turned around and walked back to my goal. I was so focused on what I needed to do. It's probably the best goal I've ever seen live, but there was nothing else going on in my head. I just turned around and walked away. I'd taken the emotion completely out of the night. We had to win this game, and that allowed me to stay calm and make better decisions.

Ruled out with strained ankle ligaments, Lennon Miller was watching on his lonesome in his Udine digs.

I was on a bit of a delay on my TV. I was getting messages into my group chat not long after the game started saying, 'What a goal.' So I knew we had scored, but I wasn't expecting that. It was still a shock seeing it, but it didn't surprise me; he's always trying stuff like that in training. I turned my phone off after that so I didn't get any more notifications through.

Scotland continued to play with force for the opening 15 minutes. High on the rush from McTominay's all-timer, the players and fans were riding the wave. The Danes were shit-feart of Gannon-Doak. He had the beating of Manchester United's Patrick Dorgu, only a year his superior, who was identified on the *Hampden Roar* podcast as Denmark's weak link by Danish commentator Peter Piil during the build-up. Joakim Mæhle's injury was a costly one. He'd terrorised Scotland from left-back in Copenhagen four years ago.

After a quarter of an hour, Denmark started to find a groove. Nothing too elaborate, but for the first time they were beginning to dominate the ball. This was slightly disconcerting but not a disaster. After all, they did that in the Parken without making us perspire profusely. As we hit 20 and Denmark continued to stroke it around, that's when disaster struck.

A stretcher was being brought on for Gannon-Doak as he switched between clutching his hamstring and face. He had started the game *on flames*, as they say at his age. His absence during the Euros and Nations League play-offs adjacent to his presence during the Nations League and World Cup qualifying groups portrayed a gruesome truth about the pace and directness this Scotland squad can offer when he isn't around. His influence cannot be understated. The muscle tear kept him out for almost five months. He'd turned 20 years old a week before.

As soon as I felt it I knew I was done. It was quite emotional for me. I knew I'd been playing well. I knew it would be an operation as well. I'd already had two so I was thinking, 'Fuck sake, am I ever going to get a year of having no problems?' Three times in a row now I've had a bad one; quad, knee and hammy. Four months, seven months and five months. I never seem to get minor injuries where I miss a week or two. It was emotional because of the game it happened in and I'd had a good start, then suddenly I was done. I take the view it's strengthening me and is preparing me for something else. I missed the rest of the first half and came back out five minutes into the second.

Any other pacey players available to Steve Clarke were not available for use on the night because, eh, there were none in the squad. Christie shuttled to the right, and McLean took his place next to Ferguson. If you saw McLean getting stripped and thought he was going to be taking on Dorgu, you haven't been paying attention. In fact, it seems even he had dozed off in class!

I could tell Doaky was in trouble so I told a few of the boys on the bench to get warmed up, the forward-type players. I was still sitting with my big jacket and trousers on, then I heard my name and saw the manager looking up at me. I got myself ready thinking, 'I haven't played wide for Scotland in ages,' but it made sense for Christie to go to the right. Denmark had started to get a hold of the game; Højbjerg drops to the left a lot, we knew that and were ready for it. Christie is incredible at knowing when to press or not so he could jump on to Højbjerg, Hickey would push up and I'd stop the pockets to try and stop their rotation. [Yeah, me neither]. It was about trying to wrestle back control of the game. With a 1-0 lead it's hard not to sit and accept what you have. Maybe we scored a bit too early.

The Danish commentary team spoke with an allusion as the stretcher came on for Scotland's starboy. 'We had less to fear when Gannon-Doak suffered his injury.'

When Gannon-Doak lay down, Christie knew immediately he'd have to change his job spec. Everyone in the team knows their role before a game, but it is challenging to assume someone else's when your preparation and visualisation aren't relevant to that in advance. It wasn't until half-time that Scotland sussed out a slight adaptation to their press. Denmark continued to pass and move. By the half-hour mark, they hadn't just grown into the game, they were dominating it. Teenage playmaker Victor Froholdt of Porto was enjoying the space afforded to him while Lazio's Gustav Isaksen looked threatening drifting from the right side. Højlund had a goal correctly ruled out for a shove on Hickey; his performative incredulity nonsensical. He missed a couple more but hadn't broken the trap on each occasion.

Scotland were skating on thin ice, terrified it would crack if they kept the ball for more than three or four passes. A few fans around me in B8 bemoaned Gilmour's absence, but BGD's injury had left the team dumbfounded at how to progress through midfield and up the pitch. Oh, it was painful viewing. Denmark were taking sweeties aff a wain, but Scotland got to the break at 1-0. Barring one of the most outrageous goals ever scored on these islands, not much had happened. Denmark had completed about four times as many passes as us. Lewis Ferguson tells us we were much more concerned than the lads on the pitch:

> You know what it's like. At 1-0 it's them that need to get back into the game so they're putting the pressure on. I thought we were decent in the first half and defended well without creating a massive amount. It was in the back of our heads we were 1-0 up and wanted to protect it. We regrouped and tweaked a few things but I don't remember feeling under massive pressure. I had

Damsgaard behind my right shoulder and Froholdt over my left. It was my job to close down their spaces, make tackles and stop them from creating much. They're good and can have possession, but without cutting us open. I was right behind McTominay for his goal; incredible athleticism. You couldn't really enjoy it too much though because there was 87 minutes to go!

Like us, Denmark were able to score multiple times against Greece because they had space in which to slip and slice into the final third. They struggled to score against us because we didn't afford them that opportunity. With their eardrums still reverberating from 'Carnaval de Paris', Denmark continued unperturbed by their unwanted and enforced 15-minute pow-wow. Gordon quickly stopped Højlund from equalising with a strong, low save ... We couldn't do this for 45 minutes. He'd have a far easier opportunity in a matter of minutes.

Robertson tripped Isaksen on the box's apex. Right on the line. Initially unpunished, Polish referee Szymon Marciniak was advised to take a second look. 'There's no way that's a foul,' muttered Robertson to Højbjerg as the referee hurried back onto the pitch. I'm afraid it was, Andy. It's a penalty.

Højlund had the ball. McTominay advised Gordon to dive to his left. He did. Højlund put it high in the opposite direction. It was 1-1. Deserved. Just more than half an hour to go. Hickey, whom like Doak is so placid it's hard to imagine him in any kind of fluster, was having to focus against someone he knows well.

I was directly up against my Brentford team-mate, Mikkel Damsgaard. I know what he's capable of and have never had that at international level before. He tried to speak to me a little bit during the game but I wasn't having it, it was very serious. Sometimes I might not look I'm nervous or excited but deep down I am.

Nerves probably wouldn't be the right word normally, it's usually excitement.

Clarke and the players could rightly reject the notion of luck dictating Scotland's successful campaign until this point. There was an argument for it – I'd certainly argue it had impacted it – but they could point to a combination of solidity – at times – and prolificacy – when it mattered – as the reasons for the ten points in their column. Now this may be subjective as well, but the red card that followed shortly after Højlund's equaliser was nothing short of shambolic. Right-back Rasmus Kristensen was booked in a stonewall sense before half-time for bringing down McGinn as he burst towards the Danish box.

McGinn did not forget.

He spun the Eintracht Frankfurtian in his trademark style midway through the Danish half and hit the deck. Replays showed no tangle of legs, no shove, no tug, no nothing, just a forearm nudge that would do well to fell a mannequin. Marciniak brandished the second yellow as Ferguson arrived on the scene, shouting, 'He's got to go!' If VAR were permitted to offer advice on second yellow cards, this would have been overturned. Kristensen had spoken at the end of the previous season about nearly retiring after a rotten campaign with Leeds United because he 'couldn't be bothered anymore'. That might tip him over the edge.

Scotland needed a goal and Clarke was true to his word. Christie and Dykes took their seats; Ché Adams was introduced along with Lawrence Shankland.

> I was warming up when the penalty got given, then they got the red card and I kinda knew at that point we needed to go for it. Naisy shouted me back up and I was ready for it. I'd been preparing for it all day. I was playing it over and over in my head and I had a feeling I was going to get a goal. McTominay said the same before the match. Sometimes you just have a feeling.

Shankland grew up in a family who supported the national team. He was now the great hope in a game that bore tension resembling one of the matches he attended as an 11-year-old. He went bananas when Gary Caldwell slide-tackled us into the lead against France and stood in the east stand behind Craig Gordon begging him to catch the ball as a last-second header bounced towards him.

> My wee cousin and I had our tops off at full time! That's what it's all about. I was greeting at full time in the Italy game and you think about all that in the lead-up to a match like the Denmark one. I went to the games as a kid and can appreciate how much it means to everyone. When you play well for your club you get folk congratulating you here and there, but the amount of people messaging in the lead-up to a big Scotland game is crazy. Everyone is pulling for the same thing which is quite unusual in this country!

The ten Danish men continued passing Scotland off the park. They'd had 17 shots on goal. We'd had one. Scotland had been disjointed for at least half of the campaign but were one goal from reaching the World Cup. Tierney came on at right-back for a shattered Hickey, a decision Clarke had informed Kieran about before the game because of Hickey's fitness levels and in order to remind KT he is viewed as a key member of the squad. Ferguson had a shot blocked. Corner.

'SCOOTTTTTTLAND! SCOOTTTTTTLAND!'

Ferguson delivered with whip and suddenly it was in the back of the net. From B8, it looked like it had gone straight in but no, it was Shankland! Scoring from a yard out, into the goal behind which he was overcome with nerves nearly 20 years ago. There is something very precious about the innocence of what he'd achieve one day, from himself and those around him unaware they were sitting next to a future hero. He ran and leapt into Ferguson's arms, who waited for him with clenched fists and arms bent like he was completing a bicep curl. Just 13 minutes remained and Scotland had what was necessary. It felt too good to be true. We waited for a VAR intervention but the moment remained pure. Scotland had needed a goal and Clarke's prophecy came to pass.

Fuck knows what Schmeichel was doing. It was like a magnetic force dragged him towards the front post while gravity grew stronger. Shankland's finish could barely have been easier but Ferguson's delivery was terrific. Hard, just high enough to beat the first man and with enough dip to land in the six-yard area. It was no accident.

> I knew straight away Shanks had got a touch on it. We worked on that exact corner the day before the game; looked at it in meetings and practiced it on the training pitch. We felt the front post area was dangerous to hit because if you miss the first man and the ball drops in front of the keeper then it's a very difficult one for him to get. Bodies can cause confusion. My instruction was basically to shoot from the corner flag.

He owed Ferguson the massive cuddle they shared towards the north stand, but this was Shankland's moment. At that point, the owner of the goal that would take Scotland to the World Cup.

> I couldn't believe it. 'Please count' was my first thought after I ran to Fergie. He was probably thinking I'd just nicked his goal, but I had to touch it. If I'd left that and it bounced past the post it would have haunted me for the rest of my life. There's one angle that shows it might have, so I'm happy I did touch it. My role was to be around Schmeichel. He doesn't like to come off his line too much now, so the thought was to get the ball around him and try and make something happen. I was alone in the six-yard box with everyone else outside it! It was a great delivery, the big defender at the near post

didn't want to touch it and I was happy to oblige. It was absolute euphoria, then I looked at the clock and realised there was still a wee bit to go so I was quickly thinking about what to do next. We were on the brink of something special.

McLean backs up Fergie and Shanks's versions of events too:

That was no coincidence whatsoever. We tried to get a lot of deliveries on top of Kasper. A lot of the boys up in Scotland know that's not his strength now and if we can identify some kind of weakness we'll try and exploit it. Fergie put the ball where we wanted it and as the gaffer said, Shanks is your man for a goal. I know him from way back in my days at Aberdeen and he's always been very good technically, but in recent seasons I think people have been seeing that more while his finishing speaks for itself. We need him as an option in the squad, he puts the ball in the net. A massive player. I didn't celebrate his goal like Scotty's, I think because I understood what was about to happen over the next 15 minutes. I arrived late to the huddle and was trying to speak to the boys and settle them down, get them back to thinking about what was needed now. Emotions are natural but we have to handle them. I felt the situation we were about to face was bigger than a celebration at that time.

After watching Denmark dominate for nearly an hour, commentator Thomas Kristensen couldn't believe it:

Things happen so quickly around Schmeichel. He was standing on the line but didn't take any action to go for the ball. That's him in that stage of his career now, he'll never go for the ball. I would never try to give him the answers, but I think a younger Schmeichel would have done something. It was only 2cm or 3cm.

Shankland was caught on camera bellowing, 'Let's keep the fucking ball!' as the players took their places for kick-off while Gannon-Doak had to be told to calm down on the bench to protect his torn hamstring. It was now Scotland's turn to defend. To defend against ten men for 12 minutes plus the five, give or take, that would be added. It wasn't really a late goal after all, was it?

The soundwaves of 'We'll Be Coming' soared around Hampden. Scotland fell back as they tried to stuff and squeeze three points into their safe before the Danes booted the backroom door down. They probed and when Morten Hjulmand gathered the ball 30 yards from goal, Scotland had all but Shankland behind the ball. Højlund held it up supremely and as he fended off McLean and poked the ball wide to Isaksen, 'We'll Be Coming' was replaced by *inevitability*. In came a cross that Scotland just couldn't clear and Dorgu – the alleged weak link – stroked it into the net. Echoes of the goals conceded in Slovenia when we allowed a play-off place for Russia '18 to disintegrate. Three minutes after taking the lead, we'd surrendered it.

Tierney lay crumpled in the six-yard area, McTominay's hands were clasped behind his head, McGinn was on his knees while Ferguson was hinged at a 45-degree angle with his hands on his own. About 47,000 surveyed the wreckage from afar. After encouraging the players to be ready for what was about to come at them, McLean was digesting the reality:

> Initially it was total deflation, but I've never felt Hampden like that before. I was on my knees but got up and looked around and a few of the lads were shouting there was still time. The energy started to come back straight away; it was a moment I wish I could have taken in more. It was like the fans understood we really needed

them now. We spoke earlier about them reacting to us or vice versa – well, that was them lifting us and saying we could still do this. A few of the boys were vocal very quickly after Dorgu scored, but it only took about 15 seconds for the fans to show their encouragement and lift the noise levels again.

Gallows humour: *grim and ironic humour in a desperate or hopeless situation.*

Hanley had Shankland and Ferguson nearby as the Scotland squad regrouped before kick-off. He tells me now that he fully believed what he verifiably told them during the assembly: 'It's alright, lads, we scored too early to hang on anyway.'

Dorgu's goal wasn't like Solskjær's in '99. There were still roughly 12 to 15 minutes remaining. We used to bemoan the lack of experience among Scotland squads; in Clarke's early days it was normal for starting XIs to have somewhere between 100 to 150. The team finishing this game had 627 caps between them, an average of 57 per player. Most of us would argue they should be able to cope more appropriately with the threat posed by a team with ten men in the minutes after scoring a vital and potentially winning goal. Then again, you (probably) nor I (definitely) have never been required to do that while the hopes of a nation crush our shoulders.

It is also reasonable to expect that with nearly 15 minutes to go, this war was not over. With a man advantage, Scotland had lost almost every battle on the field, yet they could still win this war. In the eight minutes preceding the stoppages, Scotland huffed and puffed themselves into a higher gear. Denmark understandably tried to turn every possible given inch into a mile. An inch was all McGinn missed by when he curled one towards the top corner with four of the 90 to play. McLean had his head in his hands:

To an extent it starts to become desperate, but at the same time we can't just start launching it into the box straight away because they've got two huge centre-backs who will just header everything away. We probed for a bit and switched it a lot, tried to use the extra man, and that makes the crowd uneasy because they're encouraging us to put it in from deep, but we wanted it in better areas that we'd been working on. We've seen the stats for where we're at our best on the ball; we always want to be within the width of the box for cutbacks or to fizz it to the back post instead of putting it in from too wide because unless we have Dykes on the pitch it's unlikely we'll win it. Can we get to the byline or can we keep any crosses from deep narrower?

Six minutes added; Scotland started to take a more direct flight path. Hampden had become a house of murmurs and mutterings. We'd led twice. We'd seen one of the best goals of all time. We were playing against ten men. We were going to end up in the play-offs.

'That's Troy Parrott! That is unbelievable! Right at the death, Ireland have done it!'

You might have also felt a burning envy the night before last watching the Irish celebrate their last-second winner in Hungary to seal their play-off place. Their team chased Parrott like a scene from a nature documentary, subs met them halfway and the celebrations among the pile-up reflected those in the away end. It was an absolute joy to watch.

I was watching the Ireland moment thinking it had been a while since we'd had a moment like that.

Ryan Christie's words there, who was on the bench watching this unfold in the 93rd minute. Hickey had been jealous too, watching a couple of his Brentford team-mates revel in the moment. Minutes were turning to seconds. Scotland had to score.

McGinn launches in a free kick from near halfway. First phase: cleared. Second phase: McLean scampers wide and delivers. Cleared. Third phase: McGinn puts his laces through the ball from 25 yards, which thunders off Hanley and rebounds to 50 yards from goal. Fourth phase: McLean hoists one towards the box, met by Andersen's head, returned by Ferguson's, fluffed by Hjulmand on the box's edge … and buried – breathtakingly buried – by Kieran Tierney!

Hampden Park produced a noise to overpower most that have come before. A left-back thrown on at right-back. The left-back the team used to be built around because his quality could not be neglected but was no longer a starter. The left-back so supreme whose career and impact at the top level of the sport has been blighted by injury to the extent he has returned to the comfort zone of the Scottish Premiership at 28 years old. The left-back whose only previous international goal was in a friendly against Poland. In it went from 23 yards, whizzing past a few Danish faces and his club-mate in goal. An astonishing strike.

Tierney – an introverted personality – dashed towards the family section with all in tow a la McTominay, while looking quite uncertain about what had just happened. He wasn't alone for much longer and became as buried as his own strike, under a huddle of dark blue. Emerging, he cracked a sort of bashful smile and received a hug from Clarke. His dreams were about to come true as well as ours and theirs.

'History for Scotland and Kieran Tierney!' Liam McLeod exclaimed on commentary. This was it now. This was how the 10,000-day wait for a return to the World Cup was going to climax. The boys on the bench, Dykes for the second time that night, had the perfect view:

I was right in line with it. I couldn't believe it! KT is a funny boy, he joins in with shooting at the end of training, he's never stuck one in like that. It was perfect timing, and an amazing goal and moment. It's the best I've felt with Scotland, that was the winning goal.

McLean played an important part in keeping the attack alive several times:

We regularly work on how to sustain attacks from set pieces. How to keep the ball in there, building habits so that everyone knows their jobs. My ball in was actually slightly underhit and somehow their player [Hjulmand] took a wild swipe at it – composure absolutely out the window for them. I'm right behind KT as he runs on to it and it started three yards outside the post but I knew it was coming back in. I lost my shit. I actually hit the deck. I looked up and everyone was at the dugout. What is amazing is at the start of the game, Shanks, KT and I were all discussing what we could do if we came on – that's the importance we have as a team. The manager always references the boys on the bench and who aren't stripped, it's one of the first things he says in a meeting; everyone has a part to play and should know their role.

Shankland's goal had only been the winner for a few minutes. Not that he cared. He had been loitering for the shot that Tierney eventually took.

Hjulmand had been really good that night as well. He tried to clear it and you'll see me flinching in the video. I'd expected it to fly over my head but it dropped and it's just pure football that you put a left-back on the right side of the pitch and he's able to run on to it. I was in line with the ball and could see it spinning. I knew it was in. What a feeling. It felt like Naisy was about 45 yards onto the pitch! It was just euphoria, but it lasted about 30 seconds then I thought, 'Aw, shit, still got work to do.'

Summed up well by Shanks, euphoria is the perfect word. But for all of it on the pitch and the sold-out stands surrounding it, one man between the opposite goal barely moved a muscle.

> Kieran is capable of hitting a cracker and he found the gap perfectly. He could probably never hit it better. We still had five minutes to go. I just turned around and walked back to my net. I hadn't done my job yet, we hadn't completed this. They might get a chance, so all I was thinking was: 'Be ready, switch on. They will get a chance, they will cross the ball, there will be another attacking action.' That's all I was telling myself. I couldn't allow myself to think we'd done it.

If Scotland didn't concede, they were going to the World Cup. Hampden was gripped in tension's vice. Jeers and whistles followed for four minutes after Scotland's celebrations added more time to the stoppages. Overwhelmment-induced tears trickled out my eyes as we roared encouragement for the lads to boot and head every ball as far away from our box as humanly possible. A fluorescent barrier had been constructed at short notice to prevent what felt like an unstoppable and imminent pitch invasion. Denmark had the ball midway through the Scotland half, trying to find an angle to cross and … actually … you know what? I'll just let the man of this moment take it from here …

> I saw Robbo and Fergie pressing, trying to stop the source of the cross because they had all their big men up. I moved as soon as I saw their guy cutting back and playing the blind pass, and the centre-back knows if he comes and misses it then he'll foul me and the game is

done, so he retreated. I was looking for the right pass because I knew we had spare men up, they'd given up on running back and we were one pass away from the whistle, which would have gone before we got to the corner anyway. I had Fergie to my left and Adams to my right, but when I skipped inside past Andersen I heard a few rumblings of 'Shoot!' so I glanced up and saw Kasper wasn't really reacting. I'd asked the ref about a minute ago how long was left and he said, 'One minute,' so I'm aware the game is over. The ball was actually stuck under my feet, but when I heard the shout I thought, 'Why not?' It started about a yard outside the post but I could see it coming in and Kasper was in trouble. I started running quite early and when it hit the net, the rest is a bit of a blur. I got to the corner flag well ahead of everyone. I don't know how the boys got there so quickly. All of a sudden everyone was on the pitch! The joy on their faces will not be possible to match for me.

'Shoot! Shoot! He's done him! He's done him!' BBC Scotland co-commentator Stephen Thompson urged Scotland's number 23 like a racehorse. Kenny McLean had scored from the halfway line to seal Scotland's place at the World Cup, and those inside Hampden Park were literally causing seismic activity comparable to a small earthquake. The squad that had been defying instructions by merging into a human stress ball on the sideline exploded into individual particles and hurtled down the pitch. The full-time whistle had gone while the squad clambered over each other down by the flag on the corner of south and east, where McLean's knee slide ended. A flag that McTominay plucked from the turf. Robertson was on his knees, shaking, head on the grass with his hands interlocked behind it. Three of Scotland's best goals of all time had been scored in one game. *This* was the climax.

Steve Clarke went bush with delirium and leapt around the technical area with Naismith, Irvine and the whole lot of them. He had been yelling at McLean to take it to the corner and he wasn't the only one. Ferguson's impact on the game's culmination was huge; his presence forced Hjulmand to abandon ship:

> I knew because we had the extra man I could break out because of the protection behind me. Robbo and I were tearing after him and Kenny read his pass, from there I was trying to help him by getting down the line but I had nothing left. I was giving it everything thinking, 'If he rolls this to me I'm gonna have to take it for a run.' But he has that quality to execute that. I'll never forget the feeling of running after Kenny knowing the game was over and we were going to the World Cup. As soon as he hit it, I thought it was going in. It genuinely felt like it was in slow motion. The crowd fell silent for a second then erupted. Everyone celebrating in the corner together; that's a hard feeling to match.

Christie was one of a dozen or so who tore down the touchline's turf after ignoring the fourth official's demands to take a few steps back.

> I was hoping he'd slide in Ché to take it for a run to the corner flag! The moment he shifted it onto his left and hit it I thought, 'What are you doing?!' But I quickly realised it had a chance. I was so buzzing for Kenny. He's one of the most underrated players I've ever played with and has done amazing things for Scotland. It was an unbelievable moment.

Dykes was the first to arrive on the scene. He was already sidestepping his way down the line when McLean's shot was floating:

I remember it more clearly than KT's goal because we were all down by the technical area together. Some of us were crouched down low, shouting for the ref to blow and then at Kenny to boot the ball away. It was the slowest ball flight ever but when it went in we knew it was done. Kenny is a great lad and he's a major key in what we have off the pitch as well. He still deserves to be playing with us. He's a key player for us and would be a major miss.

Shankland had been happy to sit back after his defensive diligence but started to break into a stride as soon as McLean struck the ball, keeping his habit of bending a run but on this occasion to make sure the ball was going into the net. He was soon on his way to the corner with McKenna and Ferguson.

You could not pick a better way to finish a game. I was bent over, absolutely fucked. I don't think I breathed from the minute the guy nicked the ball away from me up the other end until Kenny hit it, just thinking, 'Please do not score, I can't be the guy that gave the ball away.'

Hanley's territorial instincts are so strong that he didn't realise the game had ended and while the Scotland squad continued to celebrate was concluding 'right, let's get back in here.' He was hoping his best pal wouldn't shoot but knew it was in from the nanosecond it started to curl. Gannon-Doak had been shouting for Adams to take it to the corner before managing to hobble down and get in on the *pandemonium* without his ice pack sliding down his leg.

'Scotty, did you see how fuckin' high you went?' he asked the evening's first goalscorer.

One man's celebration and outpouring probably *hit differently* to the other lads'. Craig Gordon's guard dropped and he thundered towards the gang. He'd done it.

I remember watching '98 and coming home from school in time for the game. I was 15 years old then. Now my daughter is the same age and that's us only just achieved it again. When Kenny hit it I was right behind it and it was just outside the post. I was thinking, 'Go on, get in, get in!' and I could see it was creeping round. When it bounced it was one of the best feelings I could ever have on a football pitch and one of the best feelings for the crowd at Hampden. At that moment I knew I'd just played in a match that will go down as one of the best Scotland matches of all time. To be part of the squad that finally qualified for a World Cup was relief more than anything else. It was something I had strived towards for so long and it finally happened.

The game had everything. Six goals, three of them sensational, one in the first few minutes, two in stoppage time, two equalisers, a red card, a penalty, a disallowed goal and an injury to a star player.

Hampden remained full for around half an hour after full time while the players continued to celebrate on the pitch. Dykes's son, with whom he walked out before the game, and McGinn's nephew were on centre-stage for a few minutes and were celebrated every time they scored into the west stand's goal. McTominay lay flat on his back, starfished in the box. Even the Danish support wasn't in a hurry to jettison. TV2 commentator Thomas Kristensen filmed the history. He describes 'dark days' rather than a 'dark night', blaming the result against Belarus rather than the events he'd just witnessed.

'USA! USA! USA!'

'Letter from America' was the evening's poignant musical offering from the brothers Easton – Graham and Keith – in charge of Hampden's playlists. 'I Can Boogie', 'Bits and Pieces', 'Freed From Desire' and 'Rockin' All Over the World' are repeated before, during or after most matches at Hampden and listen, music is a subjective pleasure. Your average Status Quo fan probably doesn't pre-drink to GBX on a Friday evening. Tonight, every melody was magic. The squad took off towards the corner of north and west like fighter jets in formation and leapt as 'Freed From Desire's' beat dropped. Hey, it's not my cup of tea. In fact, I'm pretty sure I hate that song. I'm also pretty sure I didn't care in the slightest and sang every word.

'I thought we were pretty rubbish to be honest, but who cares?' asked McGinn, laughing. He didn't believe Scotland were going to do it. He thought he'd blocked Dorgu's shot. He thought he was about to give Scotland the lead in the 86th minute. He was thinking about returning to Hampden for a play-off in March, until Tierney scored. 'I will never feel like that in a football stadium ever again.'

Clarke cemented almost all the credit outside his players' door. It was all 'very simple' from where he stood: 'What a fantastic group of players.' He outlined the number of caps they've earned together, his trust in their ability and their strength of character. He's revealed before that he needed between a year or two to properly grip the handle of international management's wild ride, unswerving in the certainty that the path being followed was the correct one. 'If I give myself a bit of credit,' he teed up on BBC Scotland, 'I chose the right way.' The outlook when he took the job had no sunny intervals. Scotland had now qualified for three major tournaments – two of them automatically – and sadly stumbled in a play-off for the other. Dissenters airing grievances about performances at the two Euros had valid perspectives, but the regular complaints about squad selections rightly fell on ignorant ears. Fourteen of the players from the play-off semi-final defeat to Ukraine – plus Gilmour – were involved against Denmark three years later.

This was another play-off final in spirit. Clarke recognised Scotland froze in 2022 and made extra steps to relax the squad and decelerate their minds. 21 years after his debut in a friendly at Easter Road against Trinidad and Tobago, those were the steps Gordon took throughout the whole international break. He fulfilled the Christie role and shed a tear in front of the BBC Scotland cameras. He sounds like a proud dad in his recollections:

> I was in disbelief for a while. Watching the crowd while we walked around the park and being able to see that joy … I've won trophies with clubs, but this felt like it was for everybody. I soaked it in, watching everyone celebrating in their own ways, all the players constantly hugging each other, it was just sheer joy. I had my family there too. They'd been there not long ago in the Finland game and that was a totally different atmosphere, so to come back from that to the highest high was pretty special.

We'll be comin', we'll be comin', we'll be comin' down the road! When you hear the noise of the Tartan Army boys, we'll be comin' down the road!

That was the slogan on the T-shirts distributed with saltires and lion rampants while the players continued to make their way from corner to corner. Dykes and Robertson shared a never-ending hug. Big group picture? Check.

The goals were being replayed on the televisions inside the dressing room and were celebrated by the players on each occasion as if they were seeing them for the first time. Clarke was 'close to tears' according to one player. He made his speech, which was instantly followed by bottles of beer being sprayed all around him. The boys bounced off the four walls watching McLean's goal over and over.

> I've been so fortunate to be in the positions I've been in with Scotland. I've worked my nuts off to get there and to be given the opportunities, the backing of the manager and the trust he continually puts in me, but

of all the moments I've had in a Scotland jersey –
that tops the rest put together. I'm a Championship
player now but even for the lads that play in the
Champions League and Premier League or big teams
across Europe, this was the pinnacle as well. Those
celebrations, with your best mates? It's amazing.

Not among the mosh pit of merriment were McGinn and
Shankland. They'd been pulled in for drugs testing and missed
around half an hour. A repeat of history for John, who was also
randomly selected after winning in Belgrade. The drums, bass
and karaoke tried to perforate the walls and Rasmus Højlund
– relatively chatty with McGinn given their familiarity down
south – told the lads they could play some tunes on their phones
if they wanted.

The players – some still in full kit – ascended to the players'
lounge to raise a glass with their families. Hanley isn't normally
one to fuss over photos, but he's got the one with him and his
daughter, draped in a Scotland flag, framed in his living room.

Your family kick every ball with you. They know how
hard it is, see the sacrifices, the disappointments and
stresses. These moments are what make it all worth it.

Robertson's announcement that he'd prebooked popular Glasgow
nightclub Kong for the after-party was like testing a fire alarm
with a flamethrower. Ewan McVicar would DJ and everyone was
invited! McTominay couldn't make it as he was going home via
Manchester to see family. Flights home to Naples, Zagreb, Saudi
Arabia, London and wherever else are organised by the SFA for
the players at the most convenient time for their clubs. Hickey
enjoyed some conversations with Damsgaard upon their return,
during which he whacked accusations of luck into the boundary.
His return to the squad was crucial.

> Playing for Scotland is very special for me. It's a dream. I used to kick about down the park thinking about World Cups. It has always been a massive goal for me. To help take us there, wow. I've never experienced anything like that.

Dykes doesn't drink so there was no risk of a hangover there, but Shankland was a fragile man during Wednesday's school run. Ferguson was afforded a lie-in the morning after the celebrations before flying to Bologna in the evening. Not everyone was so lucky.

Ryan Christie had been in touch with Bournemouth's Head of Performance.

'I don't know if you watched our game tonight, but could I have a late report to training tomorrow, if not the day off? I'll just be on recovery anyway.'

'No, you're on a 6.40am flight from Edinburgh.'

> I refused to go to my bed early – there was no way I was missing any of that. I had Lyndon babysitting me and Ben hobbling around on crutches. I've seen so many videos of us that night in Kong and I have no memory of any of them. I left at about four, ran back to the Blythswood with Doaky behind me on crutches, jumped in a taxi to Edinburgh Airport and got on the flight. There must be folk out there with pictures or videos of us. I was absolutely stumbling through the airport. I went to training and got sent home at about 11.30.

There may or may not have been cameras inconspicuously making sure Christie and BGD didn't evade detection between Kong and Bournemouth's training centre. I've yet to see any evidence. We all saw the bleary-eyed Scotland players leaving the Blythswood on Wednesday morning with Sky Sports' more industrial cameras inches from their faces.

McLean went on holiday for a few days not long after the match, and unlike Ryan he was approached in the airport by natives eager to express their gratitude. His six-year-old daughter innocently queried why people kept saying hello. 'The biggest buzz for me is somehow giving other people the emotion and the elation,' he said.

Gordon's days spent digesting the achievement were local, but just as satisfying: 'I watched loads of videos of people celebrating in pubs and living rooms and people were stopping me in the street for weeks to talk about it. That really brought it home to me how massive this was.'

Almost unspeakably, Craig.

Scotland had avoided a play-off semi-final against either Albania, Republic of Ireland, Bosnia & Herzegovina or Kosovo. One of Italy, Turkey or Ukraine would likely have been around the corner following a win, but Sweden, Romania, North Macedonia and Northern Ireland were other potential opponents if they upset a Pot 1 team. Denmark ended up drawing North Macedonia and were paired to play the winner of Czech Republic v Republic of Ireland.

Intriguing, but irrelevant. That safety net could be cut loose. An amusing tweet from America-based Scottish commentator Mark Donaldson read: 'BREAKING … Ben Gannon-Doak will miss the FIFA World Cup qualifying play-offs in March. And so will every other Scotland player in Steve Clarke's squad!'

Unlike the desperate attempts to snatch a play-off spot for 2022, 2018, 2010, 2006 and 2002, our success story this time was defined by the pursuit of automatic World Cup qualification. Manipulated year after year to accommodate a calendar fit to burst – like the wallets of those making the decisions – this was football in its purest form resulting in a historic World Cup qualification. Our best against your best. Scotland had *done it*, and they had done it like *that*.

That was a long time coming.